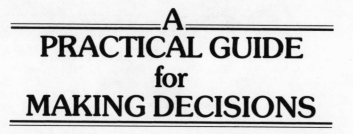

A
PRACTICAL GUIDE
for
MAKING DECISIONS

A PRACTICAL GUIDE for MAKING DECISIONS

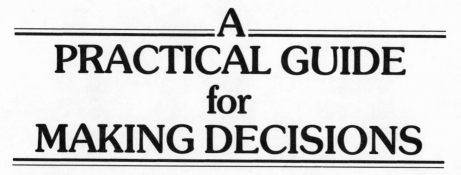

Daniel D. Wheeler
Irving L. Janis

THE FREE PRESS

A Division of Macmillan Publishing Co., Inc.

NEW YORK

Collier Macmillan Publishers

LONDON

THE FREE PRESS
A Division of Macmillan Publishing Co., Inc.
866 Third Avenue, New York, N.Y. 10022

Collier Macmillan Canada, Ltd.

Library of Congress Catalog Card Number: 79-6766

PRINTED IN THE UNITED STATES OF AMERICA

printing number

1 2 3 4 5 6 7 8 9 10

Library of Congress Cataloging in Publication Data

Wheeler, Daniel D
    A practical guide for making decisions.

    Includes index.
    1. Decision-making. 2. Success. I. Janis,
Irving Lester   joint author. II. Title.
BF441.W472   153.8'3   79-6766
ISBN 0-02-934460-3

Table 2 has been adapted from Table 3 on pages 62–63 of *Permanent Weight Control* by Michael J. Mahoney, Ph.D., and Kath-
ryn Mahoney, by permission of W. W. Norton & Company, Inc.
Copyright © 1976 by W. W. Norton & Company, Inc.

To Cathy

Contents

Preface

Effective decision making is both an art and a science. Our goal in writing this book has been to produce a practical guide to the art of decision making that is soundly based in the science of psychology. Our suggestions for improving the quality of decisions are applicable to all the important choices that people make throughout their lives. All of our advice is based on what we regard as the best available research. But this is not a book about research. We have distilled the research findings into a stage-by-stage guide that combines the art and the science.

The breadth of our approach is increased by the differences in our backgrounds. One of us (Wheeler) is an experimental psychologist specializing in practical problem solving. The other (Janis) is a social psychologist and expert on decision making. We have enjoyed working together to bring you the best from both perspectives.

The overall framework that we use is based on the conflict model of decision making developed by Irving Janis and Leon Mann. The model and the supporting research was presented in detail in their recent book, *Decision Making*, which is intended for specialists and advanced students. In this book we present most of the main conclusions from the Janis and Mann book, but we also draw upon many other sources of theory and research. The literature on problem solving, creativity, negotiation, and group processes has provided important guidelines for specific situations that arise in making decisions.

There have been major advances in the last few years in the development of formal, mathematical methods for decision analysis. These methods are becoming widely used in business and industry where the criteria can usually be quantified in dollars and where mathematically trained specialists are available to carry out the calculations. But we feel that these methods are not directly applicable to most of the vital decisions made by individuals. We recommend methods consistent with the formal theory but using reasoning rather than numerical calculations to compare alternatives. Our methods do not involve any mathematics and thus can be applied to all situations, even those where numerical estimates are not possible.

Our approach is also much broader than formal decision analysis, which focuses almost exclusively on the evaluation of alternatives. We begin with the initial challenge that indicates the need for a decision. We carry through to the final stage of maintaining the decision in spite of setbacks that inevitably occur. The prescriptions we present are based mainly on what is now known about when, why, and how errors are made or avoided by people when they have to make consequential decisions. Our approach tries to understand and to build upon research findings about the stresses of making major decisions and the ways that people seek to avoid those stresses. We try to highlight the procedures that anyone can use to avoid the errors that are most likely to crop up in personal decision making or at least to keep such errors to a minimum.

In offering a wide variety of prescriptions about how to avoid or minimize errors, we do not hesitate to present ideal ways of arriving at effective decisions. But in doing so we try to take account of the psychology of human beings with all their conflicts and imperfections that prevent them from achieving whatever ideals they may have about being purely rational decision makers. While all of our prescriptions are based on research and psychological theory, some of the specific techniques have not yet been adequately tested to prove their worth. In those cases we label the techniques as unproved and urge our readers to try the techniques cautiously to make sure they work in their particular situations.

Throughout the book we try to give vivid illustrations of each of the main points. The case histories involve personal decisions concerning careers, love life, health, finances, and major purchases as well as business and professional decisions in a variety of fields. They also include both purely individual decisions and family or group decisions. Most of the case histories are based on real cases or composites of real cases. We have changed some of the details to avoid embarrassing our friends and clients and to better illustrate the points we are making. We hope you enjoy the case histories and learn from the experiences described.

Psychologists and other human services professionals will find some new theoretical concepts as well as new practical procedures that can be applied in their consulting work, although many topics we cover may be already familiar to them. Those readers should find our book especially helpful in educating their clients.

We are indebted to Professor Lee Ross of Stanford University for a thorough critique of an early draft of each chapter. A number of other friends and colleagues who read one or more chapters gave us additional suggestions that were valuable for making revisions: Virginia Bales, Alexander George, Robert N. Hamburger, Marjorie G. Janis, Michael Kubovy, Leah Lapidus, Helgola Ross, and Suzanne Veilleux. We also wish to thank June Connolley, Linda Schwartz, and Jane Shreve for typing successive drafts of the manuscript.

1
Going through the Essential Stages

"It doesn't make any difference what I decide. My future is beyond my control." All too many people have this attitude. As long as they believe that they are only pawns at the mercy of outside forces, they are unlikely to take the kind of action that would give them some degree of conscious control over their lives. They are trapped in a self-fulfilling prophecy. Such people don't actively make decisions; they wait until they have only one alternative left to take.

Active decision making gives you a degree of control over your life. The choices you make do help to determine your future. But, obviously, it is not enough just to make decisions. Making the wrong decisions can be worse than making no decisions at all. To play an active part in determining your future, you should go through the stages that are essential for arriving at sound choices.

The central theme of this book is that you *can* go through these essential stages and arrive at sound decisions, decisions that increase your chances of attaining your major objectives. Some people already have effective decision-making skills; those who don't can learn them.

Choosing your own future

Here are some examples to show how your choices can determine your future. To appreciate the kind of problems that arise, try to imagine yourself in each of the following situations.

1

SITUATION 1.   You work in the development section of a large corporation. One day your boss tells you, in confidence, that he is fed up with the company and is searching for another job. You have worked very closely with your boss, and his departure will be a real loss to you.

- *Future A.* Two months later, when your boss leaves, you are promoted to fill his position because you have worked so closely with him. It is a great opportunity for you to make full use of your talents.
- *Future B.* Two months later, when your boss leaves, management puts in a new section head who has an organizational philosophy much closer to theirs. She reorganizes the entire section. You are fired.
- *Future C.* You realize immediately that there are real dangers for you if your boss leaves the company. You start looking for jobs in other companies and at the same time try to figure out the possibilities of other jobs within your own company. Two months later, when your boss leaves, you have a job offer from another company, and you are in a position to negotiate with your current company. Management offers you a new job. With two job offers, you can take the one that seems better for you.

These are only three of the many possible futures from the situation given. Your actions are only one of the many determinants of which future actually occurs. But it is clear that active decision making can help you avoid disasters like future B.

SITUATION 2.   You and your spouse have only a week for your vacation. Several months ago you signed up for a charter trip to Paris with a three-day side trip to the French Riviera. The day before you were supposed to leave, the travel agent called to tell you that your trip had been canceled. She offered you a choice of a trip to London or a trip to a beach resort on the island of Majorca. You want to go to London to see the museums and art galleries. Your spouse wants to go to the beach resort.

- *Future A.* You go to London. Your spouse is unhappy and bitter. Your relationship sours.

- *Future B.* You go to Majorca. You are unhappy and bitter. Your relationship sours.

In this case you don't want either future. But couldn't you do something to improve your prospects?

SITUATION 3.　You are considering investing in a retail computer store. Home computers are growing in popularity and you want to get in at the beginning of this major new field. You have the capital to open a store and keep it running for a year until it becomes profitable. But you are uncertain about the future of the home computer market. It might fizzle like quadraphonic sound. So you have also considered the possibility of investing instead in a wine and cheese store.

- *Future A.* You invest in the computer store. The market quickly becomes saturated. Demand is light. One of your major suppliers goes bankrupt, and your store can't get the equipment to fill even the few orders it does get. At the end of a year you have to close the store. You have lost a lot of your time and all your investment capital.
- *Future B.* You invest in the wine and cheese store. It goes well enough, but the computer business booms. New computer systems become available with enhanced capabilities and lower prices. Computer stores expand rapidly. You deeply regret that you didn't take the opportunity to invest in a business that would be much more interesting and profitable to you. You realize that you can't switch now. Much more capital would be required to break into the market, competition is already well established, and a new store's chances of being successful are lower.

This pair of futures shows that you cannot avoid risks. For every risky opportunity there is the corresponding risk of losing the gains from the opportunity if you decide not to take it. Effective decision-making methods can help you assess the risks involved and can enable you to pick which risks you want to take.

SITUATION 4.　You just got a large bonus. You and your spouse are considering four alternatives for using the money: (a) buying a new car, (b) remodeling the kitchen, (c) installing central air conditioning, and (d) putting the money into joint savings investments. There are good reasons for doing each of these but you have only enough money to do one of them. You feel overwhelmed by the complexity of trying to weigh the advantages and disadvantages of each alternative against the others.

- *Future A*. You and your spouse go to a car dealer to check the prices of new cars. Buying a car is so easy that you just go ahead and do it. When summer comes you suffer both from the heat and from the realization that you made a mistake. You wish you had installed air conditioning but it is now too late.
- *Future B*. You and your spouse think carefully about the short- and long-term consequences of each of your possibilities. Even though the weather is now cool you realize how important air conditioning will be to you in the summer. You get a good preseason price on the system and everything is ready by summer.

There is nothing very uncertain about either of these futures. Systematic decision-making methods can reduce the complexity involved in comparing a number of quite different alternatives.

What are good decisions?

A natural way to judge decisions is by whether they lead to success. Good decisions are the ones that lead to futures that the decision maker likes. Bad decisions are those that lead to unpleasant outcomes. The goal of improving the outcomes of decisions is certainly the ultimate reason for developing effective decision-making skills. But it is difficult to evaluate decision making in this way. Most people find that in some respects their hopes have been realized and in other respects not. Almost always, some expected gains do not materialize and some undesirable risks do. Sometimes the outcomes alternate between successful and unsuccessful, so that the evaluations depend critically on when they are done. For major life decisions we never know how long to wait to see if the decision is successful. The outcome may appear to be successful now, but failure may be just around the corner. We also can never tell how the other alternatives would have come out in the long run. Maybe some choice we rejected would have led to a huge success.

For example, let's consider a college student's decision to major in business rather than in applied mathematics. By her senior year Susan was bored with business courses and she wished she had picked the math major. After graduation she got a job as a stock broker. She enjoyed the training and was fascinated by the work. She also liked working in a field where women were an exception. Three years later she was discouraged. Although the firm was supportive of its female account executives, the clients, especially those with large accounts, didn't seem to want a woman as financial adviser. Again she wished she had stayed with applied math. So she quit her job and started writing a newspaper column of financial advice for women. This led to a consulting business helping women with their financial problems. Now Susan is glad she has the general business background she got as an undergraduate.

Did Susan's decision to major in business turn out well? The answer seems to change as the years go by. Right now it looks like the answer is yes, but it may be different next year. Would it have been better for her to major in applied math? We have no idea how the outcomes from that choice would compare to what actually happened.

Because of the difficulty of judging decisions by how desirable or undesirable the outcomes are or seem to be or might have been, we recommend that *decisions should be judged on the basis of the processes used in making them.* From this viewpoint, sound decisions are those that are made well, with full consideration of all the relevant aspects of the problem. Good decision makers carry out each of the essential steps of effective decision making carefully and completely. Unsound decisions are marked by flaws in the process, such as ignoring available factual information about known risks or failing to consider some important alternatives.

Sometimes sound decisions lead to undesirable outcomes. Making decisions must involve taking calculated risks; there is no way risk can be eliminated completely. Calculated risks will occasionally materialize and make the outcome bad. For instance, Stan and Donna Reimer took a calculated risk when they bought a house with a damp basement. Before buying, they had consulted the county engineer and a building contractor. The consensus was that the dampness was slight and was probably insignificant, although there was some chance that it might increase. Since the Reimers liked the house much better than any other they had seen on the market, they decided to take the risk and buy the house. The following spring the slight dampness was two feet deep.

Even when risks materialize, people who have used sound decision-making procedures have advantages. Although Stan and Donna now wish that they had not bought that house, they don't blame themselves and feel guilty about having done something stupid. Accepting the fact that an anticipated risk materialized, they are busy making the best decision about how to cope with it. They also have the advantage that their earlier analysis of the risk gave them a head start on figuring out what to do about it. They knew exactly what type of company to call to have the basement pumped out and which experts to consult about changing the drainage around the house to solve the problem permanently. People who fail to consider risks when making a decision often suffer considerable guilt and remorse. They have two problems to overcome, the risk that materialized and their emotional reactions to their failure.

The five stages of effective decision making

The essential steps of effective decision making can be categorized into five sequential stages. Each stage deals with different issues that are important to the eventual decision. Each stage has its own methods and its own pitfalls. If any of the stages is omitted or done poorly, the overall process will be flawed and the chances of failure will be increased.

STAGE 1. *Accepting the challenge.*   Decision making begins when people are confronted with a challenge to their current course of action. In Situation 1 (above) you were challenged by your boss's message that he was planning to leave the company. You had the choice of (a) accepting the challenge and beginning to do something about it or (b) ignoring the challenge and just letting things happen.

The challenge can be either an indication of a threat or a hint of an opportunity. Challenges come in many forms. Events provide challenges, as when the roof of your house starts leaking. Even more often communications provide challenges, such as news of gas shortages or announcements of new investments that are said to be desirable for people at your income level. Challenges can sometimes be very indirect and hidden. A change from color advertisements to black-and-white may indicate that an equipment supplier is in financial trouble. This minor change could challenge alert buyers to look further into the situation and to consider changing their orders.

The central question facing decision makers during Stage 1 is whether the threat or opportunity is important enough to warrant the effort of making an active decision about it. Ignoring or rejecting the challenge leads to complacently pursuing the original course of action without any change, simply continuing business as usual. Accepting the challenge, or deciding to decide, leads to the next stage of active decision making.

Chapter 2 covers methods for spotting challenges and assessing their importance. It also discusses how an intelligent and well-qualified executive named Mr. Bury failed to meet the challenge of Situation 1 when his boss told him that he was planning to leave the firm.

STAGE 2. *Searching for alternatives.* When a current course of action is challenged, effective decision makers begin searching for alternatives. In Situation 2 the travel agent offered you only two alternatives after the trip to Paris and the Riviera was canceled. Since either alternative would lead to an undesirable future, finding other alternatives is essential for making a sound decision and having a pleasant vacation.

Effective decision makers accomplish two things during Stage 2. They thoroughly consider their goals and values relevant to a decision. Then they use that information to search carefully for a wide range of alternatives that have some promise of achieving these goals. The more alternatives that are overlooked, the more likely it is that something better than the eventual choice will be missed.

Little evaluation of alternatives is done during Stage 2. Ideas are collected and kept in storage, so to speak, if they seem to have promise of overcoming problems raised by the challenge. The main danger is that good ideas may be missed or prematurely rejected. At the end of Stage 2, effective decision makers have generated a list of possibilities that seem to be viable alternatives to the challenged course of action.

Chapter 3 discusses ways to clarify your goals and values and suggests methods for helping you to generate alternatives. A good solution to the cancellation of the Paris trip that was worked out by a young couple named Brenda and Kevin is also described.

STAGE 3. *Evaluating alternatives.*   During this stage the advantages and disadvantages of each alternative are carefully considered. In Situation 3 the risks involved made it difficult to assess the alternatives of investing in the computer store or in the wine and cheese shop.

Stage 3 frequently involves considerable effort in searching for dependable information relevant to a decision. Effective decision makers seek facts and forecasts from a wide variety of sources about the consequences of the alternatives they are considering. They carefully weigh both the positive and the negative aspects of each alternative. They don't ignore new evidence that goes against their initial choice. At the end of Stage 3 effective decision makers have usually reached a tentative decision based on the information they have gathered.

Chapter 4 explains the balance-sheet method for keeping track of all the relevant considerations in a complex decision. Chapter 5 discusses ways of dealing with the uncertainty of the future. It explains how an intelligent woman named Mrs. Horvath effectively assessed the risks of opening a retail computer store.

STAGE 4. *Becoming committed.*   At this point the final choice is made and decision makers become committed to a new course of action. The final choice can be difficult, as in Situation 4, where the incommensurability of the alternatives for spending the bonus money made comparisons hard.

Effective decision makers reexamine all the information they have gathered before making a final decision. They also figure out how to implement their decision and make contingency plans just in case any risks materialize.

Chapter 6 explains several ways to weigh all the information to make a final choice. It also explains what Rick and Sally Thompson went through to reach the conclusion that they should spend their bonus money on air conditioning their home rather than on other attractive alternatives.

STAGE 5. *Adhering to the decision.* Decision makers hope that everything will go smoothly after a decision is made, but setbacks occur frequently. Each of the four situations given above includes a future with serious setbacks that could make you regret a decision.

It is not enough to select the best alternative. If the decision is not adequately implemented the favorable outcome will not be achieved. Effective decision makers devise plans to carry out their decisions. They anticipate the likely setbacks and are ready with countermeasures. They are also prepared to deal with serious setbacks and failure by accepting the new challenge and going through another cycle of the five stages to decide on a new course of action.

Chapter 7 explains some ways of overcoming setbacks. It also gives several case studies to illustrate special techniques that can be used to prevent avoidable setbacks and to salvage decisions that may temporarily go sour.

You probably already follow the five-stage model from time to time without being aware of it. Many people do follow these general steps for the important decisions they make, but sometimes they fail to do so. If you think back to your last major decisions, you may recall in some instances going through all these stages and in other instances not doing so.

Assessing consequences

One of the themes of this book is that in order to improve the quality of the vital decisions you make it is necessary to search for and evaluate information about all the potential favorable and unfavorable consequences that are to be expected for each viable alternative. This is an essential feature of the third stage (evaluating alternatives) but it also enters into each of the other stages to some extent.

Though the different consequences of such decisions may seem quite obvious once they are formulated, many people overlook some of the major risks that could lead to unplesant outcomes.

Sometimes people do not go very far with constructing realistic scenarios in their minds simply because they do not like to have to think about such painful things. It is generally worthwhile, however, to go to the trouble of working out those undesirable scenarios in considerable detail whenever you have to make a vital choice. Otherwise you may fail to take account of what could go wrong if you make one choice or another.

In order to remind you of the obvious implications of this point, and to call attention to some not so obvious implications, let us examine a decisional dilemma involving the issue of whether or not to get married. The circumstances are unusual but could be encountered by anyone capable of loving not wisely but too well. It is a type of dilemma that could one day confront you if you are not already happily married or if you do not remain so for the rest of your life. Suppose that you and your lover just reached the point where you admit to each other that you want to marry when a sad thing happens—your lover begins to express feelings of personal unworthiness, becomes more and more depressed, and begins to indulge heavily in tranquilizing drugs in an effort to get rid of distressing thoughts about committing suicide. After a month in a psychiatric hospital, your lover is fully recovered from the temporary depression. You hope that there will never be a recurrence but you realize from all that you have heard and read that after having once had a severe depressive episode a person faces a greater-than-average risk of recurrences of that particular type of psychiatric condition.

Here there are at least two unpleasant scenarios to be considered, not just the salient one posed by the psychiatric problem:

SCENARIO 1.   You decide to get married and after a few years your first child is born. Shortly thereafter the calculated risk unfortunately materializes: your spouse has another depressive episode accompanied by heavy drug use and then has to be hospitalized after an unsuccessful suicide attempt. Thereafter your spouse experiences only brief periods of normality between repeated episodes of suicidal depression accompanied by excessive use of drugs. The consequences of the psychiatric disorder are disastrous: your financial resources are exhausted by the high cost of the psychiatric treatments and hospitalization, you are justifiably worried about the adverse effects of the distressing family atmosphere on your child, the personality of your spouse deteriorates as drug usage increases, and ultimately your marrriage is ruined.

SCENARIO 2.   Realizing that taking each other for better or for worse could result in the disastrous outcome of Scenario 1, you decide not to commit yourself to living together. Soon the two of you drift apart. As time goes by, you become increasingly dissatisfied because you do not find anyone you love as passionately and as wholeheartedly. Meanwhile your former lover has married someone else and has no recurrence of the depressive episode that you had been so concerned about. In fact, you yourself have cause to be chronically depressed about having made the fateful decision that alienated you from the one great love in your life.

For any vital decision, whether it involves marriage, career, health, or any other important sphere of life, it is useful to remind yourself that, just as in this example, for every set of risks attached to taking an attractive course of action there is an opposite (but not necessarily equal) set of risks attached to *not* taking it. Assessment of consequences requires taking account of the possible gains as well as losses. Note that the main things that are lost in Scenario 2 are the rewards that might have been gained from marrying your lover if Scenario 1 does not materialize.

There are those who say that you should always base your decisions on Murphy's Law, which states that "If anything can go wrong, it will." In his book *General Systemantics*, John Gall advises every administrator in a large organization always to remember this law or its earlier version known to school boys as "Jellied bread always falls jelly-side down." His main point is that if you are an administrator, the larger the system in which you are functioning, the greater the probability that whatever you decide to do will be disastrous. But what Gall says is amusingly ludicrous; his book is a witty satire that is very consoling to anyone who has ever tried in vain to accomplish something in a large organization.

Whether or not you believe in Murphy's Law, there are serious reasons for trying to work out scenarios in order to see clearly and dramatically in your mind's eye the most probable disasters and the most probable gains that could ensue if the risks on one side or the other were to materialize. In the above example, the scenario for choosing the most attractive alternative involves the calculated risk of a relatively sudden dramatic disaster, whereas the calculated risk for not choosing that alternative is a long-drawn-out tragedy that could be just as bad or worse. Our choices are often structured in just that way.

It is not quite correct to speak of all undesirable scenarios as involving disaster. We have just pointed out that the second of the two above scenarios involves regret about having missed the opportunity to obtain gains or rewards by marrying your lover. For all sorts of vital decisions, it often happens that there are many such *opportunity costs.* In other words, with every alternative you decide *not* to choose you always run the risk of losing some precious gains or advantages. A full scenario about what could cause you to regret making one choice rather than another should therefore include the risks of failing to make use of opportunities for attaining rewards or gains, as well as risks of suffering losses.

What are the advantages that make it worthwhile to work out those gloomy scenarios? They are unpleasant to think about so why not just give them a quick glance? Why dwell on them? For one thing, if we don't, we remain unaware of exactly what kind of information we need. In the last example, a central problem is estimating the chances of recurrence of a depressive episode, which requires expert information from psychiatrists and clinical psychologists. Since there are likely to be differences in the forecasts made by such experts when it comes to judging any single case, it would be prudent to consult more than one such expert in order to determine the consensus of informed opinion.

For other kinds of decisions, you may have to deal with other kinds of experts, including some who do not try to live up to a code of professional standards designed to protect the public.

When you think about buying a particularly attractive house, but you hear a rumor that the neighborhood might be ruined by a stinking factory to be put up nearby, you might ask the real estate agent whether the nearby tract of land has been sold and if so to whom and for what purpose. If you get misleading information, you might make the mistake of buying the house without knowing that the tract has already been purchased by industrialists planning to put up an undesirable factory that will decrease property values.

Or, if the supposed expert is ill informed, you might make the mistake of deciding not to buy the home without knowing that the tract has already been sold to business people who are going to put up a desirable shopping center that will increase property values.

Chapter 8 deals with the problems of finding appropriate experts and making the most of what they have to offer. Specific guidelines are presented for asking experts the crucial questions you need to have answered and for getting information that is as reliable as possible.

Participating in groups and negotiating

Sometimes generating alternatives and assessing the consequences of each alternative can best be done by working together with one or more other persons in a group. One person's weaknesses—his or her areas of ignorance, blind spots, and biases—might be compensated for by another's strengths. We have already given several examples of the typical personal decisions on which you are likely to work together with a partner to arrive at a mutually satisfactory choice. At work and in social clubs or community organizations, you may from time to time find yourself having the opportunity to participate in a decision made by perhaps six to ten people, all of whom are members of an executive committee or a board of directors. Perhaps you have noticed that although there are some obvious advantages to working collectively on a decision, there are some disadvantages that may not be so obvious.

Chapter 9 discusses the main problems of participating in a group decision. It concentrates on a paradoxical phenomenon of group psychology known as *groupthink*. When bright and shrewd people are working together on a decision, the stronger their "we-feelings" of solidarity, the greater the likelihood that independent critical thinking and careful assessement of consequences will be replaced by a tendency to concur on a course of action that will preserve the unity of the group. Several dramatic examples of group decisions are given to illustrate various causal factors, such as directive leadership and isolation of the group, that contribute to the groupthink tendency. A number of specific suggestions are offered to prevent groupthink and to prevent other detrimental group reactions that can keep the members of a decision-making group from making full use of their potential for making effective decisions.

When marital partners or the members of a policy-making group disagree about the best course of action, it may be essential to negotiate in order to arrive at a mutually satisfactory compromise. Earlier in this chapter we gave an example of a husband and wife who want to have two quite different kinds of holidays and are trying to decide on the choice of a trip that will be satisfactory to both. In another example, a husband and wife are trying to decide whether to use a large bonus to buy a new car, to make certain home improvements, or to build up their joint savings account. If they were to disagree, they would have to work out some kind of compromise. In all such instances, if the partners are inept at negotiating, they could come to a disagreeable stalemate and end up feeling resentful toward each other even after arriving at some kind of settlement of their dispute. But such negotiations are relatively easy compared with negotiations between people who have widely divergent values and who are only weakly affiliated with each other, if at all. If you have ever served as a representative of one organization trying to negotiate with representatives of a rival organization (for example, in a legal dispute or in collective bargaining intended to settle a labor–management dispute) you probably know exactly what we are talking about.

There are also some in-between situations in which negotiating can be a pretty sticky business, often resulting in mutual recrimination rather than mutual satisfaction. In our very first example of alternative scenarios for typical personal dilemmas, we sketched out three different futures for a situation where your boss is going to quit. The best of the three was one in which you respond to the challenge by lining up another job, which would put you in a strong position when it comes to negotiating with your superiors about staying on. But, of course, in a delicate situation of this kind, if you were to negotiate unskillfully, you might "blow it" and lose the opportunity to get a better job.

Chapter 10 is devoted to the ticklish problems that arise when you need to negotiate, whether in a one-to-one face-off with a spouse, a business partner, a boss, a personal adversary, or as a member of an official negotiating team meeting with representatives of a rival organization. There are certain rules for effective negotiating that seem to apply across all those different situations. These rules are discussed and illustrated with cogent examples, together with a number of related suggestions designed to help readers improve their skill whenever they have to participate in arriving at a joint decision that requires negotiating.

At the end of the book we try to extract the most useful recommendations for improving the quality of your decision making. But instead of giving a conventional summary, we present in Chapter 11 the major myths that block sound decision making. Then we summarize in Chapter 12 the stages in the form of a guide for helping someone make a sound decision. That someone could be a member of your family, a friend, your boss, your subordinates in a business organization—or it could be yourself.

In every chapter of this book we attempt to make you more aware of your decision-making processes as they occur. You will be able to spot some of the common pitfalls in time to avoid them. You will also learn some new techniques for accomplishing the essential tasks of each essential stage. We believe that you will be able to improve your decision-making skills and increase your chances of success in all the decisions you make.

2
Accepting the Challenge

Decision making begins with a challenge. Something happens that makes it necessary to make a decision. A new plan must be devised. Sometimes the challenge is so direct and powerful that it makes the current course of action impossible. For example, when a firm went bankrupt and the employees were laid off with only a few hours notice, they simply could not ignore the challenge and had to start thinking immediately about what to do.

Direct challenges are frequently preceded by more subtle challenges that give warning of an impending crisis. In this case, the employees had known that the business had been losing money for over a year. The shop manager had told them to cut down on waste and luxuries in order to make the company profitable. The delays in receiving needed parts until the company paid in cash could have alerted them to the financial crisis. Some employees had heard through the grapevine that the bank had turned down a loan for the company. Each of these messages had provided a challenge or warning to the employees. If they had accepted any of the repeated challenges before the final crisis, they could have made a preliminary decision to invest time and effort in searching for alternatives. They might have been able to get out before the bankruptcy occurred. If they didn't at least they could have had the advantage of advance planning.

For every important decision there is an optimal time to make it. The optimal time is early enough so that there is plenty of time to make the decision yet late enough so that the situation is clear and the information necessary for the decision is available. When an unavoidable challenge occurs, such as a bankruptcy, the optimal time for decision making has usually already passed. Thus the first step in effective decision making is to recognize the early warning signals and to begin the decision-making process at the optimal time.

Hindsight is always clearer than foresight. When the company went bankrupt many of the employees were shocked. Yet after they thought about it they remembered all the warning signs and realized that they should have been able to see that the situation was serious enough to warrant doing something about it before the crisis. Their foresight could have been improved if they had stopped to think about the meaning of the early challenges as they occurred.

Challenges from opportunities

Challenges come from opportunities as well as from danger signals. Opportunities usually do not knock very loudly, and missing a golden opportunity can be just as unfortunate as missing a red-alert warning.

Signals of opportunities come in many forms. A neighbor may mention to a business executive that a new plant is opening in the area. If the executive waits until the announcement appears in the newspaper a competitor may already have a contract for services to the new plant. A couple looking for a house in a specific neighborhood might hear that someone was transferred to another city. The house might never be advertised for sale because someone else responded to the opportunity by making a direct offer to the current owners. A student looking for a part-time job may hear that a professor has received a large grant. Part-time jobs are always in demand on campus and are soon filled. In all of these cases, if a person does not move quickly to find out more about the possibility and to decide whether he or she wants it, the opportunity will be lost.

Sometimes opportunity doesn't knock but is still right at hand. You always have the opportunity to take stock of yourself, to reassess your career, your life style, your goals, your relationships with other people, and everything else about you. The possibility (and opportunity) of change is always there. The optimal time for considering these opportunities may sometimes be before specific challenges begin to occur. We recommend that you periodically take stock of yourself to see whether it is time to take the opportunity to change something deliberately.

The stress of decision making

Why are people reluctant to accept the challenge provided by a warning signal? One reason is that active decision making is stressful. Everyone agonizes over important decisions. We become cross, irritable, and upset, especially when the consequences are serious and the uncertainty is great. It is natural to attempt to avoid going through the stress of decision making. Sometimes ignoring a challenge works—the problem goes away by itself. Unfortunately, ignoring a challenge often leads to a more powerful challenge that cannot be ignored and must be dealt with under crisis conditions.

Everyone feels the stress of decision making to some extent. But some people are more bothered by it than others. They may be mildly upset trying to decide where to go for a vacation and panic-stricken by their major life decisions. This gives them more reason to ignore challenges. Ignoring challenges puts them into a vicious circle. It ensures that all their decisions will be made under crisis conditions. The resulting trauma will make them even more reluctant to begin active decision making when faced with the next challenge.

Is there any way out of this vicious circle? For some people an important reason for their insecurity in decision making is their feeling of inadequacy and incompetence. Learning about effective decision making may be sufficient to give them the confidence that they can do better—not always, of course, but often enough to make it worth trying. This book can be used as a step-by-step guide through the decision-making process. It doesn't take so much confidence to move one step at a time. These steps can lead anyone out of the vicious circle. The first step is to recognize a challenge when it occurs.

Is the challenge real?

Many warning signs occur without danger ever materializing. The weather bureau issues tornado warnings more often than tornadoes actually occur. Some apparent warning messages we see on television or in newspapers are gross exaggerations that are deliberately played up for propagandistic or commercial reasons. Others are merely intended for routine drills and have no actual connection with here-and-now danger. In some cities, air raid sirens are tested at noon on the first Friday of each month. When this occurs it is not actually a warning of anything. But to people who do not know this, it is a potential warning of serious danger. Some of the routine announcements by public health officials and financial experts may also sound like warnings when they really are not. How can we distinguish between real warnings and apparent warnings?

Exactly the same problem occurs in attempting to distinguish between real and apparent opportunities. The chance to buy "a $200 full-range high fidelity speaker" for only half price may turn out to be merely an opportunity to pay $100 for a $25 piece of junk. Even when no one is urging us not to miss the opportunity of a lifetime there is a good chance that what seems to be an opportunity for success is only an opportunity for failure. But if you take this attitude toward all the opportunities that come along you will fail to see and take advantage of the true opportunities when you encounter them.

If we could accurately forecast the future, determining whether a challenge is real would be easy. But even when a great deal of relevant scientific information is available, we can't tell precisely what will happen. Specific predictions about the future are notoriously inaccurate, especially in the realm of human affairs.

Fortunately we can make valid probability estimates about future events, at least in terms of rough categories such as low, moderate, and high. We can tell what will probably happen, and we can sometimes tell when unlikely events will become more likely to occur. For example, someone planning to buy a house in the suburbs realizes that the world energy crisis that became apparent during the late 1970s has made it more likely that fuel oil and gasoline may suddenly not be available when needed. Business executives planning to start a manufacturing plant or to open a retail store also need to take account of shortages in energy sources and to develop contingency plans to overcome problems likely to occur in times of energy crises. Similar examples could be given about all sorts of other precautions people take to avoid damage to their health, finances, and social standing.

What does it take to make these kinds of inferences about the future? It certainly doesn't take any complicated reasoning process. Once you begin to think about the future, you can draw upon common knowledge. One way to be responsive to important challenges

is to make a regular practice of thinking about and collecting information pertinent to the future consequences of events. A current
energy crisis, for example, can stimulate business executives to
think ahead about the consequences of other types of energy shortages. Thinking about these shortages can, in turn, suggest considering shortages in other things as well, such as raw materials, investment capital, skilled labor, and so on. The purpose of this kind of
thinking is to be prepared for the challenges that are most likely to
occur. It is equally important not to become obsessed with the dangers in a way that paralyzes action.

What goes wrong with decision making?

Four basic coping patterns can appear when people are faced
with challenges that require decisions. The pattern that appears depends primarily on their beliefs about the situation. Only when
people believe that the risks involved in the decision are serious and
that they can find a satisfactory solution do they follow an active
strategy of searching for alternatives and evaluating each one. The
other three basic patterns—complacency, defensive avoidance,
and panic—lead to serious flaws.

Complacency

Complacency results when people don't see the signs of approaching danger or when they ignore them. They continue with
their plans oblivious to the fact that they probably will run into
trouble, like a horse with blinders trotting toward the edge of a
cliff. When people are given warnings of possible disasters they
sometimes do not believe the danger is real and take the attitude
that "It won't happen to me." During a multiple tornado episode in
Cincinnati, college students refused to take shelter in the inner
parts of the lower floors. Instead, some of them watched the storm
from the windows at the top of their high-rise dormitory. Fortunately none of the tornadoes hit the campus area, but in stricken
neighborhoods nearby other people who made similar decisions
were injured or killed.

This pattern of nonresponse to challenging information is not
limited to community disaster situations. Many middle-aged men
and women who have high blood pressure know that they should

get more exercise, stop smoking, and eat less fat in order to avoid heart disease. But they do not take the warnings seriously and continue unchanged in their unhealthy way of life. Students who obtain very low grades in basic chemistry courses and still continue to plan to go to medical school are showing the same pattern.

Complacency also occurs when people don't respond to an opportunity. That is like a horse that trots past a pile of delicious oats on the way to a trough with only a few wisps of hay.

Complacency can occur even when people seem to be responding to a challenge. Sometimes people grab the first alternative that comes along that seems to satisfy the demands of the situation. This way of meeting the original challenge leads to complacency about the new plan. Consider what happens, for example, when employees fearing reprimand for a blunder confidently decide they can get away with it by lying, without realizing that the lie can easily be detected and will lead to even worse consequences. In such cases they do see the future consequences of their original plan but they don't look at the future consequences of their *new* plan, which might also have serious dangers. They make their decision without thinking about the potential consequences and without looking for other alternatives. Examples of this occur among people who rapidly remarry after getting a divorce. They switch from one unpleasant marriage to another because the relief of escaping from the first marriage blinds them to the signs that there will be lots of disadvantages to the new marriage. These disadvantages may turn out to be worse than the problems with the first one. This type of complacency is also shown by men and women who immediately accept an offer of what appears to be a better job with more opportunity for advancement without spending any time or effort to find out what they might be letting themselves in for.

Of course, for many apparent challenges, especially when nothing much is at stake, complacency is entirely appropriate. It is justified whenever there are no serious risks in failing to make the best choice among alternatives or when there is no reason to believe dire warnings of disaster. When people see a crudely written poster announcing that the end of the world is coming on next Tuesday, they certainly need not waste their time trying to figure out what to do about it. A common example of complacent acceptance of a change in plans that is appropriate would be when a policeman asks people to take a detour because the road is in danger of being flooded. Complacency is a sign of poor decision making only when the person jumps to the conclusion that there is no need to worry about a genuine threat or the loss of a genuine opportunity without any attempt to make a realistic appraisal.

Defensive avoidance

Recognizing the challenge as indicating a real danger or opportunity is not enough to guarantee that people will begin active decision making to cope with the challenge. People often see a danger and yet do nothing about it. This is most likely to happen when they believe that there is no way to avoid the danger. Unless people have some hope that there is a solution and believe that they have a chance to find it they are unlikely to begin the search. Instead, they follow a pattern of *defensive avoidance.* They deny the importance of the danger, or at least their responsibility for doing something about it. At the same time that they accept the reality of the challenge, they may deny its relevance to themselves.

Three different strategies are used for defensive avoidance, all of which involve wishful thinking. To avoid thinking about what should be done to deal with a serious threat people may resort to

1. Rationalization ("It can't happen to me.")
2. Procrastination ("Nothing needs to be done about it now, I can take care of it later.")
3. Buck passing ("I am not the one who needs to do something about it, let George do it.").

These strategies can be used alone or in combination to give people the feeling that they don't need to make any new plans to take account of a serious challenge. The choice of a defensive avoidance strategy, which often is not made consciously, depends a lot on the specific situation. It is difficult for an executive to pass the buck if he has been given clear-cut responsibility to work out a new policy. But it is quite easy to not do anything when an executive's responsibilities are poorly defined and overlap with those of others in the organization. Similar circumstances make it easy for a husband to pass the buck to his wife and vice versa when the challenge involves a family problem such as their child's failing in school.

Rationalization. This form of defensive avoidance consists of developing and clinging to beliefs that ignore or distort available information on the basis of what the decision makers wish were the case rather than relying on the evidence. Rationalizing is extremely common in all stages of decision making and often leads decision makers to have the illusion that they are doing a good job when, in fact, they are using poor procedures that sooner or later will result in gross miscalculations. Policy makers show this form of defensive avoidance when they develop justifications for their drastic actions that sound good but aren't based on careful appraisals. Some political analysts argue that this was the main flaw of "the best and the brightest" who were making policy decisions in Washington during the Vietnam war (see the discussion of groupthink in Chapter 9).

Rationalizations usually have some basis in reality. Although there may be good reasons for believing in the truth of the rationalization, something is always left out; the reasons are not the *whole* truth. A subtle rationalization can be very hard to distinguish from a sound justification.

A further difficulty is that people are blind to their own rationalizations. It usually takes someone else with a different point of view to spot possible rationalizations. In order to detect their own rationalizations people must be able to switch to other perspectives and look back at the reasons they are using to justify what they are doing. This is difficult to do. Nevertheless, recent research indicates that by using some fairly simple techniques people can become aware of inconsistencies in their own beliefs and even recognize that they are clinging to some comfortable beliefs without being able to justify them. In one study, for example, heavy smokers were asked to explore their "basic deep-down thoughts and feelings" about giving up smoking. They were then shown a list of eight statements which were typical rationalizations made by heavy smokers and were asked to see if they could recognize any of them as excuses they might be using for not taking health warnings seriously. As compared with a control group of heavy smokers given exactly the same information, the ones given the acknowledgment-of-rationalizations procedure showed a marked increase in concern about the harmfulness of smoking. They reported feeling much more vulnerable to the threat of both lung cancer and emphysema and expressed greater readiness to try to cut down.

The case of Mr. Bury, a mid-level executive in a large manufacturing firm, illustrates the variety of rationalizations someone might use to avoid dealing with a challenge. Mr. Bury works as a section leader in the development division of a large corporation. He has worked closely with his division chief in the reorganization of the division. The reorganization accomplished a lot, but the division head made many enemies in the process. Mr. Bury is regarded as a protege of the chief. Now the chief is involved in a conflict with higher management so serious that he has threatened to resign. Privately, the chief has told Mr. Bury that he is looking for another job and may leave even if the conflict is resolved in his favor. If the chief leaves, there is likely to be another reorganization and this would make Mr. Bury's situation difficult. He may even lose his job.

Does Mr. Bury start making plans to avoid these difficulties? No, he manages to persuade himself that the danger is not real. He reasons that if the chief leaves, the conflict with higher management will be resolved and the division will prosper (exaggerating advantages). He assumes that any reorganization that occurs is not very likely to touch him (minimizing drawbacks). He believes that having a new head of the division with whom he doesn't have a close relation will make him more independent (denying bad consequences). He thinks that plenty of time will elapse before there will be another reorganization (exaggerating remoteness). He tells himself that there is no reason why others in his section should expect him to be able to protect them in case the reorganization occurs and in this way minimizes the likelihood that the members of his section will show their displeasure if he does nothing (minimizing social consequences). Finally, he feels that he cannot plan to do anything about the impending crisis until higher management decides what to do about the head of his division (avoiding personal responsibility).

Each of these rationalizations is part of Mr. Bury's strategy of defensive avoidance. It will succeed for a while, enabling him to avoid the worry and bother of having to work on making a decision. Eventually, another, much stronger challenge will occur that cannot be denied. If Mr. Bury is lucky he may still be able to find a workable solution, but it may be too late.

Studying the common types of rationalization might make it a little easier for you to recognize that certain of your own beliefs need to be reconsidered carefully and perhaps brought more in line with reality. Mr. Bury used six major tactics for rationalizing. These are explained below with different examples.

- *Exaggerating advantages.* To play up the advantages of a choice, we may take a small gain and overestimate its importance. For example, in deciding to accept a job we may overestimate the importance of the fact that we already know a few people who work for the same company.
- *Minimizing drawbacks.* We may persuade ourselves that the disadvantages are less serious than they actually are. A college graduate looking for a good job may consider a high salary sufficient compensation for the routine work that will often be required. At the time such a job is offered, many applicants invent plausible-sounding reasons for ignoring the likelihood that they will be working on uninteresting tasks that will make them constantly dissatisfied with the job.

  Another way to minimize drawbacks is to believe that if things go badly we can always change our minds later. We may ignore the trouble and costs involved in changing again, including the danger that a disgruntled boss will not write a favorable letter of recommendation, and that employers are generally suspicious of people who are looking for a new position shortly after having started on a job.

  Finally, minimizing drawbacks includes minimizing the advantages of the other choices that are being given up. This is "sour grapes" reasoning. We may conclude that the more pleasant social atmosphere of an unchosen job is not very important because the employees there probably do not get promoted as quickly. We may belittle the friendly atmosphere in this way without any good evidence about the prospects for being promoted.
- *Denying bad consequences.* Disadvantages can be turned into advantages with some quick mental gymnastics. If a job is

dangerous, we can reason that it is an exhilarating challenge. Thus the bad feature is turned into a good one. For some people this would not be a rationalization; they really value the excitement of a dangerous job. But for others the danger is a disadvantage that is denied by their rationalizations.

- *Exaggerating remoteness.* Events far in the future don't seem important. Too much can happen and the events may never occur. We can rationalize a choice by considering the costs or undesirable consequences to be part of the distant future where things don't matter, ignoring the obvious fact that eventually the future becomes the present. People frequently use this type of rationalization when they buy with credit. Merchants take advantage of this type of rationalization by advertising "No payment until after Christmas" or "Fly now, pay later."

- *Minimizing social consequences.* We sometimes think that our decisions will remain secret and that no one will know about them. We ignore the social consequences that may come from the disapproval of our friends and the social pressures that may occur to get us to stick to the commitment we have made. For example, a progressive who goes to work for a reactionary organization may tell herself that her friends won't realize or won't pay any attention to the type of company she is working for.

- *Avoiding personal responsibility.* We may claim that we have no choice, that external pressures are wholly to blame for our decision. Using this tactic for rationalization, we can claim that we did not really want to make the choice we did, but there was nothing else we could do. An employee's decision to misrepresent the product he is trying to sell can be blamed either on other people ("The boss makes me do it," for example) or on the impersonal situation ("We have to do it to survive the financial crisis").

The same types of rationalizations can be used to deny opportunities as well as dangers. You may fail to assert yourself by telling yourself "I don't really want it that much" or "It wouldn't be worth the effort" or "It wouldn't be proper for me to ask for that." These rationalizations are just as destructive in their effect as those that deny dangers, but the damage they do is much less obvious.

As this analysis shows, rationalizations can be very complex and devious. They are another demonstration of the powerful creativity of the human mind. It is unfortunate when creativity is used in defensive avoidance to prevent effective decision making.

The other two tactics of defensive avoidance are less complex. But they are equally common and equally effective in blocking the beginning of the active decision-making process.

Procrastination. This is the second main tactic of defensive avoidance. It is especially likely to occur when there is no clear deadline for responding to the challenge. For example, people frequently don't do anything about swellings that could be early symptoms of cancer, even though they know that these symptoms could be danger signals. They try not to think about their symptoms and stay away from their physicians and others who could tell them what the symptoms may mean. In the typical pattern of defensive procrastination, we avoid thinking about a problem and don't actively seek relevant information. Although we may realize that we shall have to deal with the problem eventually, we don't even take note of useful information we may happen to get so that we'll have it when we need it. To acknowledge that information will be useful in the future is to acknowledge the reality of the problem right now. This type of procrastination is more than just not doing anything. It involves refusing to deal with a challenge or anything connected with it. For instance, when people are told by their doctors that they will probably have to have an operation they may suddenly stop listening and avoid obtaining any further information. They turn off the television or put down the magazine when they come across something relevant that reminds them of their condition. This active refusal to focus on the problem or to work on it is a common form of defensive procrastination.

Buck passing. This is the third tactic of defensive avoidance. It consists of turning the decision over to someone else. It is a common occupational disease in bureaucratic organizations. The responsibility for a decision can be pushed up, down, or sideways in an organization. Large organizations are not necessary for the buck to be passed; two people are enough. Husbands and wives may maneuver to get the other to make decisions. The "victor" avoids the stress of making the decision and can blame the spouse if anything goes wrong.

Buck passing is especially common in situations where there is ambiguity about who has the responsibility for the decision. In fact, in some situations turning the decision over to other people is appropriate, because they actually do have the responsibility for making the choice. But when the decision has been made at a higher level, the people at the lower level still have their own responsibility to decide whether to accept and to implement the decision. The fact that the decision was made above them will not absolve them if anything goes wrong.

In the early days of the Watergate coverup conspiracy in the Nixon administration, a number of high-level aides and assistants, including John Dean, Jeb Magruder, Herbert Kalmbach, Dwight Chapin, and many others, assumed that their acts of perjury or obstruction of justice were not illegal and were fully justified because they were responding to requests that came from the White House. Most of them were surprised when they learned that they were personally culpable and would be sent to jail. But despite the lessons of Watergate, some employees in government and business organizations still make the same kind of mistaken assumption.

None of the three patterns of defensive avoidance is effective in the long run. All three enable people to avoid the stress of decision making temporarily, but they all set up conditions for the emergence of more serious problems later. Both rationalization and procrastination result in nothing being done. Buck passing may result in some decision being implemented, but often not the one that would have been best for the people who should have decided.

Complacency and defensive avoidance are similar in that in both cases people are not actively making a decision when they should be. The difference is in the underlying beliefs and in what it takes to change them. People who really believe that there is no real threat are complacent. They are relaxed and feel no stress. People who believe in the reality of a threat but who believe that they can't cope with it show defensive avoidance. They avoid facing up to their dilemmas by indulging in wishful thinking. They become anxious whenever anyone talks about the threat. They sometimes show signs of stress, but their anxiety may be controlled and hidden most of the time so that they often appear outwardly calm. Some are even able to hide the stress of their own awareness. Only when they are forced to deal with some aspect of a threatening situation does anxiety appear.

Panic and paniclike reactions

The third basic pattern of decision making is panic or near-panic. It occurs when people are faced with an immediate threat and they believe that there is not enough time to find a satisfactory solution. When panic or near-panic is the dominant pattern, people are so upset that they search frantically for a way out of the dilemma and seize upon a hastily contrived solution. They may rapidly shift back and forth between alternatives. The state of panic or near-panic, which psychologists refer to as "hypervigilance," can prevent people from noticing the serious drawbacks of some alternatives and the availability of other alternatives. For example, in a panic during a fire people may go right past a plainly marked exit while rushing toward an exit jammed with people.

Fortunately, mass panics during community disasters are not very common, in spite of the vivid portrayals of wild stampedes in fiction and films about catastrophes. People generally rise to the occasion during a disaster. Paniclike reactions are more likely when we have to make personal decisions after a crisis has passed. Even when there is no physical danger at all, a person who has to make a personal decision, such as whether or not to try to cover up a horrible error in his work, sometimes makes an ill-considered choice in a state of near-panic. People who are in a panic or near-panic state generally show signs of a temporary impairment in cognitive functioning, such as simplistic thinking and a reduction in immediate memory span. The fear aroused by the threat interferes with the quality of their thinking, which prevents them from seeing all the complicated consequences of what they have chosen and also prevents them from keeping in mind the large number of considerations necessary for making a sound choice among the various alternatives that may be available. This can happen when people have only a very short time to decide whether or not to do what their physician, lawyer, or investment counselor recommends to avert an imminent personal disaster.

Paniclike reactions can be regarded as the extreme opposite of complacency. Worry-warts respond to too many things as challenges. They always assume that the worst is going to happen. An anonymous wit once claimed that two types can be distinguished: an optimistic worry-wart, after reading the financial news, says, "A year from now all of us will be borrowing or begging," whereas a pessimistic one asks, "From whom?"

Hypochondriacs are medical worry-warts who assume that each little ache or pain is a sure sign of cancer or a heart attack. It is usually sensible, of course, to observe worrisome symptoms and to be prepared for some probable difficulty even though it does not occur. But worrying about false challenges creates unnecessary misery and interferes with effective decision making.

Milder paniclike reactions occur in individual, nondisaster situations whenever people feel that the deadline for the decision is very close and are worried that whichever choice they make could have bad consequences. For instance, when people are heavily in debt and lose their job as a result of a general lay-off, they may get into near-panic states in their attempts to find another job immediately. In their excited state they may accept the first offer they get. Failing to notice subtle signs that they would normally take seriously, they may be blind to the disadvantages of the new job. If they weren't in a near-panic state, even without having any additional time, they could see the potential disadvantages, think about their implications, and perhaps find some way to tide themselves over while looking for a better offer. There is such a thing as constructive procrastination. Whereas the defensive procrastinator evokes the conventional admonition from family and friends, "Don't just sit there, do something!" the panicky decision maker warrants the reverse admonition, "Don't do anything, just sit there!"

Deadlines for decisions are often more flexible than people think they are. It is often possible to get a deadline changed to allow adequate time for decision making. For instance, an overworked suburbanite facing a decision about replacing his car after a major breakdown of the engine could rent one for a few days to give him time to consider carefully which one of several different models to buy. Renting a car costs money, but it may cost less in the long run than a hasty decision made in a near-panic.

Changing a deadline is not always a good idea. If the purpose is to enable the person to postpone a decision after he or she already has obtained practically all the relevant information and has had plenty of time to mull it over, the cost of the delay will have to be paid without any benefits from improved decision making. Procrastination in the face of a serious challenge is constructive only when it is used to obtain time for more thorough decision making.

Prevention is the best cure for panic. If, in response to an early challenge, you consider the risks seriously, you are less likely to find yourself in a tight deadline situation. Realizing in advance what is likely to happen can help you avoid overreacting when serious difficulty arises.

Decision by default

The three defective patterns of decision making—complacency, defensive avoidance, and panic—all lead to decisions by default. When people display these patterns they never get to the later stages of the active decision-making process and they lose the advantages they could have gained by making a decision carefully and deliberately. As long as complacency and defensive avoidance continue, people do nothing. Panicky decision makers do something, but frequently the emotional excitement results in gross miscalculations that could have been avoided by going through the later stages of active decision making.

Effective decision makers end the first stage by accepting a realistic challenge, by deciding to decide. They go on to search actively for better alternatives and to deliberate carefully about them. Other pitfalls may trap them in later stages, but none is as dangerous as decision by default. The pattern of effective decision making occurs only when decision makers believe (1) that the risks are serious, (2) that they can find a solution, and (3) that there is enough time. When these three conditions are met at the end of stage 1, people can go through an active decision-making process that results in an effective search for alternatives (Stage 2) and a careful evaluation of the available alternatives (Stage 3). Further, they evaluate the information in a relatively *unbiased* way. They also work out implementation plans and contingency plans (in case one or another of the risks materializes) before they commit themselves (Stage 4). In contrast, those who display complacency, defensive avoidance, or near-panic are unprepared for even minor setbacks during Stage 5. They develop strong feelings of regret and are much less likely to stick to their decision, even though changing may be quite costly in terms of time, money, and reputation. Many of the suggestions we present throughout this book pertain to counteracting the conditions that lead to defective decision making. All too often it is difficult for a person to relinquish a defective coping strategy. Nevertheless, there is reason to believe that practically everyone can learn to improve his or her decision-making skills and that knowledge about those skills can help to provide the confidence necessary to do well on decision-making tasks.

Taking stock of yourself

We believe that becoming aware of the pitfalls of ignoring major threats or opportunities will make you more alert to the possibility that you may be about to fall into one. To increase your awareness, we recommend that you periodically take stock of yourself. Ask yourself how you are doing in the major areas of your life, such as your relationships with others, your health, your job, and anything else that is important to you. What do you want in each of these areas? What are you doing about each of these goals? What have you done since your last stock taking? What decisions do you need to make about the future?

You should look outward as well as inward for challenges that might require active decision making. What is happening in the world around you that will have an effect on you? What is changing that will force a change in your life? Are there signs of danger to your relationships, your health, your job? Are there hints of opportunities that might be actively pursued in any of these areas?

Other questions can help you ward off procrastination. Why not now? If not now, when?

The result of the stock taking should be to focus your attention on those areas that you need to do something about. You can then accept the challenge and go through the stages of active decision making to find the best way to meet your needs.

Screening challenges

Obviously we can't expect ourselves to be responsive to all, or even to the majority of apparent challenges that we encounter day after day. If we were, we would have little time to do anything but reevaluate our past decisions. On the other hand, if we were to ignore practically all challenges until they actually materialize, we would leave ourselves open to one avoidable crisis after another, which would require us to make many urgent decisions by default, without enough time for adequate search and appraisal. The point is that we have to be highly discriminating about the potential challenges we accept and those we reject, using as many sound criteria as we can to screen all the various bits of information that warn us about losses we are likely to suffer or that make us aware of the promise of opportunities for gain that we might fail to realize if we don't change to a new course of action.

No definitive rules are available for screening challenges. But there are a few key questions you can ask yourself that may serve as guidelines each time you encounter a message containing impressive information about a threat or an opportunity.

The big question, of course, is whether or not you should take the alleged threat or opportunity seriously enough to start thinking about what you are going to do about it. This big question can be broken down into a set of smaller questions, each of which contributes to appraising a potential challenge as valid and as sufficiently important and urgent to warrant response.

Here are the key questions you can use as a guide to screen potential warnings, such as a vivid news story indicating that industrial pollution that might affect your neighborhood can cause severe illness or a disturbing rumor at your place of work that people in jobs like yours might be laid off soon.

Appraising credibility of information
- Is my source in a position to know the truth?
- If so, is my source likely to be honest or dishonest? (For example, is he trying to sell something or to make scare propaganda for his own purposes?)
- Is any evidence given that makes the predicted threat seem plausible and, if so, how good is the evidence?

- If there are serious doubts about the credibility of the information, is there a trustworthy source who could easily be consulted—someone who is an impartial expert or someone who would be willing to give inside information? (For example, a friend in the top management office might know whether the rumor about impending layoffs is true.)

Importance of the threat
- If there is some real danger, how likely is it to materialize?
- How likely is it to affect me or people I care about?
- How severe might the losses be?

Urgency
- If the danger is likely to materialize and lead to serious losses, might it happen soon or is it unlikely to occur for a long time to come?
- Even if it is likely to occur soon, will the danger develop gradually so that there would be ample time to plan protective actions if I wait to see what happens? Or is the danger likely to come on so suddenly that I will be caught short and be unable to protect myself if I postpone doing anything about it?
- If some immediate planning of protective action is urgent, could I do just a part of it now and safely postpone the rest until the first signs of danger appear?

It is seldom necessary to ask yourself all the above questions and there is no need to ask them in this sequence. Sometimes asking yourself only one or two of the questions is sufficient to dismiss a warning as just so much hot air or as too trivial to bother with. It is worthwhile to ask all the above questions only when a warning is very impressive and is starting to get through to you.

The same can be said for the equivalent questions that can be used as guidelines for screening challenges that pertain to new *opportunities*. Essentially the same three sets of questions are pertinent, but in some instances, of course, the wording has to be changed somewhat. The final question about the importance of the opportunity, for example, would be "How great might the gains be?"

If you deliberately train yourself to make use of these questions, especially for the most impressive warnings about possible losses and the most impressive promises of possible gains, you may be able

to cut down on the number of errors you make in screening challenges. You may still make serious errors, sometimes ignoring a really serious challenge that should have been taken seriously and sometimes overreacting to an inauthentic, unimportant, or nonurgent
challenge that should have been ignored. The value of asking yourself these questions can be completely undermined if you give
biased answers that express what you would like to believe rather
than what you really think is true. At times you may have to be
somewhat skeptical about whether you are being honest with yourself and perhaps suspect yourself of giving rationalizations if you see
signs that you might be indulging in wishful thinking rather than
making an objective appraisal. Nevertheless, you can probably do a
somewhat better job at screening challenges than you have been doing if you conscientiously attempt to give honest answers to the
three sets of questions about the credibility, importance, and urgency of the potential threats and opportunities that momentarily
capture your attention.

3
Searching for Alternatives

After people accept a challenge in the first stage of decision making, in the next stage they figure out their alternatives. They search for the choices available to them for meeting the challenge. Unfortunately these searches often miss good alternatives unless the decision makers deliberately try to make a thorough search for them. People often ignore alternatives because they follow conventional or unconventional advice, some of it more colorful than sound, like the three fundamental rules offered by a convict: "Never play cards with a man called Doc. Never eat at a place called Mom's. Never sleep with a woman whose troubles are worse than your own."

Missing good alternatives

When it comes to making a vital decision about your career, love life, finances, health, or recreations, you may usually believe that you are considering all the promising alternatives that are open to you. You are right in the sense that you aren't leaving out any choices that you *know* about. The catch is that you cannot know that you are leaving out good alternatives without knowing that those alternatives exist. For instance, if your flight to Paris is canceled you might accept an inconvenient substitute. But a nonscheduled group flight might be departing for Paris just when you want to leave and might still have a few seats available. As long as you think you know all the alternatives, you are unlikely to ask about flights not listed on the printed schedules.

Can we ever know that we have considered all the possible choices? Probably not. Even when it looks like the choices are limited to a definite small set, it is conceivable that other alternatives could be found by looking at the situation in another way.

At any of the later stages of decision making, if it appears that none of the choices is desirable, it is reasonable to go back to Stage 2 and attempt to find new choices to consider. Of course, it would save time and emotional wear and tear if the other choices were found the first time through Stage 2. One obvious way to avoid overlooking good alternatives in the early stages of making a vital decision is to talk freely about it to everyone who is willing to give free advice, whether or not they have any expertise. Nonexperts sometimes make excellent suggestions and are even likely to be grateful for being given the opportunity to say something useful.

What are your goals?

Before you can search for alternative ways to achieve your goals, you must know what your goals are. The challenge that provokes you to start making a new decision does not usually tell you what your various goals are; all it usually indicates is that your current course of action or inaction is running into trouble or won't work. If your current plan is directed toward some specific goals, these goals can serve as a starting place for examining the full range of objectives for the new decision.

In the example of the canceled flight to Paris we assumed that the other alternatives were other flights to the same city. But someone—let's call him Kevin—might be planning to spend half his time on the Riviera. His main goal might be specifically to have a relaxed vacation at a pleasant seaside resort as well as to see some foreign places he has never been to. Kevin's list of alternatives might include flights to other foreign resorts, such as those in Bermuda, Puerto Rico, and Mexico. Someone else—let's call her Brenda— might have a different goal. She might want to see the art treasures in the leading cities of Europe. If Brenda feels that all the available flights to Paris would be inconvenient, her list of alternatives would include flights to other European cities such as London, Munich, Vienna, and Rome. Although the challenge for both Kevin and Brenda is the same, the differences between their goals could result in completely different lists of alternatives. But if they are married and want to travel together, this additional goal would require them to do some delicate negotiating and compromising in order to arrive at a list of alternatives that would be at least minimally satisfactory to both.

Goals can be placed on different levels. On a low level, Kevin and Brenda have the same goal, traveling to Paris. But on the next level, their goals are very different. Kevin is mainly seeking the specific pleasures of a seaside resort; Brenda is looking primarily for opportunities to visit the great European art museums. On yet another level, however, both may have the common goal of staying together. For that goal, each might be willing to include possibilities that are not their first or second choices. If either Kevin or Brenda cannot find an alternative that satisfies fairly well each of his or her main goals, the trip is likely to be spoiled and the corrosive effects could even cause a deterioration in their marriage. (That threat might be removed as soon as they learn that Rome, with its great art galleries, is only a short distance away from seaside resorts on the Mediterranean.)

This discussion of goals depends on the distinction between means and ends. The ends are the goals that people want and the means are the ways that are available to try to get to the ends. Means–ends analysis is a powerful problem-solving technique that has been studied extensively by psychologists. The general method involves breaking complex problems down into parts by analyzing what can be accomplished by the available means. Then the same method can be applied to the simpler subproblems. The result is that a complex end (goal) is analyzed into a hierarchy of simple goals that can be achieved more easily.

Sometimes the same action can be both a means and an end. For example, playing tennis can be an enjoyable end in its own right as well as being a means, as part of an exercise program, to the end of better health. Even in these cases it is frequently helpful to consider the functions separately.

The why-and-how technique

This technique is helpful in applying means–ends analysis to figure out the hierarchy of goals involved in a decision-making situation. Asking "why?" takes one to the next level of goal and asking "how?" helps one to think of the alternative means on that level. Repeating the cycle of why and how questions gets you to the next level of goal and alternatives.

The example of Kevin and Brenda's air trip was a case of a joint decision in which confusion over the appropriate level could ruin a vacation and possibly a marriage. For an instructive example of an individual decision, let's consider the case of Jennifer, a freshman college student picking her courses for the first year. As a serious student, her main decisions have nothing to do with travel or marriage. She is concerned about whether to take freshman chemistry. She begins by thinking of other courses she would like to take instead of chemistry. Then if Jennifer asks herself *why* she is interested in taking freshman chemistry, the answer is that she might want to major in chemistry. Suddenly the focus of the decision has changed to the choice of a major. Another why question might show that Jennifer is thinking about a chemistry major because she wants to be a doctor and chemistry is a good major to prepare for medical school. The focus changes again. Jennifer's career plans are the central issue. Eventually the why questions reach a point where they can't go any further.

Q. Why do you want to be a doctor?
A. So I'll have a satisfying career.
Q. Why do you want a satisfying career?
A. So I'll be happy.
Q. Why do you want to be happy?

If Jennifer succeeds in answering this question perhaps she should consider being a philosophy major.

Where should Jennifer go from here? The best place to concentrate is on the lowest level that she is sure of. Suppose she is sure that she wants to be a doctor and she sees no need to reconsider that decision now. Then she can begin asking herself the how questions.

Q. How can I become a doctor?
A. By going to medical school.
Q. Any other ways?
A. No.
Q. How can I get into medical school?
A. By majoring in chemistry.

Q. Any other ways?

A. Yes. Biology.

Q. Any other ways?

A. Well, any major might do as long as I take the pre-med science requirements.

The how question leads Jennifer to begin thinking of the alternatives on the level that is most important for reaching her goal of becoming a doctor.

It is not unusual for people to try to make decisions on the wrong level. Sometimes it is a form of defensive avoidance. Working on a lower-level decision can help people ignore the possibility that something more serious may be wrong. For instance, students who fail accounting may try to decide whether to take it again during the summer or the fall when they should be considering switching to another major. The failure in accounting is a challenge to their decision to major in business, but they are ignoring it by concentrating on a more specific decision. They won't realize the need to reconsider the business major until some stronger challenge occurs. The why-and-how technique helps prevent this difficulty by focusing attention on *all* the levels of goals. It is still possible for people to pick the wrong level, but it's less likely after they have explicitly considered all of them.

Clarifying your goals

The use of the why-and-how technique assumes that you are sufficiently aware of your goals to be able to answer the why questions. This isn't always true. Sometimes you don't know what you want. All you know is that you aren't happy with your current plans. You don't seem to have any clear-cut goals. It is very difficult to make decisions without a clear understanding of your goals.

Several techniques are available to help you figure out your goals for yourself. Most of the methods involve two stages. In the first, participants are given some questions or statements to respond to. For instance, when making a career decision they may be asked to list their hobbies or their favorite activities. They are supposed to answer the questions spontaneously with little deliberate analysis. In the second stage, participants are asked to go back over their answers and try to figure out some of the implicit values and goals reflected in their answers.

EXERCISE: *"Twenty things you love to do."* If you would like to try one of the most popular of these techniques, first make a list of twenty (or so) things you love to do. Your list may include any sort of activity, just as long as you really enjoy doing it. Since this exercise is more effective when you make your list before you find out what to do with it, we have hidden the rest of the instructions at the end of this chapter. If you want to get the most out of doing the exercise, finish your list before turning to page 49 to read the remaining instructions. See also the notes at the back of the book for sources of other goal-clarifying exercises for you to do on your own.

Such simple exercises can be very helpful to people who haven't thought deeply about their own values and goals, but obviously they will not magically resolve any underlying psychological problem. Professional counseling or therapy may be necessary to work through conflicts about values and goals.

Generating alternatives

In some decisions the alternatives are obvious from the outset. For instance, anyone looking for a job in a special field would apply only to the limited number of employers who hire people in that field. In other decisions there may be an overload of choices. In a large city anyone who wants to buy a used car can always count on several hundred being available on the dealers' used car lots. At the other extreme are decisions for which there seem to be no acceptable choices at all. People who hate the type of work they are doing may stick to it because they don't see any other way to earn a living. Sometimes all the choices seem to have serious drawbacks. This section is about ways to deal with a shortage of good alternatives.

There are several useful rules for generating alternatives. Most of these rules come from brainstorming methods developed to encourage creative problem solving in business and industry. They were originally developed for groups of people working together. Although strong claims have been made for brainstorming methods, research evidence indicates that exchange of spontaneous ideas in a group can sometimes prove to be an inefficient way to try to solve problems (see Chapter 9). Nevertheless, it is possible for a person working alone to benefit from using some of the rules of the brainstorming techniques.

RULE 1. *Don't evaluate at the beginning.* Think of possible choices and write them down without worrying about what is wrong with them. Many people have a general tendency to think first of what is wrong with any new idea, even (or especially) their own. Sometimes it turns out that the drawbacks aren't really there or can be avoided. For instance, dissatisfied junior executives may think it would take years to save enough to finance the graduate study needed to advance their careers in the direction they want to go. They may not realize that in some fields there are fellowships that provide advanced students money to live on while engaging in graduate studies. If they reject the idea of going to a graduate school, they won't find out in the next stage, when they search for more information about the alternatives and consider them more carefully, that the apparent drawback could be eliminated. To avoid the inadvertent loss of viable alternatives it is important for you to consider all ideas that show any promise of satisfying your goals and to ignore (for the moment) the apparent drawbacks.

RULE 2. *Generate as many alternatives as possible.* The more alternatives you consider, the less likely you are to miss the ones that are best. It is always possible later to cut down the choices to a smaller, more manageable set that contains the most promising choices.

There is one danger in the emphasis on quantity. For some decisions people can figure out mechanical ways of generating long lists of apparent choices. For example, young people trying to decide on a career can think of an almost endless list of jobs: butcher, baker, candlestick maker. . . . Although it is important to consider a wide range of alternatives, it is sufficient to list only those that are reasonably possible for you and that have some possible appeal or potential advantage. In other words, ignoring the drawbacks does not mean that you should list all your pipedreams or any alternatives too objectionable to be seriously considered.

RULE 3. *Try to be original.* Deliberately try to think up a few far-out choices to include on your list. The choices you find when you are looking for unusual possibilities will frequently turn out to be more practical than they seem at first. This is especially likely with dilemmas that allow for few alternatives or when all available alternatives have serious drawbacks. It is in these dilemmas that a creative solution is needed most.

One method that some people find helpful in stimulating their imagination is to indulge in frankly wishful daydreams about an ideal outcome. One young man worked out a creative solution to his career dilemma on the basis of a good idea he obtained from his daydreams. He was trying to decide between continuing his career as folk guitarist (which had been launched with great success when he was still a high school student) and his new career as a counselor, for which his college training prepared him. In his daydreams, he repeatedly saw himself getting great kicks out of pursuing both careers simultaneously. In one daydream he could see the looks of adulation on the faces of his female colleagues on the staff of a leading counseling center where he would like to be employed, when they were being thrilled by hearing him perform at one of his concerts. In another type of daydream he would make a deep impression on fellow performers at a summer folk music festival, especially the young women, by giving them expert counseling when they told him privately about their personal troubles. Taking his cue from his daydreams, he began considering for the first time a new alternative, that of combining both careers. Eventually he was able to work it out in reality by obtaining a steady job as a counselor for the nine-month academic year at a junior college. During weekends he could pursue his career as a folk guitarist by making recordings and during each summer he could travel all over the country participating in folk music festivals and workshops.

RULE 4. *Modify flawed alternatives.*   Use the alternatives that you have already generated as springboards for new ideas. The old ideas can be combined, broken apart, or shifted around to avoid their flaws. What was original about the solution worked out by the young man who was trying to decide between being a folk guitarist or a counselor was the unconventional combination of the two disparate careers inspired by his seemingly unrealistic daydreams. The wild ideas that result from Rule 3 are especially good candidates for realistic modification. For instance, in trying to decide where to rent a home after arriving in a big city, a young lawyer thought of living on a luxurious houseboat because he would enjoy cruising up and down the nearby river. Although this is not a practical possibility, it led him to the idea of renting a summer cottage on the river and buying a second-hand motor boat. This was an ideal choice for his limited budget while satisfying in a modest way his interest in river cruising.

The new ideas don't have to be directly connected to the old. Someone might have used the idea of the luxurious houseboat to think of renting a house in a more remote section of the city across the river, where good rentals might be much cheaper because of the inconvenience of having to take a ferryboat ride to go downtown. Although there is no apparent connection between the two ideas, the houseboat could have suggested the city of Hong Kong, which is noted for its thousands of houseboats and also for its huge ferryboats on which hundreds of thousands of people commute to and from the downtown section on the main island every day.

RULE 5. *Ask other people.* Everyone looks at the world in a different way. Combining the ideas from several people produces a wider variety than any one person could have produced. You can ask other people individually for their ideas, or you can get two or more people together in a group to generate ideas at the same time. In fact, as we mentioned earlier, the first four rules are the same as the rules for brainstorming, which was designed to be done in a group.

It pays, of course, to consult an expert or someone with considerable personal experience that is relevant to the decision. Such people not only can supply useful information about the probable consequences of the alternatives that are under consideration but also can suggest new alternatives that the decision maker never thought of. Sometimes the original ideas pertain to the things one can do to select the best choice. For example, if a husband and wife who cannot decide whether or not to obtain a divorce consult a marriage counselor, they might learn for the first time about the separation-under-one-roof plan, which marriage counselors occasionally suggest as a means for allowing each partner to find out how he or she really feels about splitting without either taking the momentous step of actually moving out of the home. The plan requires the partners to agree that they will sleep in separate rooms in their home and will pursue completely independent lives for a fixed trial period of several months.

Obviously, a person making a vital decision can benefit from seeking out advisers who know a great deal about the type of personal problem he or she is confronting. Experts can draw upon a large repertoire of potential solutions for such problems, including the creative ones worked out by a few exceptionally talented persons as well as the folk wisdon distilled from the experience of large numbers of other people who have faced the same kind of dilemma. Chapter 8 gives some guidelines for getting the most out of consultations with experts.

Rules 1 and 4 are important not only when deliberating privately about your own decision but also when talking it over with other people, expert or nonexpert. If you immediately criticize or evaluate their ideas (contrary to Rule 1), they are unlikely to work very long or very hard on generating alternatives (Rule 2). Since their ideas come from their own point of view, the alternatives they suggest may be more suitable for themselves than for you. Still, they can sometimes come up with original ideas (Rule 3) or suggest a good starting point for modification and development (Rule 4).

RULE 6. *Use contemplation as a source of ideas.*   If you set aside some time to engage in free-floating contemplation of a decision you are facing, practically any train of thought or external stimulus can serve as the source of an idea. There is no need to try to be transcendental in these meditations. For instance, if you are trying to think of an ideal wedding present for your best friend, just looking around the room (any room) while musing in a free-floating way can suggest new alternatives. An old oil lamp on the mantle could suggest a battery-powered lantern and other equipment for the camping trip that the newlyweds are planning. Other sources for stimulating ideas are obvious, like paging through a gift catalog or wandering around in a gift shop while in a relaxed mood. Even just daydreaming about an ideal choice, as we suggested earlier, can be helpful.

As a more complicated example, consider the problem of a high school algebra teacher who had just been told that there was a well-organized cheating ring in one of her classes. A small group of students were trading answers to exam questions by using the position of their feet as signals. The teacher wanted to stop the cheating by punishing the cheaters. She knew that some of her students would welcome that. But she couldn't see any way to do it without the hassle of trying to prove who was and who was not cheating, which could have a bad effect on the entire classroom.

On the weekend, while having dinner in a restaurant, she looked at the attractive handmade stoneware dishes on the table as she contemplated the cheating problem. Although the dishes were all very similar, each piece had its own unique markings from the glazing process. This struck her as a good metaphor for the results of successful classroom teaching. The metaphor, in turn, gave her the idea of making up a somewhat different exam for each student. The forms of the algebraic equations would be the same for each student (like the forms of the dishes) but the numbers in the equations would be slightly different. Of course this solution had the disadvantage that it was a lot of work for the teacher. But she didn't evaluate that drawback right then (Rule 1); she simply added it to her list of alternatives. Later in the evening the teacher was playing cards at the home of one of her friends. As she shuffled the cards she suddenly realized that she could shuffle the order of the problems for each student rather than use different problems. Different orders of the problems would be enough to prevent the cheating because the foot signals wouldn't work without the students knowing which problem the answers were for.

Getting ideas like this teacher had is not something that everyone can do just by deciding to do it or by racking one's brains over it. But by engaging in a relaxed, meditative sort of contemplation and realizing that good ideas can come from metaphors suggested by any intriguing images, real or imaginary, people can find new and sometimes creative alternatives for the decisions they face.

RULE 7. *Avoid dichotomies.* Many decisions seem to have only two alternatives, either do it or don't do it. Examples of either–or choices are getting married, getting divorced, accepting a unique job offer, moving to another city, accepting a social invitation, or going on a diet. Although the alternatives fall into two dichotomous classes, there are always different ways to do it and different ways not to do it. Suppose that a young woman knows that the man she has been living with wants to be married to her. She may feel that she has only two choices: (1) tell him that she agrees that they should get married or (2) tell him that she doesn't want to get married. But she actually may have several more viable alternatives: (3) say yes, but set the date a long way in the future, (4) delay by postponing discussion of the issue, (5) state frankly all the issues she feels need to be resolved before they agree to get married, (6) propose a contractual arrangement that includes the equivalent of a trial marriage, (7) say yes, but only on specified conditions. These alternatives are fairly general; in an actual situation there would be more alternatives with specific details. The young man, in turn, would be considering a number of specific alternatives and might suggest some additional ones to add to her list. Some of the alternatives in the above list amount to procrastination and aren't likely to help in the long run, but others could lead the couple to a sounder marriage agreement than the original dichotomous choice.

Whenever you are faced with an either–or choice, you should try to take a broader view of the situation and consider alternative ways of solving the main problem confronting you. This could change the yes–no choice into a problem for which there may be other acceptable solutions, like the combined career of the folk guitarist–counselor and the separation-under-one-roof plan for the couple contemplating a divorce.

Dangers

There are two obvious sources of danger in connection with generating alternatives during Stage 2. The first is one that we have repeatedly emphasized—the decision makers may miss alternatives that could turn out to be better than any they are considering. Most of this chapter has been concerned with ways to avoid this. The second danger is that the decision makers may promptly adopt the first alternative that seems viable without considering its possible drawbacks. When people are upset by a challenge they sometimes seize upon the first likely alternative and adopt it immediately. After quickly making up their minds, they feel complacent because they believe they have solved the problem. They fail to foresee the possible risky consequences of their choice.

There are two ways to avoid this danger. The first is to continue generating alternatives even after one is found that is likely to work, looking for one that is better yet. The second is to be sure to continue on to the third stage of decision making and evaluate the alternatives carefully, which includes constructing scenarios about potentially undesirable outcomes. The shortcut that avoids evaluation can be a shortcut to disaster.

EXERCISE: *"Twenty things you love to do" (continued).* Instructions for the first part of the "Twenty things" exercise appear on page 42. To complete the exercise, go through your list of activities and code them as follows. (Items can receive more than one code.) Place an *A* by those you do alone, a *P* by those you do with other people, and an *S* by those you do with a special person. Put a dollar sign by those things that cost money to do. Write "plan" by those that require advance planning. Write "new" by those you have started doing in the last five years. Decide which are the five most important items and number them 1 through 5. Write down by every item the last time you did that thing.

When you finish coding the things on your list go back over it and think about what it tells you about yourself. What did you learn about what you like? Are you satisfied with the frequency you do the things you love? What does this suggest about the goals you would like to set for yourself?

4
Evaluating Alternativ

Evaluating alternatives is of crucial importance for sound decision making. It is a major determinant of how well the decision will work out in the future.

If we could accurately foretell the future, this third stage would be easy. All we would have to do is look into the future for each of the alternatives and pick the one that will have the outcome we prefer. But because our future vision is cloudy, we have to make do with our best estimates about the future, which always are of doubtful validity.

Two major problems make this stage difficult. The first is the amount of information that must be considered. As Benjamin Franklin noted, "People cannot keep all the pros and cons in mind at one time." As one group of factors comes to mind, others are lost. As the other factors are considered, the first group fades out. The choices fluctuate in their attractiveness as the various factors are considered. Franklin advised writing down the factors and then balancing off the pros against the cons. One of our main recommendations in this chapter is an updated version of Franklin's advice about constructing a balance sheet.

The second major problem is dealing with the probabilities of the uncertain consequences of the alternatives. We can easily make judgments about the likelihood of events. Sometimes our intuitive estimates are very accurate, despite the various kinds of bias that are common when humans estimate probabilities. Chapter 5 discusses ways of dealing with uncertainty and avoiding some of the common pitfalls, while this chapter concentrates on the use of the balance sheet.

Gaps in the balance sheet

A financial balance sheet lists all the monetary income and expenses of a company so that the inflow of money can be balanced against the outflow. It should give an overall picture of the financial status of the company. A decision-making balance sheet provides the same sort of overall picture of the considerations involved in a decision. It makes it possible to weigh the advantages and disadvantages of the choices against each other. But in order to arrive at a reasonably accurate evaluation of the alternatives, it is essential that there be no big gaps in the balance sheet.

Without some system, people often fail to consider whole areas of consequences. They may consider the material or tangible consequences of the choices and ignore the consequences of self-approval or -disapproval or they may only think about the consequences for themselves and forget that their decisions will have an impact on other people that they care about. When decision makers leave out one of the broad areas, they usually become considerably upset later on when relatively minor setbacks occur in the forgotten area.

All too often people leave out major areas that can make all the difference. The more gaps in a decisional balance sheet at the time people become committed to a new course of action, the more likely they will be shaken by setbacks and regret the decision. After it is too late to reverse the decision without exorbitant costs, people may realize that they selected the wrong choice because they had been blithely unaware of crippling objections to what had seemed the best course of action at the time. They may realize that they missed an opportunity that would have led to a satisfying outcome because they didn't see that one of the alternatives they were considering offered them that opportunity. This type of regret occurs frequently when men and women look back at their career choices, even among those who seem to be most successful.

Seymour Wishman, a successful criminal lawyer, for example, recently explained in an Op-ed article in the *New York Times* how he has been brutalized by his profession in ways he had never imagined in law school when he was "filled with high expectations and principles." What he had not realized was that as a criminal lawyer he would suffer from "inner damage" because he must live in a

"world filled with deceit, incompetence, aggression, and violence."
As a result of encountering so much deceit, Wishman says, he has
grown distrustful of everyone. "I automatically search for motives
and reflexively recall all prior inconsistent statements—good habits
for a criminal lawyer, if only they didn't carry over, insidiously,
into my personal life." He cannot take pride in his successes in the
courtroom because, contrary to his youthful positive image of trial
lawyers, he must violate his own ethical standards in order to be effective. "I must act forcefully, and, often, brutally. I must frequently, for example, discredit witnesses, destroy them if possible."
Furthermore, he often finds himself using all his legal skills and
clever courtroom tricks to prove the alleged innocence of guilty clients, many of whom "are monsters who have done monstrous
things," such as torturing and murdering young children. In order
to deal with his own sense of guilt about what he must do to be an
effective criminal lawyer, he has developed a sense of "profession-
alism," which "makes a virtue out of noninvolvement" and "fosters
an attitude of dissociation that can distort other parts of your life."
As for the criminal law system in which he is actively participating,
he finds that in practice it falls far short of the high ideals and tradi-
tions of the profession: "I see myself as part of a process which is arbitrary, frequently racist, and often brutal."

Like Wishman, many men and women are ignorant of the risks
of inner damage at the time they make their choice of profession.
But they need not remain so. Realistic information about what one
needs to do to become an "effective" professional in a given specialty and about common pressures to violate ethical standards could
be obtained by asking several "old pros" who are friends of one's
own family or of a friend's family to talk frankly about the way of
life imposed by their professional role. If Wishman had interviewed
a few practicing criminal lawyers before he decided to go into that
specialty, he might have corrected his romantic misconceptions by
learning what he would be letting himself in for. With the available
information added to his balance sheet, he might have decided, before it was too late, that in order to avoid self-disapproval and to
satisfy his own standards of conduct, as well as his other objectives,
he would be better off to drop his plans to become a criminal lawyer and go into some less lucrative but more soul-satisfying branch

of the law instead—perhaps to practice in a legal aid clinic for poverty-stricken people who need help to avoid getting raw deals because they can't afford a private attorney.

People choosing other careers often fail to fill the same kind of information gaps about the way of life and the inner damage to be expected. Irving H. Page, a former editor of a magazine for physicians, says: "A combination of forces has conspired against [physicians] that has destroyed their ideals of human behavior and embittered them to the point of wanting out." Among the difficulties are extreme time pressures that induce many physicians to treat their patients as things rather than as people and to develop dehumanizing attitudes. Similarly, nurses are frequently disillusioned and experience the pangs of self-disapproval when they discover that their humanitarian ideals are constantly being violated by what they have to do. Enid V. Blaylock, a registered nurse who quit her full-time hospital job, writes that "today nursing is one of the least humane of the helping professions." Underneath, she says, nurses may be humane and compassionate, but they are not permitted to act that way on a hospital ward. Medical technology and the policies dictated by hospital administrators who have an exclusively cost-accounting mentality, she says, "unwittingly conspire to block nurses' expressions of empathy and caring." Nurses on the wards end up regulating gadgets hanging over the beds without even looking at the patients lying there. A major reason why Blaylock decided to quit was her discomfort at participating in "the many ways in which patients were stripped of their privacy, dignity, and independence."

Here again, however, the deviation from humanitarian ideals is common knowledge that could have been obtained by working as a volunteer in a hospital or by interviewing practically any nurse who works on a hospital ward about the satisfactions and dissatisfactions of the job. If early in her training Blaylock had become fully aware of the extent to which nurses must devote themselves to meeting the requirements of legal regulations and cost accounting rather than to the patients' well-being, she might have selected a more satisfying nursing specialty, such as school nurse, public health nurse, or nurse practitioner. If she decided despite the drawbacks to devote herself to nursing on hospital wards, she might have been prepared to deal more effectively with the administrative pressures and to resist the dehumanization tendencies.

The same can be said about many practitioners in the mental health profession. For example, psychiatrists and psychologists who practice psychotherapy report that their work is frequently frustrating and distressing. Some become disillusioned and burn out early in their careers if they unexpectedly encounter a series of extremely disturbed, depressed, or suicidal patients who do not respond to their treatments. Other therapists who continue to find satisfaction in their work are nevertheless perturbed by unanticipated consequences of their chosen career, such as chronic feelings of exhaustion, emotional depletion, and—like the attorney we quoted earlier—difficulty in turning off their professional approach after they leave the office. If they knew about all the sources of frustration and disillusionment in advance, most therapists probably would not have changed their choice of career, but they might have been better prepared to deal with the stresses and to avoid becoming upset and demoralized.

Even in careers where one might least expect it, there are likely to be hidden drawbacks that will not be discovered until it is too late, unless one makes a deliberate effort to find out before becoming committed. Some topnotch scientists and leading experts in many different academic fields, for example, decide to accept appointments in teaching, research, or administration of training programs at institutions of higher learning. When they make that choice they expect that they will spend their lives in a congenial community of scholars. But some may soon discover, as one wit put it, that the university is a collection of "mutually repellent particles held together by a common interest in parking."

It goes without saying that there are all sorts of hidden drawbacks for every type of career, especially in the sharply competitive world of business. Sociologists have documented the conspiracies of silence that make it difficult for employees, including those recruited for executive positions, to obtain crucial information bearing on ethical standards. It is usually very easy to find out about pay rates, opportunities for advancement, and fringe benefits, but it

takes special efforts and a certain amount of courage to uncover information about the disagreeable and unethical "dirty work" that
might be demanded.

Filling out a balance sheet

One of the main reasons that people make so many erroneous decisions they soon regret is, as we suggested earlier, that at the time
of making a choice they are unaware of the gaps in their knowledge
about the drawbacks or are only vaguely aware of the gaps and
don't bother to think about them. It is much more comfortable to
concentrate on the positive features of the most attractive alternative. One way to overcome the tendency not to think about negative
aspects and to become aware of the gaps that need to be filled in is
to use a systematic balance sheet procedure. A standard list of considerations used in preparing the balance sheet for career choice is
presented in Table 1. Similar lists using the same four main categories can be constructed for preparing balance sheets on other
kinds of vital choices, including not only personal decisions about
marriage, raising children, and health problems, but also business
decisions about borrowing money, forming partnerships, buying or
selling property, and the like.

We recommend that the balance sheet be divided into the following four categories so that none of the important areas will be forgotten: (1) tangible or utilitarian considerations for the decision
maker, (2) tangible considerations for the decision maker's family,
friends, or associates who will be affected by the decision, (3) self-
approval or -disapproval, including ethical considerations, and (4)
approval or disapproval from others whose opinions are important
to the decision maker. There is a little overlap among these categories; some aspects of a decision may even have effects in all four
areas. The decision maker simply does the best he or she can to fill
out for each alternative a balance-sheet grid describing the positive
and negative anticipations expected in each of the four categories.

One executive who filled out such a balance sheet was thinking
about whether to leave his position as a production manager in a
large manufacturing plant (see Figure 1). He listed a number of
negative anticipations, ranging from long hours and constant time

TABLE 1   Considerations affecting career choice.

Utilitarian considerations: gains and losses for self
1. Income
2. Difficulty of the work
3. Interest level of the work
4. Freedom to select work tasks
5. Chances of advancement
6. Security
7. Time available for personal interests—e.g., recreation
8. Other (e.g., special restrictions or opportunities with respect to social life; effect of the career or job demands on marriage; type of people you will come in contact with)

Utilitarian considerations: gains and losses for others
1. Income for family
2. Status for family
3. Time available for family
4. Kind of environment for family—e.g., stimulating, dull; safe, unsafe
5. Being in a position to help an organization or group (e.g., social, political, or religious)
6. Other (e.g, fringe benefits for family)

Self-approval or -disapproval
1. Self-esteem from contributions to society or to good causes
2. Extent to which work tasks are ethically justifiable
3. Extent to which work will involve compromising oneself
4. Creativeness or originality of work
5. Extent to which job will involve a way of life that meets one's moral or ethical standards
6. Opportunity to fulfill long-range life goals
7. Other (e.g., extent to which work is "more than just a job")

Approval or disapproval from others (includes being criticized or being excluded from a group as well as being praised or obtaining prestige, admiration, and respect)
1. Parents
2. College friends
3. Spouse
4. Colleagues
5. Community at large
6. Others (e.g., social, political, or religious groups)

FIGURE 1 **A manager's balance sheet.**

The grid lays out the pros and cons for staying with his present job. A balance-sheet grid would be filled out for each of the other alternatives as well—for example, whether to seek a lateral transfer within the company.

EXPECTED CONSEQUENCES	POSITIVE ANTICIPATIONS	NEGATIVE ANTICIPATIONS
Tangible gains and losses for *self*	1. Satisfactory pay. 2. Plenty of opportunities to use my skills and competencies. 3. For the present, my status in the organization is okay (but it won't be for long if I am not promoted in the next year).	1. Long hours. 2. Constant time pressures, short deadlines. 3. Unpleasant paper work. 4. Poor prospects for advancement to a higher-level position. 5. Repeated reorganizations make my work chaotic.
Tangible gains and losses for *others*	1. Adequate income for family. 2. Wife and children get special privileges because of my position in the firm.	1. Not enough time free to spend with my family. 2. Wife often has to put up with my irritability when I come home after bad days at work.
Self-approval or self-disapproval	1. This position allows me to make full use of my potentialities. 2. Proud of my achievements. 3. Proud of the competent team I have shaped up. 4. Sense of meaningful accomplishment.	1. Sometimes feel I'm a fool to continue putting up with the unreasonable deadlines and other stupid demands made by the top managers.
Social approval or disapproval	1. Approval of men on my team, who look up to me as their leader and who are good friends. 2. Approval of my superior who is a friend and wants me to stay.	1. Very slight skeptical reaction of my wife—she asks me if I might be better off in a different firm. 2. A friend who has been wanting to wangle a new job for me will be disappointed.

pressures to stupid demands made by the top managers, and his own irritability at home as a consequence of job problems. Nevertheless, this man decided to stay where he was because of the weight he gave to the positive entries in the nonutilitarian categories—his pride in his role as leader of a competent team, his sense of welcome responsibility for their high morale, and his warm, friendly relationship with the others, whom he did not want to let down by leaving. He felt that his friendship with his immediate superior was especially rewarding and that together the two of them could save their team from the negligence and stupidity of the firm's top managers. But the negative aspects of the job did affect this executive's contingency plans: he was determined to find a position in another firm if the men in his unit were scattered in a planned reorganization.

Studies with Yale College seniors suggest that the balance sheet is a feasible way of stimulating people to become aware of major gaps in their information about decisions. In *Decision Making*, Irving Janis and Leon Mann illustrate with the following example how this procedure can be something quite different from a coldly intellectual exercise:

One senior who originally was planning to go to a graduate business school for training to become an executive in his father's Wall Street firm was surprised at first when he discovered that the cells in the balance-sheet grid pertaining to self-approval or -disapproval were almost completely empty. After looking over the standard list of items to be considered in those categories, he was stimulated to write down several ways in which his career as a broker would fail to meet his ethical ideals or satisfy his desire to help improve the quality of life for people in his community. As he thought about these neglected considerations, he became worried and depressed. Then, while filling out the cells of the balance-sheet grid for his second choice—going to law school—he began to brighten up a bit. Eventually he became glowingly enthusiastic when he hit upon the notion that instead of becoming a Wall Street lawyer he might better meet his objectives by being trained for a career in a legal aid clinic or in public-interest law. Finally, his mood became more sober, but with some residual elation, as he conscientiously listed the serious drawbacks (parental disapproval, relatively low income, poor prospects for travel abroad, etc.) of the new career plan he had conceived. Afterward he thanked the interviewer for making him realize he had been on the wrong track and for helping him arrive at his new career plan, which, in fact, he had worked out entirely by himself in response to the open-ended nature of the balance-sheet procedure.

What works for Yale seniors may not, of course, work for other kinds of people. However, three large field experiments have shown that it can work with other populations as well. The tests were done on high-school seniors trying to decide where to go to college and on two groups of adults deciding whether or not to diet and attend an early-morning exercise class for health reasons. Those who were asked to fill out balance sheets in making their choices were more likely to adhere to their decision and had fewer regrets afterward than those who did not use the balance sheets.

Why is it beneficial to go through the laborious procedure of filling out a balance sheet? First of all, as in the case of contrasting outcome scenarios, such a procedure counteracts complacency and promotes vigilance. Second, it makes the decision maker realize the need for contingency plans—figuring out what to do if one or another of the unfavorable consequences listed in the minus columns were to materialize. Third, it helps one to make a more comprehensive appraisal of the alternatives. By seeing all the entries, the decision maker can start thinking about possible tradeoffs, concentrate on the major differences between alternatives, and think about the degree of importance of crucial pros and cons.

Most often the value of filling out a detailed balance sheet is that decision makers become more aware not only of their own objectives but also of the gaps in their knowledge about the alternatives that need to be filled in, either by recalling what they already know or by actively seeking out the missing information. This is illustrated by the balance sheet in Figure 2, which was filled out by a twenty-two-year-old man (we'll call him Bruce Calahan) trying to decide between two job offers. Bruce has just graduated from college with a degree in printing management. He has two job offers. One is from a furniture company in North Carolina that is planning to start its own printing plant to produce advertising materials. They want Bruce to be on the management team that organizes and runs the printing division. The other job offer is from a paper company in West Virginia. After a year's training Bruce would be technical representative for the paper mill.

Bruce discussed the decision with one of the present authors and was advised to construct a balance sheet. He began by taking two large sheets of paper (one for each alternative) and divided them into quarters. He labeled the sheets as shown. As he thought of the various aspects of the job offers, he found the appropriate boxes to put them in. He jotted down the advantages in the top half of each box and the disadvantages in the bottom half. After he listed all the things that spontaneously came to mind he looked for the boxes that didn't have much in them yet and worked on finding both the advantages and disadvantages in those areas. Some of the entries in the figure summarize the result of considerable thought.

Bruce believed that one of the major differences between the jobs was in the long-term opportunities for advancement. If he was successful in the paper company he would be able to work in several different divisions and then would have a chance to move up into the executive level management of the company. In the furniture company he would have more immediate responsibility but little chance to advance into the general company management.

When Bruce started his balance sheet he didn't know whether the chance to become an executive was important to him. He hadn't thought about the kind of life he wanted to be living in twenty years. At first the secure existence as head of a printing plant appealed to him. He would be able to settle down and have time for his family and other interests. Even if he didn't continue with the furniture company the experience would make it easy to find other similar jobs. After a while Bruce began to realize that he had some other values that would not be satisfied with that kind of existence. He wanted more variety and opportunity to develop and carry out his own business ideas. He also realized that he liked risk. Instead of being an advantage, the security of the furniture company job was actually a disadvantage. The safe and secure existence did not fit Bruce's idea of what kind of person he was or wanted to be.

Next, Bruce considered the riskiness of the paper company job. Was it challenging enough? He thought he could get more opportunity to prove himself by trying to start his own printing business.

FIGURE 2 A balance sheet (plus-and-minus version).

EXPECTED CONSEQUENCES	JOB #1 Furniture company in North Carolina	JOB #2 Paper mill in West Virginia
Tangible gains (+) for *self*	Chance to show what I can do on management team setting up a new plant. Immediate responsibility. More money now. Good city to live in. Daily work activities will be interesting and challenging.	A year of training in paper manufacturing will provide me with more expertise. I like the people at the mill. The region is a pleasant place to spend a year. I like most of the other places where the company has plants. There is an established route for moving up in the company and this job provides good chances for advancement. The job requires a lot of travel, which may help me to meet single women.
Tangible losses (−) for *self*	Little chance to advance. May not be able to meet single women easily in that town.	As a trainee, I will have little responsibility during the first year. After the first year, I will have to move to another plant and may not have any choice. There seem to be very few single women in the area. Considerably more travel is involved than I want (calling on customers having trouble with the company's paper products). After all that traveling around it will be hard to settle down later on if I get married, which eventually I want to do.

Tangible gains (+) for others	My parents have friends in Greensboro so they can come to visit me and have a place to stay.	Close for my two best friends to visit.
Tangible loss (−) for others		Inconvenient for my parents to visit me. Later I will probably lose touch with friends and seldom see my relatives when I have to move to a plant far away.
Self-approval (+)	I want the satisfaction of having responsibility. I believe in the principle that "small is beautiful" and will feel better about being part of a smaller company.	I'll feel good about facing up to a long-term challenge. Opportunity for variety is something I value. I'm the type of person who wants to take risks; I will feel proud of not running away from a big opportunity.
Self-disapproval (−)	Job will offer no opportunity for trying out different roles, so it offers little chance to find out about my capabilities and to develop new interests.	Concern about pollution makes me uneasy about working for a company that might pollute.
Approval from others (+)	My parents will approve of this job slightly more than the other.	My parents will approve of this job.
Disapproval from others (−)	One of my most helpful instructors would rather I go directly into printing.	Some friends are very concerned about environmental preservation issues and will criticize me for working in an industry that destroys forests and pollutes the air.

But Bruce knew that the odds were against new businesses, especially those started with the amount of capital Bruce could hope to raise. Bruce was willing to take risks but not that much of a risk. He decided that the paper company provided about the right level of opportunity and risk.

It took Bruce a couple of days to work through these issues of security, opportunity, and risk. Then the results of all that deliberation were entered as two small entries under the "self-approval" category of the balance sheet. These written entires were enough to keep these considerations in the focus of Bruce's attention through the rest of the decision-making process.

Dividing the balance sheet into four areas helped Bruce find some important considerations that he might have missed. For example, while he was thinking about whether his friends would approve of the jobs, he realized that the environmental problems of the paper industry were an issue. Paper companies destroy forests to get their raw materials and paper mills are notorious for their air and water pollution. Bruce didn't know anything about the specific environmental record of the company offering him the job. So he called a friend who knew about the records of the different paper companies in West Virginia and found out that his company had one of the better environmental records. They had started to install pollution control equipment earlier than most of the others. This satisfied Bruce's concerns about the company's environmental impact. His friends might still be bothered but Bruce felt confident that he would be able to counter their arguments with the facts about the company's record.

Bruce accepted the job with the paper company in West Virginia. It has turned out well and Bruce feels that the balance-sheet procedure helped him make a good decision.

Other formats for balance sheets

Another way to do a balance sheet is by filling out a report card. Each of the alternatives is given a grade on each aspect that is important in the decision. This system works well in situations where the alternatives are similar so that they can all be given grades on the same aspects. Decisions about purchases are frequently like this.

For instance, in buying a car, the choices can all be rated on price, comfort, trunk space, gas mileage, and whatever else is important for the purchaser.

Another aspect of the report card system is that it does not force things to be divided into advantages and disadvantages. In buying a car the gas mileage of the Ford compact may have an advantage when compared to one competitive model, but a disadvantage when compared to another. In the report-card system the relative standings on gas mileage can be represented easily by giving the grades A, B, and C to the three cars.

Figure 3 shows an example of a report-card balance sheet filled out by a young couple, Jeff and Anne Coleman, in the process of buying a house. They looked all around the city and found three developments with new houses that met their family's basic requirements of space, location, and cost. The Fairfax Village house was a split level with three bedrooms above the garage, family room, and den. It was on a nice lot with trees and was located conveniently for both their jobs. The Oak Knoll house featured a hexagonal living room between two wings set at an angle. The Colemans found it the most exciting design. The Shady Lane House was a straight ranch house. It impressed them as being the most practical of the three houses.

Jeff and Anne could have worked separately on balance sheets so that both their views would be represented independently. But they found that they usually agreed in their opinions about the houses they had looked at so they decided to work together on a single balance sheet. They agreed that whenever they disagreed they would agree to disagree; they would give separate evaluations for that item.

The balance sheet (Figure 3) looks simple, but the simplicity is deceptive. It conceals all the deliberation and animated discussion that went into each grade. The first issue that had to be decided before the balance sheet could be filled out was how to organize the grades. The Colemans first thought of giving grades to each room in the houses. Then they realized that the houses did not all have the same number of rooms. They then thought of grouping the rooms by function. This in turn suggested function or activities as the main organizing principle for rating the utilitarian aspects of the

FIGURE 3   A joint balance sheet (report-card version).

EXPECTED CONSEQUENCES	HOUSE #1 Fairfax Village	HOUSE #2 Oak Knoll	HOUSE #3 Shady Lane
Tangible gains (vs. losses) for *self*			
Comfort and functionality			
Sleeping area	B	A	A
Leisure (TV, den)	A	B	A
Entertaining	A	B	A
Kitchen and dining area	B	B	A
Housework and utility-laundry			
Jeff	B	A	B
Anne	B	C	A
Location in relation to work, school, shopping, bus lines	B	B	C
Cost: Initial price	C	B	A
Utility costs to operate (heating, electricity, water, etc.)	B	C	B
Cost to furnish	B	B	B
Cost to keep the grounds in good condition	C	C	A
Value of the house as a short-term investment (if we want to sell in the next few years)	A	A	B
Value of the house as a long-term investment (5 to 10 years)	A	?	?
Value of the house as a very long-term investment (25 years)	A	?	?
Tangible gains (vs. losses) for *others*			
For the children:			
Bedroom areas	B	A	A
Play areas	A	A	B
Yard	A	A	B
Convenience of getting to school (bus or walking)	B	B	C
Quality of the school	A	B	B
For our friends—entertaining at home and accommodating visitors	A	A	A
For our parents—ease of visiting	B	C	C

houses. Their six major categories of activities around the house were sleeping, eating, entertaining, housework, leisure, and indoor play for their two children. They used these categories to rate each house.

The first step in rating a house on one of these categories was to figure out what the pattern of that activity would be like in the house. Jeff and Anne Coleman could not assume that their current habits would remain unchanged. For instance, in their current apartment they had a small kitchen and a single small dining area. All three houses had provisions for multiple dining areas. One house had a breakfast nook; the others had the family room next to the kitchen so that the family room could be set up for informal dinners. Before Anne and Jeff could decide how to rate a house they had to predict how they would organize and use the house. After discussing the issues about the eating areas, they decided that they would probably set up a single eating area that would serve for both family meals and company. Then they considered the individual houses.

EXPECTED CONSEQUENCES	HOUSE #1 Fairfax Village	HOUSE #2 Oak Knoll	HOUSE #3 Shady Lane
Self-approval (vs. *self*-disapproval)			
Style–image of house	B	A	C
Our preference for avoiding flight from the city to the suburbs	B	C	B
Opportunities the neighborhood offers for the life style Anne wants	A	A	?
Opportunities the neighborhood offers for the life style Jeff wants	A	B	C
Approval (vs. disapproval) from *others*			
The children	A	B	B
Anne's closest friend	C	A	C
Jeff's closest friend	B	B	A
Our social circle	A	B	B
Jeff's parents	A	?	?
Anne's parents	A	C	B

The Shady Lane house had a dining area attached to the living room. It was around the corner from the kitchen and impressed them as inconvenient. In other words, they predicted that if they moved into that house the location of the dining area would be a continuing source of annoyance rather than something they would get used to.

How else could they solve this problem? Jeff suggested that they could put the dining table in the family room. There was an open bar between the kitchen and family room so that eating in the family room would be convenient. But there were other consequences of this plan. They wouldn't want the television set in the dining area because their young children frequently finished dinner early and watched television, which allowed the parents to eat in peace. Maybe the television set could go in the area originally designated the dining room. But then the television would interfere with entertaining friends in the living room. Then it occurred to Anne that they could ask the builder to extend the wall and add a door to separate the living room from what would be their television den.

Finally Anne and Jeff were ready to rate the Shady Lane house for the eating function, including preparation, eating, and cleaning up. They took into account their plan for the use of the space, the organization of the kitchen, the storage space for food and utensils, et cetera. They both thought the house was good in these matters and they put an A on their report-card balance sheet. They also wrote down on another sheet the assumptions they made in giving the grade of A. When they considered other areas, it was important to remember that they planned to add a wall so as to use the dining area as a television den, which would increase the initial cost of the house.

Jeff and Anne filled out the rest of the report-card balance sheet in a similar fashion. They decided for each of the four areas on the balance sheet what were the aspects they should take into consideration. In the grading process they kept track of the assumptions they made in assigning the grades. At the end they double-checked to make sure they made the same assumptions all the way through.

When they finished the balance sheet Jeff and Anne both felt that the Fairfax Village house was best for them. It seemed to have better grades in the areas that were most important to them. The only rating that they worried about was the B they gave the Fairfax Village house in style or image. This was important to them and they felt it might become more important in a few years. But they decided that the superior style of the Oak Knoll house did not outweigh its disadvantages and that they were fairly comfortable with the style of the Fairfax Village house. So they went out the next day and signed the papers to buy it.

The report-card balance sheet helped them because it enabled them to compare the houses directly on each aspect. Whenever something occurred to them about one of the houses, the same aspect of the other houses could also be graded.

One drawback of the report-card type of balance-sheet procedure is that it entices decision makers into using a grade average or some other oversimplifying rule to arrive at their final choice. The procedure has other shortcomings as well. The report card format might not have been good for Bruce to use for his job decision because the advantages and disadvantages of his job possibilities did not match as closely as the aspects of the houses. The plus-and-minus balance sheet enabled Bruce to get a good evaluation of each job without having to distort his view by forcing them into the same mold. The plus-and-minus format can be used for any decision. But the report-card format makes it easier when the alternatives being considered have similar aspects.

There are two different ways to fill out the report-card balance sheet. The first is to take each aspect of the alternatives in turn and rate all the alternatives at once on that aspect. This is called the *breadth-first approach*; the full breadth of alternatives is considered from the beginning. The other way is to begin with one alternative and give it grades on all the aspects before considering the other alternatives. This is called the *depth-first approach*; each alternative is considered in depth one at a time.

Jeff and Anne Coleman used the breadth-first approach. This approach has a powerful advantage. When grades are assigned for all the alternatives at once only the relative standing on the aspect being considered matters. It was easy for the Colemans to give the Oak Knoll house an A in style and the Fairfax Village a B. This reflected their clear preference for the style of the Oak Knoll house. But if they hadn't been comparing houses they would have found it difficult to give grades to each one. They didn't have an absolute standard against which to measure a single house to determine what grade its style deserved. There is abundant psychological evidence that relative judgments are easier and better than absolute judgments.

There are occasions on which the depth-first approach has strong advantages. These occur when the information about the alternatives is available for only one alternative at a time. It is better to make the ratings while you can examine the alternative closely and get more information if needed. For instance, when buying a car you can test-drive only one make at a time. It is better to do the ratings during the test drive or immediately afterward. Your memory for individual aspects of the cars is apt to be confused after test-driving several different cars. Thus the depth-first approach is superior when the alternatives can be examined only once, one at a time. The three houses could be reexamined by the Colemans several times, which enabled them to make comparative ratings on each aspect, as required when the breadth-first approach is used.

What about your personal feelings?

People are often concerned that if they work out a balance sheet of any kind, they will become so coldly analytical that their emotional reactions to the alternatives will be left out of the picture entirely. John Stuart Mill, the great nineteenth-century philosopher, said, "The habit of analysis has a tendency to wear away the feelings." But as an extraordinarily rational and analytical man, Mill may have underestimated the persistence of the emotions aroused when vital choices have to be made. A recent commentator points out that the reverse of what Mill said might be closer to the truth: "With most people, rather, it works the other way round; as long as their feelings are involved, they are incapable of analysis."

We believe that it is a gross exaggeration to set up any such dichotomy, to assume that either you have strong feelings or you engage in rational analysis. Even when emotions run high, most people can adopt an analytical approach, at least for a short period of time, by following the simple procedures of filling out the entries in a balance sheet. Furthermore, they do not need to leave their emotional feelings out of the analysis and probably should not. Twinges of emotion, in fact, often occur while people are writing down specific entries. Vague feelings of uneasiness as well as more specific apprehensions about certain risks can be recorded in the balance sheet if the person expects that he or she will suffer that kind of subjective discomfort from choosing a particular alternative. Similarly, people can write down expected feelings of shame or guilt and take them into account as an important part of the overall picture while thinking analytically about the choice that would suit them best.

Sometimes the emotional reactions people experience while filling out the balance sheet can play a crucial role in making them realize that they must be leaving out something very important. A person may be surprised that he is still strongly attracted to an alternative that has relatively few pluses and many minuses in the balance sheet. It may induce him to ask, "Why do I feel that way? What am I leaving out of the picture?" The surprising reaction may be a strong "irrational" feeling of aversion toward the alternative that looks like it might be the best one. Either reaction shows that something important must be missing from the balance sheet or that the intuitive feelings are being influenced by some irrelevant factor. These discrepancies between one's gut feelings and the picture that emerges from the record of pros and cons can stimulate one to engage in intensive self-scrutiny or to talk about the conflict in a less inhibited way with close friends. This may lead to fresh discoveries of specific reasons for being attracted to one alternative or for being repulsed by another. Here we are referring to wishes and fears that psychologists describe as "preconscious" sources of conflict—considerations that people remain unaware of unless they are stimulated to think about the discrepancy between their conscious appraisals and their gut feelings.

There are other ways in which the balance-sheet procedure can prove to be much more than a simple bookkeeping operation for making a record of what you already know. We have just cited examples of people who were induced by the balance-sheet procedure to reflect more fully on their priorities, to make more careful judgments about which objectives were really most important to them when buying a house or choosing a career. Examining the listed considerations in this way can have the beneficial effect of making decision makers somewhat more aware of their uncertainties about the future. It can help them to focus their subsequent search for information on ascertaining the likelihood that the most important outcomes will or will not materialize. All entries in a balance sheet are forecasts about what is likely to happen in the future if one or another course of action is adopted, and no one can ever be completely certain about such forecasts. When one focuses on the crucial considerations in the balance sheet it is difficult to avoid asking oneself, "Can I really count on this happening? How likely is it that this positive (or negative) consequence will actually occur?" This type of self-questioning has the healthy effect of increasing the desire for pertinent information that could improve one's probability estimates of the most crucial gains and losses. (In Chapter 5 we shall discuss the various types of information that decision makers can obtain to make reasonable forecasts of the future.)

Slicing up residual problems into manageable pieces

Big complicated decisions sometimes can be divided, or "fractionated," into a series of smaller and easier decisions that can be made separately, one at a time. This is referred to as the "slicing-up" or "salami" tactic. The same tactic can be used after a basic decision has been made when there are still some big obstacles to be overcome that would make it difficult to implement the decision. After a decision maker has figured out how the residual problems can be sliced up into more manageable pieces, the balance sheet procedure can be used for each of the separate decisions. We have found this use of the balance-sheet procedure to be effective especially with men and women who are somewhat discontented with their marriages or careers but have decided not to take the drastic step of separating from the spouse or switching to a different career.

You might occasionally find it useful to use this type of procedure on your own when you feel somewhat dissatisfied with a decision that is still sufficiently satisfactory to make you reluctant to change. It may also be applicable at times when you feel just about ready to start on a new course of action but you have cold feet because of worrisome costs and risks. That is to say, the fractionating balance-sheet method might be especially useful for dealing with anticipated minor problems after a new fundamental decision has just been made. This can be illustrated by the case of a thirty-year-old man who decided (with the aid of the balance-sheet procedure) to take night courses at a law school in order to change his career from insurance salesman to attorney, with the expectation of eventually becoming an expert on the legal problems of insurance companies. This change would offer him the opportunity of a much better job with better pay, higher status, and greater security in the event of a general decline in insurance sales. But there were numerous minuses on his balance sheet that posed residual problems—for example, he would have to borrow money to pay for his law school training; there was no law school in his town so he would have to commute to one in a nearby city; the insurance salesmen with whom he was friendly would probably regard him as "some kind of nut" if he gave up his current, lucrative job.

The minor residual problems could be worked out one at a time, using the slicing-up approach. The salesman worked out a new balance sheet for each problem, noting down the pros and cons for each of the available alternatives he thought of when dealing with the challenge posed by each of the minor problems that he would have to face in order to carry out the fundamental new decision successfully. As this example suggests, the completion of the balance-sheet procedure can be followed by the use of a new series of balance sheets to deal with each of the residual minor problems that need to be solved.

Using the balance sheet

We hope that these case histories of the use of the two types of balance sheets have been sufficiently clear so that you can use them yourself without further instructions. You should, however, keep some important points in mind as you do your own balance sheet.

First, make sure you pick a form for the balance sheet that fits your style and the demands of the decision that you are working on. If the pros-and-cons format seems awkward, try the report-card form. If neither one works for you, make up your own. Any system for keeping track of the different aspects of the alternatives will work as long as it is easy to use and covers the four essential areas.

Second, remember that the balance sheet for decision making is not just a bookkeeping device; it is a tool for exploring the alternatives you are considering. You should try to solve the problems that you uncover as you do the balance sheet. You should also expect to discover that you need more information about some aspects of your alternatives. You will have to delay completion of the balance sheet until you find out what you need to know. Thus you should not expect to finish the balance sheet in one work session. For very complex decisions it can take months to obtain all the information needed to complete the final balance sheet.

Third, pay attention to your intuitions. They are essential in making the entries on the balance sheet. Pay special attention to discrepancies between your feelings and the way the balance sheet seems to be coming out. These conflicts are hints that either your rational side or your intuitive side has left something important out of consideration. In either case, figuring out the source of the conflict can lead to better analysis of the alternatives.

5
Forecasting the Future

In this chapter we continue our discussion of Stage 3 (evaluating alternatives) by focusing on the problems of estimating the probable outcome to be expected for each of the alternatives being considered. We shall explore the implications of our earlier statement that the entries on balance sheets consist of forecasts about the future. When Bruce Calahan considered the possibilities for advancement in the company to be a strong advantage of the paper company job, he was essentially forecasting that he would be able eventually to move up to a higher management position if he took that job. Jeff and Anne Coleman were forecasting how they would feel about each aspect of the houses they were considering after they had settled in for a while. None of these forecasts is certain to come true.

The uncertainty principle

As Bertrand Russell said: "Seeing that the future cannot be foretold and that there is an almost endless variety of possible beliefs about it, the chance that any belief (about the future) which a man may hold may be true is very slender. Whatever you think is going to happen ten years hence, unless it is something like the sun rising tomorrow that has nothing to do with human relations, you are almost sure to be wrong. I find this thought consoling when I remember some gloomy prophecies of which I myself have rashly been guilty."

In view of this human uncertainty principle, Russell urges us to be especially reluctant to decide upon any action that could have very harmful results for ourselves or others if our calculations about future consequences turn out to be wrong. If we admit our uncertainty we can use it to our advantage. Russell suggests that the uses of uncertainty are most obvious when we make minor decisions that depend upon the weather, such as driving out to the country for a family picnic on a slightly overcast Sunday afternoon. If we feel certain about a favorable forecast, we won't bother to take rainwear along. But if we admit that it could rain, we can allow for that possibility and manage to salvage the excursion if that undesirable event happens. We can also apply the same sort of contingency planning to major decisions to obtain a similar advantage. Whenever we can overcome our wish for certainty by admitting the possibility that we may be mistaken and that the outcome of our chosen course of action might turn out to be the opposite of what we think is most likely, we can be prepared for unexpected opportunities that might enable big gains to be made as well as for unexpected setbacks that may require immediate action to prevent drastic losses.

Uncertainty about the future paralyzes some people at the time of a vital decision. To get rid of their painful doubts, they figure that since their guesses about the future are likely to be wrong they will pay no attention to future consequences. Since the future won't happen the way they expect, it's better to ignore it. This generates a self-fulfilling prophecy. Since they don't think about future consequences they are frequently surprised by the turn of events. Each surprise confirms their belief that the future cannot be usefully foretold. Soon they are afraid to make decisions because nothing seems to come out right for them.

The fact that the future is uncertain does not mean that we cannot have valid knowledge about the future. We can anticipate most of the general possibilities for the future even if we can't anticipate the details. We can also make reliable judgments about which possibilities are most likely. Decision makers who use information about the future to make intelligent gambles increase their chances of getting what they want and increase their chances of being prepared for either trouble or unusual opportunities.

Formal decision theory

Experts in decision making use some fairly simple mathematical techniques for taking into account the probabilities of success of the alternatives being considered. Unfortunately these techniques require that the alternatives be quantified with numerical estimates of both the probabilities and the values of the outcomes. In some situations, such as marketing decisions in which dollar values can be used, these numerical estimates are easy to come by. In these cases the formal methods applied by decision-making experts can be well worthwhile. But these formal methods are not useful for most of the vital decisions that we discuss in this book. For decisions that do not involve purely financial considerations, we suggest using more informal and intuitive methods. This section on formal decision theory is included mainly to help clarify the goals of sound decision making and thus to make clear what the informal methods are attempting to accomplish without the need for precise quantification.

Formal decision theory originated in the analysis of games of chance. Thus it is appropriate to use gambling examples to explain some of the basic concepts. Two examples are presented in Boxes 1 and 2. (These boxes are intended for those readers who want to know the essential steps that enter into the calculations made by formal decision theorists and who can follow simple mathematical computations that involve a little arithmetic.)

Experts using formal decision theory apply methods very much like those shown in the two boxes to decide among alternatives in real-world decisions. For each alternative they figure out all the possible outcomes. Then they estimate the probabilities and the values for the outcomes. Finally they calculate an overall numerical value for each of the alternatives being considered. When they are finished, the decision itself is easy. All they have to do is pick the alternative with the highest overall value.

Two important distinctions have been ignored in the discussion above. The first is the difference between value and utility. Value refers to how desirable or undesirable an expected outcome is. If desirable, it has a positive value; if undesirable, a negative value. The amount of value an outcome has can occasionally be measured in objective units, such as units of time or number of dollars. But values often have to be assessed in terms of desirability from the subjective standpoint of the decision maker. Subjective values, positive and negative, are referred to as utilities. (Organizations can also be

Box 1　A simple example of formal decision theory.

Consider a simple game in a gambling casino in which the player plays against the house. The player pays $1.10 to toss two coins and the house will pay him $1.00 for each tail. Formal decision theory enables a player to analyze how good this game is for him. There are four steps.

1. The first step is to figure out all the possible outcomes. There are only three: zero tails, one tail, and two tails.

2. The next step is to figure out the probability of each outcome. Simple probability theory predicts that when two coins are tossed they will land with zero tails one quarter of the time, with one tail half the time, and with two tails one quarter of the time.

3. Next, the value of each of the outcomes must be determined if they are not already known. In this game the value of each outcome, measured in dollars, is the same as the number of tails.

4. The final step in analyzing the game is to combine the information to produce a single overall measure. It is obtained by multiplying the probability of each outcome by the value of the outcome and then adding them up across all of the outcomes. The resulting number is called the expected value of the game. It is the average amount that any player can expect to win each time he or she plays the game. Calculations show that a player can expect to gain a dollar for each game played in the long run:

Outcome	Probability	Value	Product
Zero tails	1/4	$0.00	$0.00
One tail	1/2	$1.00	$0.50
Two tails	1/4	$2.00	$0.50
		Expected value	$1.00

Gambling casinos do calculations like these for each of the games they offer. Then they charge the players slightly more than the expected value to play the game so that the house comes out ahead in the long run. In this case they would be likely to charge a fee of $1.10 per game in order to make a profit of $100 for every thousand times customers play this game. Customers might be willing to play this game because once in a while, if they are lucky, they can win $0.90 a game ($2.00 prize minus $1.10 fee). But, of course, if they play a large number of times, they should expect to lose an average of $0.10 per game.

Box 2   Decision-theory analysis of a more complex game.

Suppose you are playing the game described in Box 1 with another player. You start off taking turns tossing the coins so that each of you has an equal chance of winning from the other. Suddenly the other player suggests another similar game. One of you would toss four coins and the other would pay (in dollars) according to the difference between the number of heads and the number of tails. For example, if either zero heads or four heads comes up the absolute difference is four and the player would get four dollars. The expected value calculation is as follows:

Tails:Heads	Difference	Probability	Value	Product
Zero:four	4	1/16	$4.00	$0.25
One:three	2	1/4	$2.00	$0.50
Two:two	0	3/8	$0.00	$0.00
Three:one	2	1/4	$2.00	$0.50
Four:zero	4	1/16	$4.00	$0.25
			Expected value	$1.50

Now suppose that the other player also suggested that on each turn you would get to choose which game to play. How should you choose between the two alternatives? Since your goal is to maximize the money you receive in the long run, the rational choice is to select the new game every time it is your turn. The expected value of playing this game is fifty cents more than the game described in Box 1. So you will receive an average of fifty cents more per game by choosing this game. Of course if both of you do this each time, you will break even.

---

said to have utilities, but in such a case the organization is being treated as an individual.) Roughly speaking, utility has to do with how useful the outcome is to one particular person (the decision maker) at one particular time (right now, when he or she is thinking about the choices). For example, utility measurements reflect the usefulness of an outcome in a way that takes into account the fact that on some days the same number of dollars may be more subjectively valuable to a person than on other days. If Chris needs money for food today, the difference between being broke and having five dollars determines whether Chris will or won't go hungry until tomorrow. But the same five-dollar difference between having five dollars or ten dollars determines only how well he can eat. If Chris were asked to give numerical ratings of utility, he might rate five dollars as having a utility of eight units and ten dollars as equivalent to nine units. In other words, at that moment ten dollars in only slightly more useful to Chris than five dollars.

There is no reason to require that utility estimates be consistent from day to day or from one person to another. Suppose two men injured in an auto crash are still unable to work three months after the accident. Each is offered twenty thousand dollars to settle his accident claim out of court. The utility of that sum will depend partly on the current income of each man. It will be less for the man who has a substantial investment income than for the man who has no income at all when he is unable to work.

When utilities are positive they are referred to as expected benefits or gains. When utilities are negative, they are referred to as costs or losses. Experts have methods for getting people to make positive and negative utility ratings that (the experts hope) are internally consistent for each decision maker. They use these ratings instead of objective value measures in their calculations. Thus they calculate expected utility for each alternative rather than expected value.

The other important distinction we ignored above is the difference between objective and subjective probability estimates. The exact probabilities are known for the coin tosses in the games described in the boxes. In most real decision situations the actual probabilities are not known. Instead, subjective estimates of the probabilities are made using rating techniques like those used for the utilities.

The general approach combining both distinctions is called the Subjective Expected Utility (SEU) model of decision making. Experts using this approach carry out the rating procedures and the calculations to pick the alternative with the highest SEU. Experts on applications of formal decision theory agree that whenever the theory is applied to real life decisions all sorts of errors can enter into the assumptions that are being made about expected utility values as well as about the probability estimates. The experts have worked out techniques for keeping the errors within tolerable bounds for certain kinds of decisions, but the techniques are quite complicated. We recommend leaving these methods to the experts. That is to say, if you think that applying formal decision theory could be useful for certain of your financial or other decisions that are amenable to quantification, consult an expert on formal decision theory for guidance on each step. Where can you find an expert in formal decision theory? Try at the nearest university, in the department of economics or in the school of business. (See also Chapter 8 on consulting experts.)

We strongly recommend that you keep the two central ideas of formal decision theory in mind whenever you make a vital decision, even though you do not attempt to apply the specific techniques of the theory. The first central idea is that in order to make a sound decision it is necessary to make the best estimates of the probability that each of the expected consequences will occur. The second is that a sound decision requires taking into consideration the relative importance of each of the anticipated favorable and unfavorable consequences—their expected utility value from your own standpoint. If you keep in mind these two ideas you are more likely to arrive at a choice that you will not regret even though you do not use any of the mathematics of formal decision theory. You will be less likely to overlook serious drawbacks or to give undue weight to vivid considerations that are really not essential to you or that are unlikely to materialize. You will be in a better position to make a choice that meets your main objectives, gives you the best chance of overall gains, and keeps unnecessary costs and risks to a minimum.

Using scenarios of the future

A good way to deal with the uncertainty of the future is to think in terms of scenarios. A scenario, as we pointed out earlier, is a sketch of what might happen in the future if a particular choice is made. It usually isn't a complete sketch; it may cover only a small aspect of the future. The actual future may include parts of several scenarios. For instance, to decide about a vacation at a national park, separate sets of scenarios could be developed for daytime activities and evening entertainment. The possibility of having compatible fellow vacationers at the lodge might not matter much in developing different daytime scenarios about hiking and fishing in the wild, but companionship might be important to consider for evening activities. When a person is undecided about a vital decision involving his or her career, love life, health, or future welfare, it may be worthwhile to set aside a block of time to think up three plausible scenarios for each alternative: (1) the worst possible outcome that could happen, (2) the best possible outcome that could happen, (3) the most likely outcome, which might be a mixture of desirable and undesirable consequences. As a result of constructing these scenarios, the person may become aware of some potential risks and some potential gains that he or she had not thought of before, which can be added to the balance sheet.

In some ways, the generation of scenarios is like the generation of the possible outcomes in formal decision theory. But scenarios do not provide a basis for the use of the SEU model. We can never generate all the possible scenarios for any given alternative, nor can we make sufficiently good estimates of the probabilities for the scenarios. These uncertainties make it impossible to use the scenarios to make specific predictions about the future consequences of alternatives. They do, however, make it much easier to think about the possibilities of the future, rather than the probabilities. We can be fairly sure things will turn out worse than our best scenario and better than our worst. Scenarios also help us make contingency plans to avoid the pitfalls and take advantage of opportunities that may occur.

Examples of scenarios about alternative outcomes

For more extensive examples of the use of scenarios, consider the case of someone deciding whether to open a retail computer store. Mrs. Horvath had been a computer programmer specializing in accounting and inventory systems for retail businesses. She was very interested in opening a computer store but she also considered the possibility of opening a wine and cheese store. She completed a preliminary balance sheet for three alternatives, the computer store, the wine and cheese shop, and continuing in her present line of work. The balance sheet showed that the computer store was the most attractive alternative, but Mrs. Horvath felt that she hadn't adequately explored the possibilities for the future. So she decided to make up a series of scenarios for the computer store she was planning to open.

At the time Mrs. Horvath was working on these plans, retail computer stores had been around for only a couple of years. The potential size of the market was very uncertain, and there was already one computer store in the town where she lived. Her basic idea was to open a store selling a wide range of consumer electronic products as well as computers. She planned to offer video games, calculators, digital watches and clocks, and telephone message recorders. She expected that these items would bring people into the store who didn't know about home computers but who could be interested in them. For instance, customers who came in to look at a fancy video game might be willing to pay a bit more to get a computer that would not only play games but would also balance their checkbooks and help their kids with math homework.

Mrs. Horvath started with scenarios for the successful future of her store. In the first scenario she imagined the future of her business proceeding as she planned, initially with sales primarily of home products and with a gradual shift to computers as the market developed. Her next scenario explored variations on the way the market for personal computers might develop. One possibility lay in education. She could sell computers to schools for use in mathematics and science programs and to families with children seriously interested in these subjects. She saw herself developing this market by giving talks and demonstrations to the science clubs at the high schools, to PTA meetings, to teacher groups, and to the town school board. She thought of giving one of the systems to a couple of the largest high schools. After they had learned how to use this system, both the schools and the students would be more likely to buy more of her system than to shift to something new.

Mrs. Horvath's next scenario concentrated on a completely different market—home control systems. A small computer could be easily set up to control heating and air conditioning systems to reduce energy consumption and to monitor a burglar alarm system at the same time. It could also control other household items as well; it could turn on the coffee pot in the morning and turn off the hi-fi after people had gone to bed. In Mrs. Horvath's scenario she imagined herself working with a burglar alarm company and with a heating contractor to develop a combined system that would cost very little more than good conventional systems, yet provide sophisticated features not currently available. She worked out more details of what a successful business in this area would be like, including selling computers for telephone answering systems and automatic plant watering systems.

Mrs. Horvath worked out several other scenarios for successful variations on the business and then turned to scenarios that involved failures. The general strategy for developing unsuccessful scenarios is to ask "What could go wrong?" with each of the successful scenarios. This process involves identifying the assumptions that were made in projecting the successful scenarios. Sometimes these assumptions are explicit and can be easily identified, but often they are implicit and difficult to bring to awareness.

The central assumption in all of Mrs. Horvath's success scenarios was that a market for home computers was sure to develop. At the time she was deciding about her store, home computers were just beginning to appear. She knew that the growing interest in computers could fizzle. The home computer market could become rapidly saturated if very few people wanted to have their own computer. Mrs. Horvath's scenario for this situation involved shifting the emphasis of the store to the other consumer electronic products and phasing out the computer line. There were several variations on this scenario depending on which of the products would sell best. The store might end up as an electronic game and toy shop or it might become a calculator and clock store. Mrs. Horvath would be disappointed in any of these outcomes but not seriously so. She would have a successful business that she could sell if she really got tired of it.

Another important assumption was that the computer products would be available for her to sell. The home computer market had been plagued with product delays and cancellations. Mrs. Horvath's scenario for this case involved developing the local market and then discovering that she couldn't get enough computers delivered to her to maintain the volume of business she would need to make a profit. One version of the failure scenario was that she neglected the non-computer part of the business because the computers would take all of her time and would seem successful right up until the time that either supply or demand would go down to zero. This scenario ended in bankruptcy. Mrs. Horvath was stimulated to develop some contingency plans that would reduce the likelihood of the occurrence of this scenario. She committed herself to maintaining the non-computer part of the business even if the computer part went well. She planned to carry a variety of computer products so that she would not be dependent on a single manufacturer and could satisfy public demand for a momentarily popular model. Finally, she would be alert to delivery problems so that if they occurred she could act quickly to develop new plans.

Mrs. Horvath's next scenario considered what might happen if there were a general recession in the next few years. A recession might decrease the market for both computers and the other products that she planned to sell. This scenario would lead to continued losses and eventual failure of the business. Mrs. Horvath didn't see any way to avoid this difficulty if a serious recession occurred.

In addition to the scenarios for variations in market conditions, she also thought up little scenarios for the more specific assumptions she was making. These pertained to the financing for the store, the business location she was considering, the competition she faced, and other details of her business plans.

The actual future was unlikely to be exactly like any of Mrs. Horvath's scenarios. But since she did a good job of considering all the major possibilities, the actual future would probably turn out to be something like one of the scenarios or perhaps a combination of two of them. Mrs. Horvath's advance planning would enable her to take appropriate actions to make the successful scenarios rather than the failures come true. The scenarios gave her the power to choose her own future from a wide range of possibilities.

Techniques for generating scenarios

Generating scenarios requires imagination and creativity. A background in writing fiction or fantasy would be helpful, but we don't all have these talents. Furthermore, we have all sorts of psychological blocks against considering certain possibilites. Fortunately, there are some simple techniques for overcoming these problems. These methods involve role playing. When people pretend to be someone else, they frequently find that they know things that they did not know they knew. After the role playing they can use the newly found information in the construction of scenarios.

The first method is to have an imaginary conversation with an intelligent person who takes a different point of view. For instance, Mrs. Horvath might pretend to have a conversation with an imaginary uncle who is opposed to her going into business. As people take on the role of an opponent to their own point of view they frequently find that they are able to think up arguments that they would have missed otherwise.

This procedure can probably be used with considerable benefit at the point where your are ready to choose the best course of action. You can test the reasons for the choice that you have been taking most seriously by considering what someone who opposes your conclusion might say in refutation. It may be easiest to do this if you can imagine having an actual conversation with a particular person—it could be a famous writer or a skeptical but shrewd relative or acquaintance. The important thing is to do your best at creating a realistic conversation with someone whose opposing views are not the least bit silly or stupid. Bertrand Russell, who advocated imaginary conversations as means of overcoming unwarranted feelings of certainty, said, "I have sometimes been led actually to change my mind as a result of this kind of imaginary dialogue, and, short of this, I have frequently found myself growing less dogmatic and cocksure through realizing the possible reasonableness of a hypothetical opponent."

The imaginary conversation method is similar to the type of cognitive role-playing technique that social psychologists have found to be an effective means of changing opinions and attitudes via self-persuasion. Numerous social-psychological experiments show that when people engage in the debate type of improvised role playing they think up and take seriously new arguments they had not considered before, sometimes to the point of persuading themselves that their initial position on the issue was wrong, which leads to marked changes in attitude. One way to engage in a debate with oneself is to write an essay in favor of whichever position seems most attractive and then a second one against it, in support of a rival alternative.

A related role-playing technique is to imagine yourself a few years in the future meeting an old friend you haven't seen for years.

Imagine that everything possible has gone wrong and that you take the opportunity to cry on your friend's sympathetic shoulder. What miserable disappointments might you need to talk about? When people try to imagine the worst possible outcomes, their hidden fears sometimes come out so that they can be used constructively. You can also do the opposite. Imagine the best possible outcome. What great things might you tell your friend? This version is especially useful for people who don't easily see themselves as successful, especially those who tend to be pessimistic about any new venture.

Although awareness of uncertainty can be used in a constructive way, it can have detrimental effects if it leads to procrastination and vacillation at a time when action is necessary. If a deadline is at hand and a choice has to be made, a person has to muster up his or her courage and select whatever seems to be the best available choice, even if keenly aware of all the uncertainties about possible outcomes. At such a time, a decision maker might gain a bit of comfort from the thought that having made careful contingency plans, he is not so unprepared for adverse consequences as he otherwise might be. If that consolation is not sufficient, perhaps it would be helpful for the decision maker to have another imaginary conversation, this time with a fantasy companion who is much more keen on carrying out the least objectionable course of action.

Errors in estimating probabilities

It is not enough to know what the possibilities are for the future. It is also necessary, as decision theorists emphasize, to know as much as you can about how *likely* those possibilities are. Mrs. Horvath knew before she began generating scenarios that there was some chance that she would fail. To make an intelligent decision about whether to invest her time, energy, and money in opening a retail computer store she needed to determine whether her chances of success were sufficiently greater than her chances of failure.

Unfortunately, judgments of probability based on scenarios are frequently badly in error. Scenarios provide the possibilities but not the probabilities. In order to make reasonable probability estimates, even rough, nonquantitative ones, decision makers must look at other kinds of evidence.

One reason probability estimates based on scenarios are so bad is that most of us use very simple strategies for making probability judgments. One common strategy relies on judgments of "representativeness." To judge whether it is going to rain this afternoon we check whether the current weather is a reasonable example of the kind of weather that precedes rain, which could affect a decision about whether or not to go on an outing. If it is representative, then we judge the probability of rain to be high and decide not to go. We usually are not aware of how we make our judgments of probability. We just feel intuitively that certain things are likely to happen without an explicit analysis of the representativeness of the current situation.

Several of Mrs. Horvath's judgments about the likelihood of the various outcome scenarios were based on representativeness. Her overall judgment that her plan was likely to succeed was based on what she knew of typical successes and failures of retail businesses. Typical business successes have some unique selling point, are adequately planned and financed, and provide good service with attention to all details. Typical business failures are poorly planned and badly organized so that they don't provide good service to their customers, are underfinanced so that they can't last through the initial period of loss, and either enter a very competitive market (such as book stores) or a nonexistent one (such as cactus stores). Mrs. Horvath thought that her business plans were more representative of those that turn out to be successful than of those that fail.

Mrs. Horvath made similar judgments about the future of the market for home computers. Was it a technological advance that would become popular like stereo? Or would it flop like the attempt to replace stereo with quadraphonic sound? In answering these questions, Mrs. Horvath judged the current computer market to be very much like the early hi-fi market. The first hi-fi components appealed only to an avant-gard with specialized interest and knowledge, but soon systems were developed to appeal to a much larger group of people. Mrs. Horvath believed that this was already happening with computers. Since this pattern is typical of developing markets, she concluded that a sizable retail market for computers would soon develop.

Why are judgments of probability based on representativeness so bad? They leave out a number of factors that should be taken into account. The most important is the prior probability of a successful event. In other words, how likely is the desired type of event in general without considering the evidence bearing on representativeness? If a pair of collaborating authors decide to prepare a magazine article to be considered for publication they may think that their material is much more representative of articles that are accepted than of those that are rejected. Therefore, representativeness would lead them to expect their article to be accepted. But most magazines receive many more articles than they can publish. Suppose magazines that publish articles like theirs accept only 10 percent of all articles submitted. This base rate suggests that they only have a 10 percent chance of getting their article accepted. The fact that their article is representative of the articles accepted makes it more likely that theirs will be among them, but it may still have only a 20 percent chance. It is much more likely to be rejected than accepted.

Sometimes there is no information about the prior probability. Mrs. Horvath didn't have any idea how to estimate the prior probability of home computers becoming a large market. But she did know something about the base rate of success of new retail stores—that a very high percentage of all new businesses fail within the first year. This means that Mrs. Horvath should realize that although her plans looked typical of those that succeed, which improved her chances at least a bit, she still faced an appreciable chance of failure. The base rate may provide a better basis for estimating the probability of success than the degree to which Mrs. Horvath's plans are representative of successful businesses.

Psychological experiments have shown that people tend to ignore base rates when they have other information, even when the other information is irrelevant. For instance, when people are asked to guess whether someone is a brain surgeon or a lawyer they do not take into account the fact that there are many more lawyers than brain surgeons. Even when people are reminded of this fact they make their judgments as though it were equally likely for someone to be a lawyer or a brain surgeon. They ought to judge that it is much more likely for the person to be a lawyer unless they have specific information about the person's training or daily work activities. Similar errors are likely to be made when people are wondering whether or not to trust a salesman's promises about delivery and guarantees when they are about to buy an expensive piece of equipment. This requires judging whether the salesman is trustworthy or not. Here again people are likely to make the mistake of ignoring the base rate and of giving undue weight to diagnostic cues, such as whether he has a friendly smile and looks one straight in the eye.

In many decision-making situations the relevant base rate information is easy to get. People planning to start a new business can find out the success rate for new businesses of that specific type. Students planning to go to graduate or professional school can ask what proportion of students actually graduate at the schools where they are applying. Medical patients can ask their doctors about the base rates for the success of the treatments being considered. Automobile buyers can find out from consumer magazines the base rates for serious repairs for each make of car. In all of these cases the base rate information can be obtained without serious difficulty. The information about the specific alternatives being considered can then be used to modify the base rate prediction to make a specific forecast.

In contrast to base rates, there are other kinds of information that people pay too much attention to. This is most striking when people have experienced a single vivid case. It is very difficult to persuade a survivor of a plane crash that air travel is as safe as the record indicates it is. Even people who have not experienced a traumatic airplane accident have seen vivid reports in the news. This contributes to the greater anxiety many people feel about air travel as compared to automobile travel when the objective probabilities of serious accidents should lead to the opposite.

The vivid-example problem is one of the reasons scenarios that make one aware of possibilities can be misleading when it comes to estimating probabilities. The scenarios that seem most real and, therefore, most likely are those that are similar to the cases we have experienced. This experience can be our own direct experience or it can be the vicarious experience of hearing about someone else. If Mrs. Horvath had a close friend who had recently been very successful with a new business, the success scenarios that were similar to the friend's actual experience would seem more likely. The opposite would be true if the friend's business had failed. Actually, whether or not Mrs. Horvath knew anyone who had succeeded

with a new business would hardly affect the probability of her succeeding in her own business. Thus, this kind of vivid-example evidence ought to be given little or no weight, yet it has a strong influence on human judgments of probability

The vivid-example problem is a special case of a more general
limitation on human inference. When considering evidence, people
disregard the characteristics of the sample on which the inference is
based. They often ignore the size of the sample and also fail to consider the likelihood of bias in the selection of the sample. Since
probability is defined in terms of all possible cases, any dependable
probability estimate requires a large number of relevant cases to use
in the following formula:

$$\text{Probability of an outcome} = \frac{\text{Number of times that outcome occurred}}{\text{Total number of all relevant cases}}$$

More weight ought to be given to evidence from large samples than
to that from small samples, and to random samples more than to
specially selected ones.

For example, consider Ellen and Jim Wilson's decision about
whether to go to a mountain resort. The Wilsons have several extra
days in the Seattle area, and they are trying to decide whether to
make reservations at Mount Rainier or somewhere else. The crucial
factor is the weather. They have heard that it is often very rainy
and foggy on Mount Rainier. If the weather is bad they will not enjoy the trip at all. The Wilsons' friend Jack has said that during the
summer he lived in Seattle he had made three trips to Mount Rainier and that it was beautifully clear each time. On the basis of this
evidence the Wilsons decide that the chances of good weather are
sufficient for them to make their plans to go.

A sample of three cases is not very large. The fact that Jack was
lucky enough to be there on three clear days should not lead to the
conclusion that the chance of rain and fog is low for the time the
Wilsons are planning to be there. Suppose that the Wilsons feel that
one chance out of three that their vacation will be spoiled is too
large for them to risk. Calculations of the probabilities involved
(which we won't show) indicate that even with one out of three
days of rain, 30 percent of the people who go three times will have
clear weather all three times, 44 percent will have clear weather

twice, 22 percent will have rain twice, and 4 percent will be rained out all three times. Thus it is not unusual for someone to have three clear days in spite of a probability of rain that the Wilsons find unacceptably high. They should not take Jack's experience as indicating that the chance of rain is low enough for them to go. They should find out what the weather records indicate. The records provide a large sample for a much more reliable estimate of the chances of rain while the Wilsons are there.

There are methods, called Bayesian statistics, for calculating how much consideration ought to be given to Jack's report of his three trips to Mount Rainier. These methods are applicable only to very limited kinds of decisions, such as investment decisions for which all the objectives can be specified in terms of monetary value. We should not allow ourselves to be comforted by the fact that even the experts who use Bayesian statistics in their professional work fall victim to ignoring the sample size when they are using their everyday reasoning powers rather than their statistical tools. Experiments have shown that even researchers who know the relevant statistical methods often place too much reliance on results from small samples.

In addition to the problem of sample size, Jack's weather report also presents serious problems of sample bias. The probability calculations we reported above hold true only when the sample is a random sample of days on Mount Rainier. But Jack didn't select his days on Mount Rainier randomly. Since he was living in Seattle Jack could wait until he heard the weekend weather prediction before deciding to go. Thus Jack had a very good chance of visiting Mount Rainier on three clear days. The fact that he was successful does not indicate much about the Wilsons' chances for good weather. The Wilsons might do better by following Jack's method. They could have contingency plans for something else in case the weather is bad. They could then wait until the last minute to make the final decision about whether to go the Mount Rainier.

People are fairly good at spotting some kinds of sample bias. We know that we should be suspicious of samples presented by people with ulterior motives. Any statistics presented by a salesman are suspect. But we miss many other possible sources of sample bias. Some of these can be spotted by looking skeptically at each important piece of evidence bearing on probability estimates and by thinking about likely sources of bias that might reduce its predictive value.

Another bias in estimating probabilities comes from the availability of the images a person has of favorable and unfavorable outcomes. People tend to base their estimates of probability on their intuitive judgments of how easy it is to imagine the various events. For instance, in the earthquake areas of California and elsewhere many people think the danger of earthquake damage is greatest in the hills, and they are inclined to decide that it is more secure to live in the valleys. They can more easily imagine the hills moving and shaking than the "solid" flat areas. In fact, the flat areas in the valleys often suffer the most damage because the loose soil can shake like jelly and tear apart the buildings on it. When the hills move, they move as a unit and buildings are less likely to be torn apart.

The process of generating scenarios is subject to this availability bias. The scenarios that are created are the ones that are relatively easy to imagine. It is always possible that there is a likely scenario that for some reason is difficult to imagine. Mrs. Horvath attempted to reduce this possibility by generating as wide a range of scenarios as possible. Another way to combat this danger is to ask someone else for help. People differ in how easy it is for them to imagine different things. Experts' knowledge makes them able to imagine a lot more possibilities. Anyone facing a complicated decision like Mrs. Horvath's might find it useful to consult an expert to help create scenarios in the areas where she or he lacks some of the background knowledge.

Considerable evidence from psychological research shows that all sorts of people, including statisticians and scientists, often make the various types of errors we have described in this chapter—overestimating the likelihood of events that can be easily and vividly imagined, giving too much weight to information about representativeness, ignoring information about base rates, relying too much on evidence from small samples, and failing to discount evidence from biased samples. An excellent summary of the research findings and discussion of their implications can be found in *Human Inference* by Richard Nisbett and Lee Ross. This book reports that many people are likely to acknowledge that others make all the various kinds of errors but exempt themselves. The authors suggest that such people try out the following thought experiment:

> Let us suppose that you wish to buy a new car and have decided that on grounds of economy and longevity you want to purchase one of those solid, stalwart, middle-class Swedish cars—either a Volvo or a Saab. As a prudent and sensible buyer, you go to *Consumer Reports,* which informs you that the consensus of their experts is that the Volvo is mechanically superior, and the consensus of the readership is that the Volvo has the better repair record. Armed with this information, you decide to go and strike a bargain with the Volvo dealer before the week is out. In the interim, however, you go to a cocktail party where you announce this intention to an acquaintance. He reacts with disbelief and alarm: "A Volvo! You've got to be kidding. My brother-in-law had a Volvo. First, that fancy fuel injection computer thing went out. 250 bucks. Next he started having trouble with the rear end. Had to replace it. Then the transmission and the clutch. Finally sold it in three years for junk." . . .
>
> The logical status of the cocktail party information is that the number of Volvo-owners has been increased from several hundred to several hundred and one, and the frequency-of-repair record should, perhaps, be shifted by an iota on a few dimensions. We trust that readers will recognize that their own response to the encounter would not likely be so trivial a statistical adjustment or the calm observation that "every now and again one does sample from the tails of the distribution."

The final common flaw in estimates of probability is excessive reliance on intuition to attempt to predict the unpredictable. Gamblers on the stock market sometimes think their intuitions that certain stocks are going to go up will enable them to win. A less extreme form of the flaw occurs when people can obtain only a little bit of evidence relevant to the judgment and think that the best thing to do is to rely on shrewd hunches. Under these circumstances, people tend to be more confident about the future possibilities than is warranted by the low degree of predictability. For instance, people try to predict from intuitions based on interview impressions who is going to be successful in a management trainee program. Although the interview may produce reliable information about the relative competence of the candidates right now, casual observations from a brief interview are usually not sufficiently valid to make long-term judgments about people, especially when they are about to go through a program designed to change them. People change too much to make accurate long-term predictions about them when one has to rely on intuitive judgments based on a single conversation.

Using probability estimates

With all these flaws and biases is it really worthwhile to use probability judgments in decision making? We believe that it is. In spite of all the problems, your rough estimates of the likelihood of events can be sufficiently good to be taken into account in making many types of decisions. After generating the scenarios and looking for sound evidence about the probabilities, decision makers can go back to the balance sheet and fill in entries for the potential gains and losses that are judged to have low, moderate, or high probability of materializing for each of the alternatives being considered.

Creating the scenarios has important effects other than setting the stage for making estimates of probable outcomes. New alternatives sometimes emerge within a scenario and change the original choices being considered. The probable risks that are imagined in one or more of the scenarios can lead to contingency plans for troubles that are most likely to arise. The more detailed specification of favorable and unfavorable outcomes, although raising more doubts, can induce the decision maker to obtain more specific information that makes it easier to evaluate the leading alternatives and to work out implementation plans.

6
Choosing and Becoming Committed

As decision makers consider alternatives and gather information about them during Stage 3, one alternative may emerge as clearly the best. For instance, one choice might be better on some aspects and at least as good as other alternatives on all the other aspects. If so, the best alternative has no disadvantages, so there are no trade-offs to consider that might lead to some other choice. All the decision makers need to do is to check over the adequacy of their search and make plans to implement the decision. In these rare instances, the decision makers can move rapidly through Stage 4 (becoming committed).

Sometimes, of course, the choice seems to become more difficult after the relevant information has been gathered and the person may take a long time to go through Stage 4. This is especially true when one alternative is clearly better on some important aspects and another alternative is clearly better on others. Then the decision makers are stuck on the horns of a dilemma. It would be nice if there were some simple procedure to apply to the balance sheet that would tell which choice to take. It is tempting to count up the number of pluses and minuses for each alternative and to take the one that has the greatest excess of pluses over minuses. With the report-card form of the balance sheet the equivalent procedure is to average the grades and to pick the alternative with the highest average grade.

But these procedures may turn out to be shortcuts to disaster. They don't take into account the difference in the importance of the factors. They count a minor gain as much as a major gain. What we need are procedures for summarizing the balance sheet and comparing the alternatives to each other as wholes.

Psychologists and other behavioral scientists in the past few years have begun studying how people eliminate alternatives and select the one they consider to be the best when making personal or business decisions. Many different rules have been proposed, both as descriptions of what people actually do and as prescriptions of what they should do. Most of this work has been done using the Subjective Expected Utility model of decision making, which we explained in Chapter 5. Such complex procedures may be useful in making business or military decisions where the aspects of each alternative can be given numerical estimates. But we do not recommend these methods for making personal decisions or even for many business decisions where the alternatives have complicated consequences involving social and ethical considerations. We have no confidence in the ability of people (ourselves included) to make the kind of estimates necessary for the numerical methods unless they do so under the direct guidance of an expert each time they make a decision.

If you are intrigued by the possibility of applying the mathematical formulas of decision theory to your own business, administrative, or personal choices, we suggest that you take a university course on applications of decision theory. This will give you experience with many practical exercises, and you will become sufficiently expert to know exactly what to do each step of the way, especially when the information for the problem at hand is not too complicated or too sparse for proper application of the decision theory formulas.

Maximizing versus satisficing

The methods we have discussed so far all have as their goal the selection of the one "best" alternative. This process is referred to as maximizing. Herbert Simon has argued that sometimes it is more reasonable to choose a satisfactory alternative than to continue searching for the absolute best. The time, energy, and expense of finding the best possible choice may outweigh the improvement in the choice. Simon coined the term "satisficing" to refer to a strategy that involves setting minimum standards for each aspect of the alternatives. The first alternative that meets the minimum standards is selected. This strategy guarantees a satisfactory choice with a minimum of effort but it requires the decision maker to give up hope of finding a significantly better alternative. Satisficing is appropriate in some circumstances. For instance, most people stopping for the night during a long automobile trip will pick the first acceptable motel. If they searched further they might find a wonderful country inn at half the price of the motel, but generally the effort involved in the search outweighs the chances of finding anything significantly better than the first acceptable motel.

Satisficing is a perfectly good method for many minor decisions. When none of the alternatives is likely to be much better than merely acceptable and when the cost of further search is high, the satisficing strategy is fine. But for major decisions that can have very serious consequences the satisficing method is rarely appropriate.

The informed intuitive approach

Many people make important decisions on an intuitive basis, without consciously using any particular decision rule. Sometimes human intuition seems to do a pretty good job of taking the importance of the various factors into account. We believe that when people take the time to review carefully the relevant information about expected consequences, their intuitive judgments provide a reasonable weighting of the alternatives against one another. All the decision maker needs to do, then, is to go over the balance-sheet entries again to keep them fresh in mind. If one alternative seems clearly better it is selected as the tentative choice.

Rick and Sally Thompson used the intuitive method to decide what to do with some money they got as a bonus. Their main alternatives were (1) buying a new car, (2) remodeling the kitchen, (3) adding central air conditioning, and (4) putting the money into a savings account. After careful deliberation both of them felt that adding central air conditioning was the best alternative. The key step in making this intuitive decision was the review of the balance sheet. They made this decision in late winter, and their first inclination was that remodeling the kitchen would be best. But looking over the balance sheet reminded them of Sally's suffering from hay fever in June as well as the discomfort of the midsummer heat, which had resulted in very important pluses for the air conditioning alternative. After they were reminded of this, it felt right to both of them that the air conditioning alternative was best.

If the Thompsons had lived in a slightly cooler climate and if Sally had not been allergic to pollen, the air conditioning and kitchen alternatives might have come out essentially equal. Under these circumstances, they might feel comfortable making either choice by any means, including flipping a coin. But this random choice is appropriate only after one has made a carefully itemized balance sheet and has determined that both alternatives are good and nearly equal in overall evaluations, not just on a first intuitive guess.

The rank-ordering method

Sometimes intuition says that the intuitive method hasn't succeeded. Perhaps the balance sheet is so extensive that all the considerations can't be kept in mind at once. The first entries may be forgotten by the time the end is reached.

In cases like this it helps to rank-order the balance-sheet entries based on the importance of each pro or con listing. The result is a new balance sheet with the most important entries at the top. But more is accomplished than just a new arrangement of the balance sheet. The process of rank-ordering the entries forces decision makers to become more aware of their values. After rank-ordering, the informed intuitive method is tried again. The additional work with the balance sheet will usually make it succeed this time.

The two most important advantages that Rick and Sally Thompson listed for remodeling the kitchen were (1) the increased ease and pleasantness of cooking and eating and (2) the increase in the resale value of the house. In order to decide which was more important they had to think about their future plans and their values. It was fairly unlikely that they would be moving to another home within a year or two. The most important advantages for the air conditioning alternative were (1) eliminating temporary discomforts (hayfever and summer heat) and (2) the relatively slight increase in resale value of the house. The crux of the decision, then, involved these important considerations. In the end they decided that eliminating acute discomforts was more important than any of the other advantages. This made it easier for them to choose among the alternatives.

When optimists rank-order their balance-sheet entries they tend to put the aspects with the most positive outcomes near the top. They are apt to pick the choice that produces the maximum possible gains. Pessimists tend to rank the aspects with potential negative outcomes as the most important. They usually prefer the choice that has the least danger. When carried to extremes, both approaches add undesirable biases to the decision. But mild tendencies in either direction represent legitimate differences in values.

What if none of the methods works?

Sometimes none of the methods works. There are two possible causes for this. One is that the alternatives are so closely matched that they are essentially the same. In this case the choice doesn't really matter. The other possibility is that the earlier stages have not been completed adequately. The alternatives may not seem to be equivalent, but it's hard to tell which is better. If one decision rule points to one particular choice and another decision rule points to a different one, the person is in trouble because he or she cannot feel confident about either choice. But at least the person will realize that more time has to be spent thinking about the complicated questions involved and maybe he or she will get a good idea about what additional information is needed that could help to settle the issue (Stage 3). Perhaps it would help to consider some new alternatives (Stage 2).

The first time Rick and Sally Thompson tried to decide what to do with their money, they found that they couldn't decide. They went back to Stage 2 and considered some new alternatives. Originally they had been considering window air conditioners as a possibility instead of central air conditioning. They assumed that they would not be able to afford the central unit. Window air conditioners would be cheaper to install if put only in four critical rooms and cheaper to run since they could be turned on individually. So Rick and Sally didn't include central air conditioning on their original list of alternatives.

When they went through Stage 3 (evaluating alternatives) for the second time, they found out that central air conditioning was not so expensive as they had thought and that it would do a much better job of eliminating pollen to prevent Sally's hay fever. In addition, the increase in value of the house would be somewhat greater, so that part of the cost could be considered an investment. After these changes in Stages 2 and 3, the Thompsons had no trouble making a tentative decision after completing their new balance sheet.

The first version of a balance sheet is frequently an excellent aid to the problem-solving processes involved in finding new alternatives. The negative entries on the balance sheet identify the essential problems posed by drawbacks of the current alternatives. By trying to solve these problems, decision makers increase their chances of finding an alternative without serious drawbacks.

When price is a major consideration

When one is buying a house or making any other fairly expensive purchase, the amount of money it will cost is obviously a crucial consideration. In one way or another, all the decision rules we have discussed require the decision maker who is making a purchase to specify an acceptable price that he or she is willing to spend or an upper limit beyond which the item to be purchased would be too expensive. For major purchases many people strain to set a relatively high upper limit because they want the best they can afford. But, evidently, their financial calculations about what they can afford are often so erroneous that they make disastrous mistakes. At the end of 1977 an estimated ten to fifteen million Americans were hopelessly in debt, and tens of millions of others were in serious financial difficulties. One out of every twenty families that takes out a loan to buy a new car or to make some other purchase such as furniture or a washing machine cannot keep up the payments.

One reason that so many husbands and wives misjudge how much they can afford to pay is that they assume a steady flow of income and stable expenditures. They do not take into consideration the need for keeping reserve funds to meet special financial burdens that arise from time to time. When deciding that they can make regular payments on a mortgage or loan, they use, in effect, an oversimplified formula. They assume that the difference between the family's monthly income and its monthly fixed costs is what the family can afford to spend each month on repaying a loan. This formula fails to take into account all sorts of contingencies that could require sizable expenditures such as the need to make major home repairs every few years or to replace outworn furniture and essential equipment like the furnace or refrigerator, and to pay for expensive medical care if an illness strikes one or more members of the family. Borrowers also sometimes underestimate the size of the payments they will have to make because they do not fully understand the interest rate and the extra finance charges, which may be hidden in the fine print of the loan agreement.

Another factor that contributes to ill-considered decisions to make expensive purchases is the ease of buying on credit with little or no down payment. "Buy now, pay later" is a remarkably seductive idea even when it is not being pushed directly as an advertising slogan. As one commentator put it, "The affluent society is built on plastic, the shiny plastic of the innocuous-looking credit card. The small embossed chips give entree into a world of glittering material goods and exotic faraway vacations. But all too often, the cards also open the door to harrowing concerns over how to pay off mountains of overdue bills. . . . 'Debt entanglement is a major social problem.' " Obviously, the more expensive the purchase you are planning to make, the more carefully you need to check it out before committing yourself.

Checking out the decision

The tentative decision made during Stage 4 marks the transition from the evaluation of all the alternatives to the beginning of commitment to one choice. Three sorts of substeps usually occur during this stage. First, the decision makers reach the point where the decision feels right both in the final choice and in the process used to make that choice. If the decision makers feel that there is too much uncertainty or that their search and appriasal have not been thorough enough, they can decide to go back to the earlier stages. Second, the decision makers use the scenarios they developed to make more explicit contingency plans for the things that might go wrong when they implement their new course of action and for the unusual opportunities it might yield. Third, the decision makers begin taking steps that lead them to become more and more committed to the decision. These three aspects of Stage 4 are not necessarily sequential. Sometimes all three go on at once.

There are several key questions you can use to check out a tentative decision. The most basic is "How do you really feel about the choice?" If, after considerable search, appraisal, and deliberation about the alternatives the choice feels right, it is usually a good sign that it's time to make the commitment.

More specific questions deal with the processes used in reaching the decision. Are there any important alternatives that were left out in Stage 2? Are there other consequences not considered in Stage 3? Even though you may have spent a great deal of time on it, do you think your search was effective enough so that if you went back to the earlier stages you wouldn't find anything new? If everything about the process seems right, you are ready to move a step closer to commitment.

A major area of concern during Stage 4 is the likelihood of unknown consequences. There is something paradoxical in asking about unknowns. If they are unknown, we don't know what they are. In spite of this it is usually possible to estimate how likely we are to be surprised by some unanticipated consequence of our choice. What we are actually estimating is our uncertainty or lack of information about the choice. But it isn't just uncertainty about whether certain possible consequences will actually occur—that kind of uncertainty is taken into account in the balance sheet during Stage 3. Rather, the uncertainty is about consequences whose possibility is not even anticipated. In situations where we have less general knowledge, we feel that we are less able to anticipate the consequences. If you have never been to Kenya, you are more likely to be surprised by unanticipated aspects of living conditions in Nairobi than you are by another city in your home country.

Concern about the unanticipated consequences of a decision is a major cause of hesitation and vacillation during Stage 4. This hesitation is usually a good thing. It gives decision makers time to work through the important issues involved. The impasse may be resolved by returning to Stage 3. More information might be obtained that suggests new possible consequences. Many a person who feels almost ready to invest in a get-rich-quick business proposition worries about the hidden catch, seeks out additional financial and legal advice, and ends up discovering that there actually are serious risks, deeply buried in the fine print of the agreement he or she was about to sign—risks that could result in the loss not only of the entire investment but of other assets as well. In such instances of constructive procrastination the new negative entry transforms the balance sheet so drastically that the decision makers completely discard the unwise choice they were about to make. In other instances, a little longer information search is enough to enable the decision makers to overcome the fear of the unknown and to feel comfortable moving on to commitment.

Making contingency plans

Murphy's Law, you may recall, says that if anything can go wrong, it will. Although life isn't so bad as this pessimistic saying indicates, occasions where everything goes perfectly well are certainly rare. It is wise to be prepared for something to go wrong.

The scenarios developed during the evaluation of the alternatives can form the basis of contingency planning. Sometimes all that is needed is a quick review of the things that were in the scenario. In other situations the details of the contingency plans have to be worked out and other preparations made. If you do not want to miss out on gaining the full advantages of unusually good outcomes, it is worthwhile to make some plans about how you could make the most of the favorable outcomes you visualized in your most optimistic scenarios, just in case something like that might come true. It may be even more important to work out contingency plans that take account of scenarios that show what the bad outcomes could be.

The following case history illustrates the value of contingency plans in cases of major decisions made by organizations. The outbreak of Legionnaire's disease on one of the wards of a hospital created a major decision-making crisis. One patient had died and three more who were recovering were diagnosed as having Legion-naire's disease. The physicians on the staff were not worried about the medical consequences; now that the organism responsible for the disease is known, effective treatment by antibiotics is possible if the diagnosis is made early. What the hospital staff was concerned about was the possibility of a loss of public confidence in the hospi-tal. It could be closed by a panic among the patients or among po-tential patients who would choose to go to other hospitals. This was the fate of the hotel in Philadelphia where the first outbreak oc-curred.

After considering a number of alternatives, the staff decided on a plan that involved being open and honest about the occurrence of the disease. The county health commissioner would make the an-nouncement to the press and present it as a general health problem rather than as a hospital problem. The hospital physicians would be given credit for their skill in diagnosing the problem. At the same time, a factual letter explaining what was going on would be given to all patients and staff to cut down on rumors.

If this plan worked, the hospital would emerge as the hero of the story rather than the villain. But some scenarios discussed by the staff indicated that there could be serious trouble ahead. What if investigative reporters really pushed the issue of the hospital's re-sponsibility? The contingency plan involved having the spokesper-son ready with a lot of factual information about the disease itself, the kinds of transmission paths that had been ruled out, and the measures that were being taken at the hospital to check for the source of the disease. The spokesperson spent a great deal of time during Stage 4 preparing for this contingency.

Other contingencies for which the staff made plans included the occurrence of more cases of the disease, inquiries or even protests from the employees' union and from upset patients. For each of these, the staff had a general idea of how they should respond, and someone on the staff was designated to take care of these tasks. The staff even developed a plan for unforeseen consequences—someone was put in charge of getting the group of key people back together if further decisions were needed. But the crisis was not like the worst scenario, and only the first part of the contingency plan was needed. It was implemented promptly, and the hospital emerged safely from the crisis.

An important part of the hospital's plan was the division of responsibilities among the members of the decision-making group. Contingency plans are usually much more informal when only one decision maker is involved, but they are still just as important. The value of making contingency plans for vital personal decisions emerges in Stage 5, adhering to the decision.

Becoming committed

Commitment does not usually come about in a flash. There is no magic moment in which everything suddenly becomes so clear to decision makers that all at once they publicly announce their choice to all interested parties. First is the tentative decision that begins Stage 4. Then commitment develops in a series of small steps. Some of these steps are internal to the decision maker. As positive answers are made in checking out the decision, the internal readiness to act increases. But the important part of commitment is external. Most decisions are implemented in a series of acts. First the decision maker lets his or her close friends know the tentative decision. Then others are informed and preparations for further implementation are made. Finally there may come a moment when the commitment becomes complete, sealed by a legal contract, as when a couple says "I do" in the marriage ceremony.

Each of the external steps of commitment changes the balance sheet. The cost of undoing the steps taken is added to the disadvantages of each of the other alternatives. These costs can be material, as when a deposit cannot be refunded. Or they can be in the form of social disapproval that would be expected if one were to back out of a commitment. These changes in the balance sheet tend to swing the evaluation even more strongly over to the side of the tentative decision and help make the following steps of commitment easier.

Consider a young woman's experience in becoming committed to making a parachute jump. Betsy Evans was looking for something adventurous to do when she saw a movie about skydiving. Both the challenge and the aesthetic experience appealed greatly to her.

After researching what was involved in the sport, Betsy made a tentative decision that she wanted to try it. The first step of the tentative decision was to tell her close friends that she was planning to do it. Her adventurous friends thought it was a great idea. They admired Betsy for doing something that they felt uncomfortable doing themselves. Her less adventurous friends were less than enthusiastic about Betsy's plan, but they were generally supportive of her decision to do it.

At this point Betsy's mental balance sheet gained entries reflecting the social and self-disapproval she would feel if she changed her mind. Being fearless was an important part of her self-concept. She and her friends both would view her as fearful if she changed her mind and decided not to try skydiving.

The next step was for Betsy to sign up for ground training and her first jump. Then came a series of small steps: showing up for the training, getting the equipment together for the first jump, climbing into the plane, hooking up and standing in line in the aisle waiting for the jump master's signal. Then there was the final step out of the door of the plane. As Betsy looked down just before the final step she had a sudden strong feeling of fear. But, as in the case of many other parachute jumpers, her commitment carried her through and she began to feel exhilarated as she floated down to earth.

Going down the path of commitment

The major danger with the process of commitment in small steps is that you may gradually become committed to something that you wouldn't have agreed to if the decision were made without the prior steps leading up to it. Psychological research has clearly shown that in many circumstances getting people to make a small commitment, like signing an innocuous petition, increases the chances that people will make a larger commitment, even one that has some strong disadvantages. High-pressure salespeople take advantage of this all the time. They have their unwary victims make a series of small commitments, such as agreeing to receive a free gift, before they press for the final commitment to buy a nine-hundred-dollar vacuum cleaner with a built-in television set.

People get themselves into commitments they don't intend making even without the help of high-pressure salespeople. Bob Scanlan joined the skydiving club at the same time Betsy Evans did and went through ground school with her. But Bob hadn't gone through the same kind of decision-making process beforehand. He came to the first meeting just because he happened to be with a friend who was going. He hadn't made any decision about whether he wanted to try skydiving. He signed up for ground school mostly to find out more about the sport. He figured that he didn't have to jump even if he completed ground school. He really enjoyed watching the parachutes, but he also found out that he was uncomfortable with heights and very tense about the tumbling roll he was taught to do as he landed on the ground. When the time came to sign up for the first actual jump, everyone else in the class signed up. Bob didn't want to chicken out. Besides, he wanted to watch the parachutes from the plane and he figured if he were too nervous he just wouldn't jump. But Bob no longer felt that he had any real choice when the instructor pointed to him and motioned him through the door.

As soon as the blast of air hit him, Bob realized he had made a mistake. He was panic-stricken, paralyzed by fear. Fortunately, the parachutes of beginning jumpers are rigged to open automatically. The ride seemed to last forever, yet the ground seemed to be approaching all too fast. The landing was rough because Bob forgot what he was supposed to do and for over an hour he was in a state of emotional shock. He had been so inept that he was lucky not to be injured. This type of reaction is by no means uncommon. Studies of sport parachutists show that after making their first jump large numbers of them regret having committed themselves. They commonly say things like "I never, ever want to go through it again." A study of 2800 men who volunteered for sport parachuting found that 85 percent dropped out after the first jump and of the 15 percent who returned, only a minority continued after the second or third jump.

Like many other young people who are attracted to skydiving, Bob didn't make an active decision to jump. He made a series of small decisions for each of the small steps of commitment without fully realizing where they were leading him. Bob could have avoided the disaster by applying better decision-making procedures at several points, but the earlier he started the easier it would have been.

Becoming a criminal inadvertently

An especially dangerous type of situation is one in which the preliminary steps of commitment lead to a major illegal act. Stepwise commitment can be seen in a number of Washington bureaucrats during the Nixon administration who gradually became more and more involved in the illegal actions known as the "White House horrors" and "the Watergate coverup." One such bureaucrat, Egil ("Bud") Krogh, started off agreeing to set up a secret operation to watch political opponents for the White House, even though he and his superiors realized that it could prove to be embarassing because it was not authorized by law. The next step was giving his approval for at least one burglary by members of his unit—the break-in at the office of a psychiatrist who had treated Daniel Ellsberg. Then, under pressure to cover up his various illegal activities, he committed perjury at a grand jury inquiry, for which he was sent to prison.

Krogh and other White House aides made a series of such decisions partly because the demands from higher authorities to engage in illegal acts were made in the name of a "good" cause. In many business organizations, executives and other employees from time to time are exposed to similar pressures and some of them give in, displaying a similar sequence of step-by-step commitment to carry out first a minor unethical act, then an escalating series of more and more serious violations. A minor deception leads to a larger deception, then a small fraud, and finally a major criminal act. Each step along the way seems to be, at the time, the last step that will be needed. But each time it turns out that a next step is necessary to keep the earlier steps from becoming known. It is very hard to break this cycle because doing so may require admitting the earlier illegal steps.

Even when decisions involve perfectly legal activities, many people find themselves caught up in a similar escalation cycle. They may end up doing things that they deeply regret—acts that they would never have carried out if it weren't for the prior stepwise series of commitments, which may have started with a seemingly innocuous initial commitment, such as doing a little favor for a couple of friends out of compassion for their unhappy predicament. It is the first part of the road to hell that is paved with the best intentions.

From commitment to implementation

The last steps of commitment are those that actually implement the decision. If contingency planning and checking out of the decision are completed before this transition, the person is less likely to regret the decision in the final stage, discussed in Chapter 7.

7
Overcoming Setbacks

The last stage of decision making is in many ways the same as the first. Most decisions are part of cycles. People follow one course of action for a while but lose their initial enthusiasm. Then as conditions change, a clear-cut challenge occurs and the discontented decision makers change to a new decision. After that they follow the new course of action until it, too, meets a challenge that begins the next round of decision making. No decision lasts forever; we change and the world changes. Thus the stage of sticking to one decision is inevitably also the stage of evaluating challenges to start the next cycle of decision making.

Why do we have five stages instead of four? We could have said that people go back to Stage 1 immediately after Stage 4. But the stage looks different from the perspective of the decision that has already been made than it does at the beginning of the cycle of decision making. When we described the first stage in Chapter 2 we were primarily concerned with the danger of missing a challenge, of failing to recognize that a change was needed. Here we are mainly concerned with the opposite danger of overreacting to a challenge and impulsively changing the decision when it is actually still a sound course of action.

A similar problem arises when the challenging sources of dissatisfaction with one's job or love life are feelings of boredom or of being tied down, which are likely to become prominent after one begins to take the satisfactions for granted.

To avoid overreacting to challenges and making ill-considered changes it is necessary to reevaluate the decision carefully by giving an honest answer to the question "Is the current decision still best, all things considered?"

The major theme of this chapter is that setbacks can often be overcome. Even with perfect decision-making procedures setbacks will occur—the uncertainty of the future guarantees that. Sometimes the losses will be serious. But usually a lot can be salvaged and the losses may not be so serious as they originally appeared. To make the best of a bad situation, decision makers must look at the whole situation, not just at the part that failed. The emotional feelings connected with failure often make this a difficult thing to do.

Decisions as plans

The analysis of failures is made easier by considering the prior decision as a plan for action. When a couple decides to buy a house they have adopted a plan for where they are going to live for an extended period. Such plans are the basis for the scenarios developed in Stage 3 and for the contingency plans developed in Stage 4. It is helpful to talk about Stage 5 in terms of changes in plans without getting into hassles over semantic issues such as whether the decision has been reversed or merely modified.

Plans frequently have an intended time span. A decision to give a party results in a plan that covers a relatively short period of time. A decision to go to college covers a much longer period, usually four years for the traditional bachelor's degree. Many people regard the decision to get married as involving an even longer time span, a plan to stay together "till death do us part." At the opposite extreme are those who seem to regard marriage as a tentative plan for some indefinite period, until they feel like changing. They are likely to agree with Ambrose Bierce's definition of "perseverance" in *The Devil's Dictionary:* "A lowly virtue whereby mediocrity achieves an inglorious success."

Plans vary in how easy or difficult it is to reverse them. After a couple gets married there is the possibility of divorce or even annulment. Although these will undo the marriage commitment, considerable time and high costs are involved. At the other extreme are decisions such as going on a diet. These decisions can be reversed almost instantaneously.

Dealing with failure

The best-laid plans of mice and men often go awry. And when the plans go very badly awry, decision makers frequently do too. The failure of a plan produces a threatening situation that puts considerable stress on each person involved. The feeling of having failed to anticipate the difficulty adds to the stress, especially if the decision maker feels personally responsible and if he or she thinks the difficulty could have been avoided.

When a major setback occurs unexpectedly, a person is likely to overreact not only by exaggerating how badly the decision is working out but also by vowing that he or she will never again make such a terrible mistake. Here is a vivid case study of this type of reaction, which illustrates how self-defeating it can be when carried to excess in a state of anger.

This example is to be found in an autobiographical account by Boswell, who in recent decades has become as famous for his pithy journals about his own life as he used to be for his classic biography of Samuel Johnson. In his *London Journal*, written during 1762–1763, the young Boswell gives the sordid details of an ill-fated liaison with Louisa, a beautiful young actress who suddenly became, in Boswell's eyes, nothing but a "dissembling whore."

During the six months that Louisa was his mistress, Boswell regarded her as a truly "fine" woman, and for her sake he confined his active sexual life to relations with her. Before meeting her, he had had no intention of becoming a monogamist; he was always open to fresh intrigues with actresses and ladies of fashion, usually pursuing several at the same time while continuing to have his customary street affairs with prostitutes. He apparently bolstered his renunciation of affairs with other attractive ladies by idealizing Louisa. In conversations with friends he constantly played up her "many endearing qualities" to the point where they thought she was much too good to be true. They "doubted of her existence, and used to call her my ideal lady." As for giving up his habitual pleasures with prostitutes, he now prided himself on being completely safe from the risk of venereal disease.

This honeymoon period came to an abrupt end one rueful day when Boswell discovered that he had unmistakable symptoms of gonorrhea, a disease especially dreaded in those days because of the prolonged and excruciatingly painful treatment inflicted by physicians in their attempts to cure it. Bitterly disappointed and aggrieved, his ecstatic image of the lady rudely shattered, Boswell confronted her with the bad news. Louisa readily admitted having once been infected long before meeting him; but she had felt certain of her full recovery. Fervently and tearfully, she assured Boswell that for the last six months she had had nothing to do with any man besides him. But Boswell refused to believe any of her pleadings or tearful explanations. This lady, who had been so ideal a love object, overnight had become detestable and dangerous—"a most consummate dissembling whore."

Boswell apparently displayed, at least temporarily, a characteristic "never again" reaction that encompassed his entire policy regarding liaisons with women. As soon as he was able to resume his sex life following an agonizing cure and convalescence, he resorted to picking up the "lowest" kind of streetwalker and then "could not but despise myself for being so closely united with such a low wretch."

In Boswell's account of his episode of posthoneymoon disillusionment, there are numerous indications that his idealization of the object of his passion set the stage for what can be described as an extreme overreaction to negative feedback. His disappointment and rage may have been quite commensurate with the magnitude of the bad news; but his fear of being deceived by Louisa's assurances and his plunge into self-abasing promiscuity were clearly excessive. . . . [Similar] examples of such behavior are commonly seen by attorneys who specialize in legal problems of marriage. They are consulted by husbands and wives who have discovered, shortly after getting married, that their spouse has misrepresented or withheld crucial information—for example, that he or she is a bigamist, a chronic alcoholic, a drug addict, a criminal, recurrently psychotic, diseased, sadistic, sexually impotent, or frigid. When such a discovery is made, the red-hot cognitions evoked in the disillusioned person, just as in Boswell's case, move the person to disavow the partner and expunge as thoroughly as possible all signs of prior commitment. The heroine in the musical comedy *South Pacific* epitomizes this tendency when she sings "I want to wash that man right out of my hair," following the discovery that her fiancé neglected to inform her that he already has a wife and children.

The "never again" reaction, which is so apparent when a disillusioned partner's love turns into hate, also occurs when new employees discover that their job has a hidden catch, that the boss expects them to lie, cheat, or in some way prostitute themselves. Like Boswell, the angry employees feel that they have been "had." They may impulsively walk out on the job without even waiting to find another one and without discussing the offensive demands with the boss to see if he or she might be a sufficiently decent person to withdraw the demands and perhaps to respect the rights of employees who refuse to violate their moral standards.

Months and even years after a distressing outcome, the "never again" reaction may linger on, like a traumatic neurosis. Each time the person faces a similar choice, he or she may immediately think, "Last time that didn't work, so this time I shall do the opposite."

Analyzing what has gone wrong

Although men and women who encounter unexpected setbacks may be inclined to act in a thoughtless, impulsive way to reverse or undo the decision as quickly as possible, they are usually capable of controlling this tendency if they *delay* action long enough to allow their intense rage, anxiety, or remorse to subside.

After a distressing setback like the one that impelled Boswell to break off completely with Louisa, a decision maker needs to wait until he or she calms down before considering whether the whole plan should be thrown out or whether it can somehow be remedied and salvaged. In order to learn from any such hard knock, it is also essential for the person to analyze as objectively as possible exactly what went wrong, which particular assumptions or which steps in arriving at the prior decision were in error. The disillusioned person's impetus to avoid ever making the same horrible mistake again can then be channeled into a constructive direction. This is illustrated by the way President John F. Kennedy reacted to the most shattering defeat of his career, the Bay of Pigs fiasco. In the midst of the humiliation of the complete failure of the attempt by the United States to invade Cuba on April 17, 1961—which practically everyone subsequently realized deserved to be a fiasco because it was so badly planned—he kept asking over and over, "How could I have been so stupid to let them go ahead?" One of his closest aides reported that "his anguish was doubly deepened by the knowledge that the rest of the world was asking the same question." He resisted the temptation, to which many heads of state succumb at such a time, to direct his rage against his advisers—the two CIA chiefs who had developed and urged the ill-fated invasion plan and other top-level government officers, including members of his White House team, who had supposedly checked it out and unequivocally recommended that it be put into operation. He announced to the press that he was personally responsible for the crucial decision and he opposed attempts by his followers to shift responsibility to the others who had participated in the deliberations. Although he was outwardly composed, his closest associates realized that he was deeply perturbed for many days. Soon his question about having been so stupid was replaced by a more constructive question: "What can we do to avoid being so stupid again?" One of President Kennedy's first public acts after the Bay of Pigs debacle was to set in motion a governmental inquiry to find out what had gone wrong with the planning and deliberation that led to approval of the faulty invasion plan. He took a keen interest in the work of the commission of inquiry he set up and studied their reports carefully. Then he introduced a number of major changes in the policy-planning procedures that he and his team of advisers would follow in order to increase their problem-solving efficiency. Some of his innovations broke with traditional practices. For example, he changed the strict security rules that were limiting the circulation of documents containing secret plans so as to allow all participants in the deliberations to have full access to relevant information. Other innovations, which he introduced to promote independent thinking among the members of policy-making groups will be discussed in Chapter 9 when we talk about what can be done to curtail the influence of groupthink. The important point here is that President Kennedy's handling of the debacle is an example of how the impetus to avoid making the same kind of mistake again, which is a central feature of the "never again" reaction, can be channeled into realistic planning that could result in genuine improvements in decision-making procedures.

When an ill-considered decision works out badly, the decision maker is likely to try to compensate in some way for his error.

> Regret can . . . function as a prod to higher-level conceptual thinking—stimulating the decision maker to move from the concrete level of retrospection about a past mistake to abstract generalizations that can help him avoid making similar mistakes in the future. In a sense, then, such

regret can be an important educative experience, leading to insightful intellectual analysis and enriching the person's repertoire of coping capabilities. This seems to be what people vaguely have in mind when they speak of having learned their lessons in the proverbial "school of hard knocks." But the educational potential of decisions that knock one about often fails to be realized.

Salvaging a decision after a setback

Total disasters like the Bay of Pigs debacle fortunately are rare. Usually the basic plan can be salvaged after a setback, even a major one. But all too often people immediately reverse a salvageable decision even though the defect might be corrected with persistent effort. Before people can grapple effectively with the external crisis posed by a failure, they must first grapple with the internal crisis— curbing the strong emotional impulses to take drastic action that arise in a state of acute anger, fear, shame, or guilt.

Dr. Dobbs, a successful dentist, went through just such a twofold crisis when one of his plans for improving the efficiency of his professional practice went awry. A few months earlier he and his partners had reached the point where they needed to add a new clerical employee to handle the increasing load of paperwork. Dr. Dobbs had suggested that they try instead one of the new inexpensive computer systems. So they bought a system complete with a set of programs for use in a dentist's office. The transition to the new system went very smoothly. The receptionist liked the new system and enjoyed learning how to use it. With it she was able to do all the paperwork without feeling rushed. The computer kept track of appointments and patient accounts with just a few simple entries on a display terminal. It printed out schedules, bills, and appointment reminder notices.

Late one afternoon as the receptionist was entering a patient's appointment into the system, the display screen went blank. The system had "crashed." Dr. Dobbs was not upset because he had been told by an expert that all computer systems occasionally have momentary failures. He reloaded the programs into the computer and ten minutes later the system was operating again. Then he discovered that the system couldn't read the magnetic disk of appointments. Somehow in the system crash the contents of the computer file of scheduled appointments for all the partners had been destroyed.

Dr. Dobbs had a sudden sinking feeling in the pit of his stomach. He realized that they had absolutely no record of the appointments they had made with any of their patients. They wouldn't know who was going to show up or when. They wouldn't be able to make appointments for anyone because they wouldn't know what times they had free and what times were already taken. The chaos would last for six or seven months because they had already made appointments that far in advance.

Dr. Dobbs went back to finish a patient's filling that he had been working on when the receptionist called him about the computer. As he worked he slipped and narrowly missed hurting the patient. He began to realize some of the further ramifications of the situation. He had always prided himself on running a very professional and businesslike practice. This reputation was important to him. He feared that the confusion about appointments would change this reputation and cause him to have worse relationships with his partners, his staff, and his patients. He might even face a malpractice suit. He would be more likely to make mistakes in the confusion. His worsened reputation would also make his patients more likely to sue over things that weren't actually his fault. Dr. Dobbs had trouble putting these thoughts out of his mind as he finished the filling. It was fortunate that the patient was the last of the day because Dr. Dobbs was in no shape to continue working.

Dr. Dobbs's bad feelings were exacerbated by the fact that he felt personally responsible for the mishap. He was the one who had suggested they get a computer in the first place. As senior partner he felt more responsibility than the other two partners for the decision to get the computer. He had also been more involved in the operation of the computer and the training of the receptionist to use it. He even remembered being told by the person from the computer company about the importance of keeping backup copies of all information stored in the computer system just in case something like this occurred. But Dr. Dobbs had not taught the receptionist to keep backup copies as part of the standard operating procedures.

Dr. Dobbs met with his partners that evening to work out a plan to deal with their crisis. Keenly aware of feelings of shame and guilt as well as fear about the damage to his professional status, Dr. Dobbs started right off saying that he regretted ever having suggested that they get a computer. He thought that getting the computer was a mistake and that they ought to hire another person to work in the office. They could go back to the old system of running the office. The new person would be able to help immediately in straightening out the mess of the unrecorded appointments and over the long run the extra person would be needed for the routine paperwork. Dr. Dobbs said he hoped that the computer could be sold for only slightly less than they paid for it so that the overall financial loss would not be great.

Dr. Dobbs was displaying the classic symptoms of impulsive reversal. The logic that he used was simple. If one course of action was wrong the opposite must be right. Perhaps "simpleminded" or "psycho-logic" would be better terms for this kind of reasoning. Dr. Dobbs was ready to act on a new decision without going through all the stages of effective decision making.

The impulsive reversal is really a variation of the paniclike reaction discussed in Chapter 2. This pattern of faulty decision making is not uncommon when people are confronted with a sudden and unexpected challenge and they feel that there is not enough time to find a better solution before things will get much worse.

Fortunately for Dr. Dobbs, his partners saw that no immediate decision needed to be made about the computer, certainly not that night. The immediate problems were how to operate without an appointment list and how to reconstruct one as soon as possible. They considered a number of possibilities, including writing to all the patients or telephoning them. They eventually figured out a way to use the patient files to determine who was likely to have an appointment in the near future. These patients were called and the rest got letters. The computer helped keep track of the letters and calls.

After the crisis was over, Dr. Dobbs realized that the original decision to buy a computer had been a good one. Instead of making only negative statements about how bad the decision had turned out to be, he began saying positive things to himself that took account of the real advantages that made it worthwhile to continue using the new computer system. He realized that the only mistake had been the failure to keep backup records. Now that they had changed their procedures they weren't in danger of a repeated crisis.

Losses from the crisis were not so severe as Dr. Dobbs had originally feared. This commonly happens when people are in a panic-like state during a crisis. They overestimate the losses that will occur and forget about all the positive things that will not be lost. They assume the worst. Even when the real losses are severe, the future usually does not turn out to be so bleak as it seems during the onset of an unanticipated crisis.

What can you do to avoid impulsive reversals? Unfortunately, the same psychological state of near-panic that contributes to unsound decision making also makes it very difficult to recognize what is happening and to change it. In the midst of a crisis, decision makers are likely to fail to realize that they are in a near-panic state. Even if they recognize the state, they are likely to forget what they learned about it. Even if they remember, they are likely to believe that their crisis is an exception; it's *really* bad and rapidly going to get worse. They don't think that what they have learned about exaggerations of disasters or impulsive reversals applies to them. These considerations suggest that getting help from someone else is most important in this kind of situation. Boswell immediately condemned Louisa and broke off with her without discussing with her or with anyone else the crisis posed by his venereal disease. It was help from his partners that prevented Dr. Dobbs from carrying out his impulsive decision to get rid of the computer. Dr. Dobbs was lucky because he did not have to make a deliberate effort to seek help. His partners already had a say in the decision and Dr. Dobbs had to consult them. If he had been in practice alone he might not have had sense enough in his excited state to seek out someone else to help him with the decision.

Decisions requiring continuous commitment

There is a special class of decisions that presents exceptional difficulties in the fifth stage of decision making. These are the decisions that require constant vigilance to maintain. Decisions to lose weight or give up smoking are typical examples. The success rate of people who make *firm* decisions in these areas is not very high. Backsliding is so easy; one piece of cake or one cigarette won't matter. Soon they are back to where they began. Numerous studies have shown that many people who come to an antismoking clinic or a weight-reduction clinic for counseling are successful at first but that the positive effects are generally not sustained after the clients are no longer in contact with the counselor. A very high percentage of people who temporarily give up smoking or who go on a diet have a relapse between the first and second month. The points we have made so far in this chapter about coping with failure and salvaging as much as possible apply in a general way to these decisions. But special techniques may also be needed to cope with the small failures that are almost certain to occur and that all too often lead to total defeat.

Two factors characterize these decisions and make them so hard to maintain.

The first is that the gains from the decision are long-term gains that aren't immediately apparent, whereas the losses are short-term and very obviously present. Backsliding produces immediate benefits by canceling the short-term losses. Strawberry shortcake will do wonders to cure the deprived feeling people get when they are dieting.

The second factor is that the steps that undo the decision are very small. Each one does not seem to have much effect on the long-term goal. The goal can still be obtained in spite of backsliding; it just takes a little longer. A portion of strawberry shortcake has only 350 calories. Dieters often rationalize a splurge with the argument that they will make it up by eating less the next day. Even if they don't eat less the next day, the strawberry shortcake will delay their goal of losing a certain amount of weight by less than a day. The problem, of course, is that if the first step backward doesn't really matter to the person, the next one won't either. Pretty soon the person is not on a diet at all.

There are two general techniques for making it easier to stick to decisions like these. The first is to make a detailed plan with specified subgoals. When people deviate from the plan, the failure is more obvious than with vague plans and distant goals. Another value of planning is to have contingency plans already formed for dealing with moments of temptation, such as when strawberry short-cake is served at a dinner party.

An experiment conducted with overweight women in a weight-reduction clinic showed some positive effects from encouraging the dieter to focus on a short-term, day-by-day time perspective. The dieters were told to approach the low-calorie diet with the plan of living up to it for one day at a time. The counselor suggested that each day they successfully followed the diet could be seen as a separate accomplishment for which they justifiably could feel pride. This day-by-day perspective was compared with a long-term perspective that emphasized the necessity to follow the diet as long as necessary to achieve the goal of losing the amount of weight each dieter wanted to lose. The clients given the day-by-day perspective were found to be much more likely to express hopefulness about succeeding and a strong sense of personal control than those given the long-term perspective. They also complied better with the request to send in weekly reports about their dieting behavior. Two months later, a subgroup of the women who had been given the day-by-day perspective were found to have lost more weight than the corresponding subgroup of those given the long-term perspective. These research findings show that the day-by-day perspective was effective for those people who were fairly self-confident about achieving the goal but did not help those who were lacking in self confidence.

Identifying root causes of failure

Figuring out effective day-by-day plans is easier for people who understand accurately why they have failed in the past. If they know what temptations or situations caused their previous failures they can devise plans to avoid them. But it is difficult for any of us to make effective use of our own personal "hard knocks" because of the necessity to curb anger and the other strong emotional reactions we have just mentioned and because there is a tendency for all of us to misjudge the causes. Once we know that a plan has resulted in an undesirable outcome, we are prejudiced in our evaluation of what went awry. With hindsight, everything about the decision may seem to have been wrong. We are likely to think we "blew it" because we are just no good at making that kind of decision, which is demoralizing and can lead to buck passing or other forms of defensive avoidance when we subsequently have to make similar decisions. Or else we may blame the persons who advised us and mistakenly cross them off our list for future decisions when they could be helpful.

Despite all the difficulties, it may still be worthwhile to try to determine, as objectively as we can, what specifically were the main causes of the miscalculations and to figure out what could be done to prevent them in the future. One formal method is to construct what is called a "fault tree," a list of possible root causes that might account for what went wrong along with a sequence of faulty branches stemming from each root cause. After listing all the candidates that one can think of, the next step is to see if there are telltale signs that correspond to the detailed effects listed on each branch that stems from the root cause. One can make an inference that a given causal sequence is the probable cause of failure if all (or most) of the telltale signs are present for that sequence and none (or few) are present for any of the others.

An example of a typical fault tree, constructed by a woman, Mrs. Holmes, who temporarily failed to stay on a diet, is shown in Box 3. Also listed are the solutions she worked out to avoid backsliding in the future. They consist of a new set of implementation rules for moving in the right direction toward successfully resisting temptation. Each of the rules shown in the right-hand column of Box 3 would lop off one of the poisonous branches of the fault tree and prevent the growth of the flower of evil at the top (giving in to the temptation to overeat). If Mrs. Holmes were to follow her first new rule (A^1) she would not need to apply any of the other new rules because the poisonous branches (B, C, D, and E) would not grow at all. If one day she were to break four of the new rules (A^1, B^1, C^1, and D^1), she would find herself at the top of the poisonous tree, but she could still nip the evil flower in the bud by following the fifth rule (E^1). Rules D^1 and E^1 involve using "positive self-talk," which we discuss in detail on pages 129–133.

When a decision is failing to work out well, a person might be able to analyze the causal sequence to explain what went wrong and develop a set of new rules to avoid the causes of failure without

Box 3 An example of a fault-tree model.

Mrs. Holmes had followed a low-calorie diet conscientiously for two weeks but after that failed to continue on the diet. The solid lines represent one causal sequence that she singled out as an explanation for her backsliding because she recognized that her own behavior had corresponded closely to each step in the causal sequence. Once Mrs. Holmes inferred the faulty causal sequence, she worked out a set of rules that would lead her to resist the temptation to eat fattening desserts. The rules are shown in the right-hand column (A^1 to E^1) and are represented in the figure by dotted lines.

THE FLOWER OF EVIL
(Going off the diet)

BRANCHES OF THE POISONOUS SEGMENT	RULES FOR PRUNING THE POISONOUS SEGMENT
E = Saying to herself at meals the next day, "Now I'm off the diet."	E^1 = Avoid going off the diet by saying to myself, "I'm back on the diet again even though I gave in to temptation."
D = Saying to herself, "Now I blew it, I have no will power; there is no point in trying to diet any longer."	D^1 = Avoid feeling defeated by saying to myself, "Nobody's perfect; I got off the diet this one time but I'm going to go right back on it starting with my next meal."

126

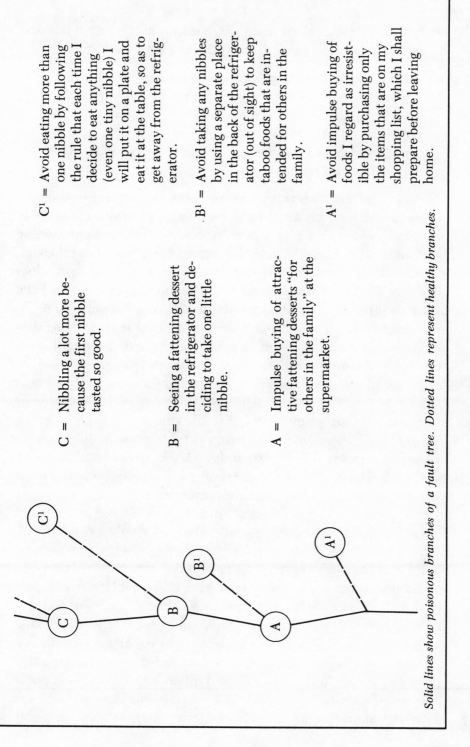

C^1 = Avoid eating more than one nibble by following the rule that each time I decide to eat anything (even one tiny nibble) I will put it on a plate and eat it at the table, so as to get away from the refrigerator.

B^1 = Avoid taking any nibbles by using a separate place in the back of the refrigerator (out of sight) to keep taboo foods that are intended for others in the family.

A^1 = Avoid impulse buying of foods I regard as irresistible by purchasing only the items that are on my shopping list, which I shall prepare before leaving home.

C = Nibbling a lot more because the first nibble tasted so good.

B = Seeing a fattening dessert in the refrigerator and deciding to take one little nibble.

A = Impulse buying of attractive fattening desserts "for others in the family" at the supermarket.

Solid lines show poisonous branches of a fault tree. Dotted lines represent healthy branches.

using a fault-tree analysis at all. Perhaps for some people it would be sufficient merely to answer the following two questions:

- What are the main problems I encountered that contributed to my failure to carry out the plan the way I had intended (for instance, to stay on a low-calorie diet)?
- What could I do from now on to solve each of those problems (for instance, to avoid the particular situations where there are strong temptations to overeat)?

One of the main advantages of using the fault-tree model is that it gets the decision maker to focus on a variety of different possible causal sequences that might account for the failures by providing reminders of specific problems that otherwise might be overlooked. It also calls attention to the prior steps leading up to each problem situation. For instance, if Mrs. Holmes had simply answered the above two questions, without using a fault-tree model, she probably would have thought about solving the problem of eating desserts when she sees them in the refrigerator but she might have overlooked the problem of buying such desserts in the first place.

To identify a causal sequence like the one shown in Box 3 as a major source of failure, you will have to do a great deal of preliminary work constructing all the possible causal sequences you can think of. Only then will you be ready to try to pinpoint one or more of the sequences that led to an undesirable outcome by looking for the telltale signs. After identifying such a causal sequence, you must do a lot of creative thinking, and some trial-and-error testing as well, to develop a feasible set of rules to prevent the growth and flowering of the poisonous segment of the fault tree.

Fault-tree analysis has been shown to be an effective tool in technical fields like engineering. It helps find the trouble in electronic or mechanical systems that aren't operating properly. Its value in personal and business decision making is less clear. The causal connections are more fuzzy than in electronic equipment. Still, a fault tree can provide a model that could sometimes be useful for analytically minded people. It can serve as a framework for identifying specific sources of error in a past decision and might even on occasion point quite specifically to a probable cause that can be taken into account the next time a similar decision has to be made. We recommend that you try the fault-tree method only if it appeals to you as a way of analyzing a specific situation you face. If it seems to work for you, then you could adopt it as a standard technique.

Positive self-talk

Some clinical psychologists advocate using an encouraging form of self-talk for decisions that you want to stick to despite setbacks and temptations that make for backsliding—like doing daily exercises, staying on a diet, cutting down on smoking, or undergoing unpleasant medical treatments that are essential for your health. They also advocate it for other types of decisions, since success in all enterprises is generally dependent on self-confidence about being successful. Some people are very self-confident and do not need any such encouragement. But most people at times are haunted by concern about failing when they try out a new course of action that is known to be difficult. Those concerns can turn out to be self-fulfilling prophecies: expecting failure begets failure just as expecting success begets success. A person who constantly thinks about failing is not likely to notice or to interpret correctly the subtle signs showing that all is going as well as can be expected; every little setback is magnified to the point where he or she is ready to throw in the towel. People are more likely to keep going if they can maintain a positive self-concept about their ability to succeed despite occasional failures. It is helpful in this respect if they can realistically attribute their failures, past and present, to specific external events rather than to something fundamentally defective in themselves, like "lack of will power." Although it is difficult for people to change their negative self-concepts, many seem to be able, with a little encouragement and effort, to modify their self-talk about a new course of action that requires self-control—replacing negative statements that are likely to be demoralizing with realistic positive ones that build up and maintain warranted expectations of success.

One variant of the positive self-talk approach is a coping method that involves focusing on the positive features of a decision and deliberately stating them to yourself each time something unpleasant happens that might incline you to reverse the decision. This technique has been tested in an experiment with surgical patients and has been found to be effective in helping patients to surmount the stresses of the postoperative period that lead some patients to regret having agreed to undergo the operation and to refuse to undergo the further treatments prescribed for full recovery. We shall describe the procedure used in some detail so that readers can judge for themselves whether it might be applicable to some of their own decisions that could entail suffering in the short run in order to obtain good health or other important goals in the long run.

The general approach is to encourage people to focus their thinking on the positive aspects of their experience, which helps to keep them from thinking constantly about the most distressing aspects of the unpleasant events they encounter. This approach is in keeping with experimental evidence on the effectiveness of positive self-talk, distraction, and a sense of being in control of the situation when stressful events occur.

What were the actual procedures used in the study of surgical patients? In brief counseling sessions, a counselor encouraged the patients to direct their attention to the more favorable aspects of their situation whenever they anticipated or experienced discomfort. This made the expected gains salient and was an active means of coping with stress under the patient's own control. Each patient was informed that he or she could initiate it at any time and in any situation. But first the counselor explained that most people are somewhat anxious before an operation and that they can usually control their own emotions if they know how. Next, the counselor reminded them that nothing that happens is either all positive or all negative—a well-known bit of folk wisdom—and that a wise person can find alternative views of threatening situations to avoid becoming overly emotional. Patients were then asked to generate examples from their own lives and to present positive alternative views of the events to be expected. After that they were encouraged to use the coping method in their own self-talk while in the hospital. If there are indeed at least two ways of interpreting every experience, the counselor pointed out, there must be a positive non-stress-provoking view of going through the experience of surgery. Attention was called to the positive or compensatory aspects of undergoing surgery in a good hospital, focusing on the improvement in health, the extra care and attention the patient will receive, the rare opportunity to relax, to take stock of oneself, to have a temporary vacation from outside pressures, and the like. Each patient was asked to work out an optimistic interpretation of typical unpleasant experiences that are to be expected when one is in the hospital for a surgical operation. The counselor suggested that the patients rehearse these realistic positive aspects whenever they started to feel upset about the unpleasant aspects of the surgical experience. They were assured that this kind of self-talk is *not* equivalent to lying to oneself.

The coping method certainly is not intended to encourage denial but rather to encourage maintaining a realistically optimistic view by taking account of the favorable consequences to be expected and reinterpreting the unfavorable ones. Thus, without encouraging denial of realistic threats, the coping method helps the person to feel confident about being successful in the long run.

The field experiment to assess the effectiveness of the coping method was carried out on the surgical ward of a hospital with patients who had already decided to accept a physician's recommendation to have a major surgical operation. Half the patients were taught the coping method and half were not. Patients who used the method showed considerably less anxiety, both before and after their operations, and needed fewer pain-killing drugs and sedatives during convalescence.

Similar procedures to guide self-talk in preparation for comparable future crises might be used to foster perseverance among people facing other types of postdecisional stress, such as those entailed by marital and career decisions as well as by all sorts of health decisions. But it may be difficult to develop the right kind of positive self-talk. One problem about trying to use the positive self-talk method entirely on your own is that it can easily be subverted into an excuse for not thinking at all about what can go wrong with a planned course of action. If you merely think up reasons for believing "There is no need to worry; everything will work out just fine," you are likely to be especially vulnerable to setbacks because of failure to develop appropriate contingency plans.

Another source of vulnerability to setbacks can be the lack of what is called stress inoculation. Evidence from many studies indicates that setbacks and losses have a less disruptive impact on a decision maker if he or she has been warned about them in advance. For example, it has been found that if job applicants are given realistic warnings about the stresses to be expected on the job, they are likely to stay with the firm much longer. This process of psychological preparation is called stress inoculation because it may be analogous to what happens when people are inoculated against a viral disease: resistance is built up in advance of expected attack. Probably the most effective warnings for purposes of stress inoculation include not only realistic descriptions of the stresses to be expected but also reassuring recommendations about ways to cope with them. Such warnings may provide decision makers with positive self-talk that is realistic when setbacks occur.

If positive self-talk is made up of flimsy rationalizations on the order of "Nothing really unpleasant will happen to me," it becomes useless the moment something really unpleasant does happen. H. L. Mencken remarked that "the most costly of all follies is to believe passionately in the palpably not true. It is the chief occupation of mankind." That popular occupation has to be renounced somehow after making a vital decision that entails any real suffering. For self-talk to be effective, decision makers must make *robust*, positive statements based on reality, not on wishful thinking, in order to withstand the common, garden-variety challenges that beset anyone who decides to undergo surgery or painful medical treatments or any unpleasant deprivations.

Positive self-talk is regularly used in a similar way to prevent backsliding among people who decide to go on a diet. The technique was developed by clinical psychologists who use an approach they call "cognitive-behavior modification" to help people develop self-control. They use it in combination with several techniques— avoiding situations where temptations to overeat are strongest, self-monitoring of eating behavior, relaxation training, and supportive help from the family, as well as thought-management exercises. When clients come for help in carrying out their decision to lose weight, one of the first things they are asked is "What do you usually say to yourself at times when you are having trouble sticking to a low-calorie diet?" Clients often report self-defeating statements, such as "I don't have the will power to do it" and "I'll never make it." They are encouraged to replace these unhelpful statements with positive self-talk that will encourage them to keep going despite set-backs. Clients are given a large number of examples to look over, in order to enable them to recognize the unhelpful negative statements they often make to themselves and to replace them with helpful positive statements. Table 2 shows illustrative positive and negative statements that are used for this purpose. A similar set of statements pertaining to smoking is used with clients who have decided to cut way down on cigarettes.

If positive self-talk proves to work well for preventing backslid-ing among persons who are trying to cut down on eating or smok-ing, it would probably work well for decisions to drink less, to exer-cise more, to reform work habits, and to make all sorts of other changes in life style that are difficult to stick to. Although no sys-tematic evaluation studies have yet been carried out with smokers or overweight men and women, clinical observations suggest that it does work for at least some people. So it is worth trying, especially since it does not require much effort and could be done entirely on your own.

The buddy system

There is one method that has been found to be effective for deci-sions requiring continuous commitment, but it does require consid-erable effort and elaborate arrangements with another person. It is the buddy system. The buddy provides support for the whole deci-sion-making process, but especially in moments of temptation.

An important part of the program offered by organizations such as Weight Watchers and Alcoholics Anonymous is their use of the buddy system. These organizations assign members who have al-ready succeeded to function as buddies for the new members. The buddies serve as models of success, as counselors for teaching the techniques to the new members, and as sympathetic listeners who have been through the troubles and know what it is like.

An experiment conducted in a clinic for heavy smokers showed markedly positive effects of the buddy system among men and women who had decided to cut way down on cigarette smoking or to stop altogether. In this study, the partners were asked to tele-phone each other every day for about ten minutes and to continue

TABLE 2 Negative and positive self-statements made by dieters.

PROBLEM CATEGORY	UNHELPFUL NEGATIVE STATEMENTS	HELPFUL POSITIVE STATEMENTS
1. Pounds lost	"I'm not losing fast enough." "I've starved myself and haven't lost a thing." "I've been more consistent than Mary and she is losing faster than I am—it's not fair."	"Pounds don't count; if I continue my eating habits, the pounds will be lost." "Have patience—those pounds took a long time to get there. As long as they stay off permanently, I'll settle for any progress." "It takes a while to break down fat and absorb the extra water produced. I'm not going to worry about it."
2. Capabilities	"I just don't have the will power." "I'm just naturally fat." "Why should this work—nothing else does." "I'll probably just regain it." "What the hell—I'd rather be fat than miserable; besides I'm not that heavy."	"There's no such thing as 'will power'—just poor planning. If I make a few improvements here and there and *take things one day at a time*, I can be very successful." "It's going to be nice to be permanently rid of all this extra baggage—I'm starting to feel better already."

3. Excuses	"If it weren't for my job and and the kids, I could lose weight."	"My schedule isn't any worse than anyone else's. What I need to do is be a bit more creative in how to improve my eating."

3. Excuses	"If it weren't for my job and and the kids, I could lose weight."	"My schedule isn't any worse than anyone else's. What I need to do is be a bit more creative in how to improve my eating."
	"It's just impossible to eat right with a schedule like mine."	"Eating doesn't satisfy psychological problems—it creates them."
	"I'm just so nervous all the time—I have to eat to satisfy my psychological needs."	"Job, kids, or whatever, I'm the one in control."
	"Maybe next time . . ."	
4. Temporary Failures	"Well, there goes my diet. That coffee cake probably cost me two pounds, and after I promised myself no more sweets."	"What is this—the Olympics? I don't need perfect habits, just improved ones."
	"I always blow it on the weekends."	"Why should one sweet or an extra portion blow it for me?"
	"Fine—I start the day off with a doughnut. I may as well enjoy myself today."	"I'll cut back elsewhere."
		"Those high standards are unrealistic."
		"Fantastic—I had a small piece of cake and it didn't blow the day."
5. Food thoughts	"I can't stop thinking about sweets."	"Whenever I find myself thinking about food, I can quickly change the topic to some other pleasant experience."
	"I had images of cakes and pies all afternoon—it must mean that I need sugar."	"If I see a magazine ad or commercial for food and I start thinking about it, I can distract my attention by doing something else (phoning a friend, getting the mail, etc.)."
	"When we order food at a restaurant, I like to think about what I have ordered until it arrives."	

doing so for five weeks. The partners were free to talk about anything they wanted to during the phone conversations, but it was suggested that they concentrate on discussing their efforts to stop smoking. These partnerships were set up in the context of a five-week program that involved having the partners come to the clinic for a meeting once a week with a psychologist to discuss their smoking problems. Pairs of smokers in the control group had exactly the same kind of meetings with the psychologist, but they did not have daily telephone contact.

The results showed that one year after the sessions with the counselor had ended the partners who had been instructed to make daily telephone calls during the first five weeks had succeeded in cutting way down on smoking (from an average of thirty-one cigarettes to only about seven cigarettes per day). Those in the control group, who started out with about the same average of thirty-one cigarettes per day, did not cut down significantly at all. The daily contact of the partners appeared to be the crucial factor that prevented backsliding.

Similar results indicating the effectiveness of daily telephone contact with a partner were obtained in an experiment conducted with dieters in a weight-reduction clinic. In this study the dieters assigned as partners were instructed to phone each other once a day for three weeks. Three months after they had started, those partners had lost significantly more weight than the ones in the control group, who had not been in daily contact.

An important feature of the two studies of the buddy system is that the clients were also in weekly contact with a professional counselor who constantly reminded them about their commitment to abstain from smoking or overeating. Additional findings show that when the buddies have no such contact it is much more difficult for them to succeed. There is even the danger that when one buddy gives in to temptation he or she will encourage the other to do likewise, to share the guilt. In view of this problem, if you decide to apply the buddy system on your own it is a good idea to choose someone who you think will be very conscientious about sticking to the commitment. Both of you had better agree to take on the role of monitor for each other to remind each other of your commitment.

Otherwise having a buddy is not likely to be at all beneficial. Buddies have to work hard to make the buddy system work.

Another noteworthy feature of the two studies is that the clients were told truthfully that the partners could *not* be closely matched on all the attitudes they had expressed in a preliminary questionnaire. The findings indicate that in order to benefit from the daily phone calls, the partners need to realize that they have somewhat different problems to start with, that they are likely to react somewhat differently to whatever deprivations they undergo, and that in other respects as well they cannot expect each other always to be on the same wave length.

One of the main reasons for the success of both the day-by-day time perspective and the buddy system is that they provide more short-term gains for sticking to the decisions. When people have a plan that specifies a certain subgoal for today they get an immediate feeling of success from accomplishing that subgoal. A helpful buddy will praise them each day for sticking to the plan and for achieving that subgoal. The short-term losses for failing to stick with the decision are also increased. People get an immediate sense of failure from missing a subgoal. It is even worse with a buddy. Then they have to confess to the buddy that they failed on that particular day. These are clearly negative consequences that can help deter backsliding. More than that, a buddy can provide social support. That is, when someone is temporarily failing, a buddy can prevent the person from becoming demoralized by expressing confidence in the person's ability to succeed in the long run and by encouraging the person to try again despite initial failures.

Setting up your own buddy system

It is possible to set up your own buddy system. But to do it you must take the lead in figuring out what would be helpful for your buddy to do and in working out an arrangement with your buddy to ensure that he or she does it.

A young man we shall call Alan Bromfield provides an example of someone who successfully planned and used the buddy system. After finishing law school, Alan moved back to his home state, where he planned to join a law firm. He signed up to take the bar exam on a date three months away. Since he wasn't working, he figured he would have plenty of time to study for the exam. After a month Alan realized that he had reviewed only one-sixth of the material he needed to cover. At that rate he realized that he would be only halfway through the material by the time of the exam. He had spent a few too many afternoons fixing up his new apartment, sailing, or just plain goofing off. Alan realized that he had to change if he wanted to pass the bar exam and become a lawyer.

Alan's first step was to find a buddy. He thought of finding someone else who was studying for the same test. Then they could have been buddies for each other. Besides helping each other maintain commitment, they could help each other with their studies. But Alan didn't know anyone else studying for the same test. His next thought was to find someone who had been through it recently. He had a cousin who had passed the bar exam the year before. But his relationship with his cousin involved so much rivalry that Alan didn't think it would work well.

Next Alan considered his girl friend. In some ways she was part of the problem; much of the time when Alan should have been studying was spent with her. If she were his buddy, she would better understand Alan's need to spend less time with her. But it would put her in conflict. As buddy she would have to help him spend less time with her when what she wanted was more time with him. Alan decided that their relationship was not quite ready for this.

Finally Alan considered his sister. They were good friends and frequently did favors for each other. She was willing to do what she could to help Alan study for the exam. Alan decided that she was the best person to do it.

Alan's next step was to work out the details of his plan. He knew from law school that about three hours was the longest he could study at one sitting and that he could study well at night but not in the morning. He figured that two three-hour study sessions a day, one in the afternoon and one in the evening from nine o'clock to midnight, would be enough to cover the material. That would leave his dinnertime and early evenings free to be with his girl friend. He figured that one study session would be enough each day on weekends.

Alan developed the plan further with help from his sister. She suggested that the plan be modified to allow one full afternoon a week for sailing whenever conditions were good. Sailing was the best form of recreation for Alan and to cut down on it as drastically as his plan did would have made it hard for him to stick to it. A common fault is to devise plans that are too strict. When there are failures to follow an overly strict plan (as there usually are) it is easy to rationalize giving up the whole plan because it is too difficult. Thus, the flexible afternoon off for sailing strengthened Alan's plan. He could have added a morning session or another weekend session to compensate for it, but he didn't think it was necessary.

The most likely time for backsliding was at night. It was sometimes very difficult to get back to work after dinner, especially on those evenings when he had dinner with his girl friend. Alan and his sister decided that Alan should check with her every evening just before beginning his study session. Thus she would know that Alan had failed to keep his commitment if she hadn't received a call from him by nine o'clock. This specific deadline coupled with the commitment to his sister made it much easier for Alan to get back to work at night.

The next step was to form contingency plans for the difficulties that were likely to occur. What should he do if he missed a session? It was inevitable that at some time he would have a headache or that he would have to go to the dentist or do something else. He decided that when he missed a session he would make it up the next morning. He would add a two-hour morning session between ten o'clock and noon. This wouldn't completely replace the missed session, both because it was two hours instead of three and because studying in the morning was less efficient for Alan. But Alan felt that if he tried to have a three-hour session in the morning he wouldn't be able to study so efficiently the rest of the day. Nine hours was just too much studying to do in one day.

The next set of contingency plans was designed to deal with temptations. Alan anticipated three types of temptations that he would have to deal with. They were spending time making love and talking with his girl friend, going out with his other friends, and attending special events, such as concerts, that he loved to go to. His main defense against giving in to these temptations too often was his strict schedule of study sessions. He would tell the others (and himself) that he must stick to his schedule and resist temptations. He expected his friends and his girl friend to accept this reasonably well. But it wouldn't always be that straightforward. His friends were likely to ask him to go with them to the beach in the mornings with the plan that they would be back in time for Alan to study. Of course, when it was time to come home nobody would want to leave. Alan would feel bad asking the others to give up their pleasure to get him home to study. Alan's contingency plan for this situation was to go alone in his own car. That way he could leave before the others without stranding them at the beach.

Although Alan expected his girl friend to accept the necessity of sticking to his schedule, he also expected her to feel a bit rejected. He really was not going to be able to spend as much time with her as he had in the past. His contingency plans involved figuring out ways to make the time they did have together more "special" and to do things to reassure his girl friend that he still loved her just as much as before.

Alan talked these plans over with his sister. They seemed fine to her. She was excited about trying out the buddy system and was really committed to doing what she could to help Alan. So Alan put the plan into effect. He called his sister daily and reported how he was doing.

Everything worked fairly well, although there was at least one close call. It turned out not to be hard for Alan to stick to his study schedule. But there was one especially rough time during the two months when Alan encountered an unexpected temptation. A friend who was a serious racing sailor wanted Alan to join his crew for a series of races. Alan would have enjoyed the racing and especially the opportunity to learn more about it from someone who was really good. The races and practice would not take much time, only two or three afternoons a week, depending on the weather. Alan's plan already allowed one afternoon for sailing. Alan started figuring out all sorts of seemingly good reasons for changing his schedule to allow for the racing. But he called his buddy, and she helped him realize that he was rationalizing and that he should resist the temptation. Opportunities for racing would come again, but if he messed up on the bar exam the consequences would be very serious for his lifelong career. So he resisted the temptation. When the exam time came, he passed without difficulty.

This case history illustrates how people can set up buddy systems for themselves. But it isn't always easy. Most people are reluctant to ask this kind of favor from others. They are also reluctant to admit their weaknesses, both the weakness that they are trying to overcome and their weakness in needing help to overcome the first weakness. In spite of these difficulties, it is worthwhile to line someone up to help you stick to commitments when you know that backsliding is all too tempting. If at all possible, get a buddy to help you to stick to decisions of the kinds that are notorious for backsliding.

8
Consulting Experts

Sooner or later, almost everyone needs expert help in making an important decision. If it involves complicated medical, legal, or technological issues, we may not be able to understand fully the situation we are in or the problem we face. We may not know the alternatives that are available or their likely consequences. Fortunately, myriads of experts are available to help us in these situations. This chapter describes how to make the best use of experts when you need their help in making a decision.

There are three major errors people make in situations requiring help from experts. First, they can err by not getting the help of an expert. Second, they can get the wrong expert. And, third, they can misuse the expert so that they do not get the advice they need.

These three points of potential difficulty were successfully avoided by a young couple, Jerry and Jenny Smyth, who had recently purchased an older home. In the fall they had a furnace company come to the house to clean the furnace and ducts in preparation for the winter. After finishing the job the furnace man told them that he thought he had detected a slight gas leak from the combustion chamber into the heating ducts going through the house. He said that they probably wouldn't be able to notice anything, but he warned them that if it suddenly got worse some winter night they "might not wake up in time." He gave them an estimate on putting in a new furnace "just in case they wanted to make sure."

The Smyths were upset by this information. They were expecting their first child in a couple of months and didn't want to take any chances. The furnace *was* fifteen years old, and they *had* noticed a bit of odor when they had first turned the furnace on, but they hadn't suspected that it was dangerous. Their first inclination was to go ahead with the new furnace, even though it would use up all their savings, because they didn't want to take any risks. But Jerry felt that they didn't know enough about furnaces to make a good decision. So they started looking for an expert.

Their first idea was to call another furnace company, but they realized that it would be better to find an expert who didn't have a conflict of interest. They needed someone who didn't have anything to gain by telling them they needed a new furnace. They decided to call the gas company and found out that the company did provide an inspection service for possible safety hazards. Furthermore, it was even a free service. Thus the problem of finding an unbiased expert was solved.

Before the company inspector came, Jenny wrote down a list of questions they wanted answered. She realized that if she wasn't ready with questions the inspector would probably make a quick statement and then leave. If there was danger she wanted to know if repairing the furnace was feasible. If the inspector reported no leakage she needed to know whether the trouble might be intermittent. Jenny obviously couldn't think of all the questions she might want to ask, because some of them would depend on what the inspector said, but her preparation reduced the chance of missing some important question.

When the inspector came, he gave the furnace a thorough going-over and tested for gas leaks using sensitive instruments. He reported that everything seemed fine and that there was no sign of a leak. Jenny then started asking questions and found out that intermittent leakage was possible but not likely. In any case, the smoke detectors they had installed would go off before the fumes reached a dangerous concentration, so there was really very little danger, even for a baby. Jenny also found out that the odors when they first turned on the furnace were from the dust that settled in the system over the summer. It wasn't a sign of anything dangerous.

Jerry and Jenny were pleased with the information Jenny got from the inspector. They had saved themselves the price of a new furnace. The additional information Jenny had received by asking questions left them with no doubts about their decision. Instead of calling the furnace company, they called the Better Business Bureau and filed a complaint about the tactics the man from the furnace company had used to try to sell them a new furnace.

When do you need an expert?

We know, most of the time, when we need an expert. Whenever we face a problem that we know requires technical knowledge that we lack, the need for an expert is obvious. The danger lies in those situations in which we don't know that we don't know enough. Our ignorance about a potential danger prevents us from knowing that we need an expert to deal with the danger.

Unfortunately, there is no powerful technique for determining which apparently simple situations have hidden dangers and which are actually simple enough to be handled by yourself. The best suggestion is to remain alert for the possibility that an expert is needed in every major decision you make. Ask yourself at every stage of decision making whether the knowledge of an expert would help you. Also ask yourself and your most knowledgeable acquaintances who the experts are for the decision you are facing. These questions are what enabled Jenny and Jerry Smyth to realize how important an expert was in their situation and to find an appropriate expert.

Even when the eventual outcome is that expert help is not needed, decision makers can benefit by considering the possibility of consulting an expert. Consider, for instance, a young man suddenly facing a much more complex income tax situation than he had dealt with in the past. He had always done his own income tax returns, but this year for the first time he had received consulting fees and royalty income that would require reporting on additional forms. He considered going to a tax expert. Either a lawyer or an accountant specializing in the tax problems of the self-employed would be able to provide the required expertise. After reading the instructions for the forms and a tax guide, filling out the return seemed relatively straightforward. So he decided that he didn't need an expert. He had learned enough to know that his return did not involve any of the more complicated issues, such as home office expenses or depreciation, where there are options about how to report the expenses that would make a big difference in his tax. If his return had involved any of these issues, consulting a tax expert might have resulted in saving a considerable sum of money.

Selecting an expert

After you have decided that you need an expert, the next step is to find a good one. This can be very difficult. It takes an expert to evaluate an expert. But at the very least it should be possible to avoid choosing someone who is not professionally qualified.

The most commonly consulted type of expert is the physician. All of us face the problem of finding a doctor we can trust, both personally and as an expert in medicine. Therefore we shall first discuss briefly the problem of selecting a good physician and then indicate how the same considerations apply to other kinds of experts.

Quite often when an adult patient goes to a general practitioner of medicine or to a specialist in internal medicine that physician will decide whether the patient needs to be examined by a specialist and, if so, will give the name of an appropriate one. It is doubly important, therefore, to choose a general practitioner or an internist in whom you have considerable confidence not only with regard to making an accurate diagnosis and giving standard medical treatment but also with regard to referring you to the best available specialists in the event that you need surgery or some other specialized treatment.

But how can one find a topnotch physician? Relying on what your friends and relatives say may enable you to find someone who is a pleasant and considerate person but is not necessarily a highly skilled practitioner. The only useful information that satisfied patients can be trusted to supply is limited to the physician's bedside manner because patients are not competent to judge a physician's technical skills and they cannot tell whether their own satisfactory improvement occurred because of or in spite of what the physician did.

One great advantage of belonging to a health plan recognized by a state government or endorsed by a university medical school is that you can feel certain that the physicians associated with it have been selected for their competence. If you do not belong to any such health plan, it is necessary to obtain the essential information about competence before selecting a physician. If you happen to know some physicians personally, it would be a good idea to ask them to recommend someone (provided that you have reason to believe that they are themselves topnotch and you think they will talk candidly to you about their colleagues). Physicians usually resent it when relatives, friends, or acquaintances ask them at a social gathering for a medical opinion about symptoms that require careful examination of the patient in the physician's office. But, in our experience, most of them do not seem to mind being asked to recommend a well-qualified physician.

If you have the name of a medical specialist who has been recommended to you by a friend and you want to make sure that he or she is qualified, you can usually find out by phoning your local county or state medical society and asking whether that physician's name is listed in the roster of physicians who are board-qualified. Their rosters are official lists of men and women with M.D. degrees who are qualified to practice in every state in the United States and who have passed the national board examinations that qualify them as specialists in their area of expertise.

Even if you do not have a physician's name to start with, you can phone your local county or state medical society and ask if they can give you the names of qualified physicians in your neighborhood. Usually they will give you two or three names so that you can make a choice. Suppose they tell you that Dr. Able and Dr. Baker are board-qualified in internal medicine. Then, if there is a university in your vicinity, you could find out if Dr. Able or Dr. Baker is regarded as topnotch within the profession by phoning the university hospital (or a local hospital affiliated with the university) and asking if either one has "privileges" at the hospital (that is, permission to treat his or her patients when they are hospitalized there). If you want to know whether a particular surgeon is considered by fellow professionals to be one of the very best available, you could phone the department of surgery at the local medical school and ask whether Dr. So-and-so is on their regular clinical faculty (this is an honor reserved only for the very best). Similarly, if you want the same kind of information about an internist, an obstetrician, a pediatrician, a psychiatrist, or any other medical specialist, you could ask the same question of the appropriate department in the medical school.

Essentially the same considerations that enter into the selection of a physician apply to the selection of other experts for certain other kinds of problems. For example, if you need a legal counselor, you can try to find out from a local county or state legal society the names of two or three lawyers in your community who are on the accredited list of attorneys. You might be able to find out through another phone call which ones are affiliated with the university law school. If you have a marital problem or any kind of psychological problem and are inclined to seek the advice of a clinical psychologist, you can phone the state psychology association for some names of psychologists in private practice who have been licensed by the state. A second phone call to the department of psychology at your local university might enable you to find out if a particular psychologist is one of the selected few appointed to the full-time or clinical staff in that department or in the medical school.

Compatibility and "emotional distance"

To obtain the fullest value from consulting an expert it is desirable that he or she should be someone whom you find compatible as a person in addition to being well qualified as a professional in his or her specialty. Recent research has emphasized the importance of matching professional consultants to clients so that they are compatible with each other. Although complete matching is never possible, matching on basic features can make a big difference in how well a client understands and uses the information obtained from a physician, attorney, or any other professional. It would seem sensible to select an expert, from among those you know are well qualified, who is likely to share your values and whose life style is similar to yours. If there is a good match, both of you will probably find it easier to level with each other and to avoid misunderstandings.

The issue of compatibility is especially important for people who belong to groups against which there exist strong prejudices, such as blacks and women. They must be very careful to find an expert who won't talk down to them or take over the responsibility that should be theirs. This does not mean that women ought to go only to women experts (or blacks to blacks). Women experts can be just as demeaning to another woman as any male expert. When a woman needs an expert she should find one, female or male, who treats her with consideration and respect.

If you happen to know an expert personally, there are some obvious advantages, but also some nonobvious disadvantages that might incline you to choose a stranger rather than a friend as your expert consultant. Without being fully aware of it, an expert may give biased answers to questions and withhold some crucial information in an attempt to avoid saying things that will displease or upset a client who is also a personal friend. Lawyers, physicians, marriage counselors, and other professional consultants are only human. If they are emotionally involved with the person, they may be much less objective and informative than they usually are with clients or patients from whom they have more "emotional distance."

Is consulting one expert sufficient?

For the most consequential decisions, the ones that could most drastically affect your future, it is realistic to feel insecure about relying on only one expert. People who have been through the mill as patients suffering from cancer or other life-threatening diseases emphasize the importance of being firm about getting more than one expert opinion, whether your physician likes the idea or not.

During the week of January 24, 1977, a week-day talk show on NBC titled "Not for Women Only" was devoted entirely to the topic of breast cancer, featuring physicians who presented scientific information and knowledgeable women who described what it is like to be a breast cancer patient. On two mornings the entire program was devoted to conversations with three patients—Rose Kushner and Betty Rollins, each of whom had written a book based on her personal experiences, and Debre Hamburger, a twenty-five-year-old student who had recently undergone a mastectomy. These three women emphasized a number of themes that could have direct effects on the decision making of members of the audience who might have cancer symptoms. One theme emphasized by all three patients was that even when a trusted physician tells you that you must undergo drastic surgery to save your life, you should take an active role as a skeptical decision maker. You should try to get a second opinion from an independent cancer specialist as to whether surgery is essential, and if so, how extensive it should be. Then, if you decide to undergo the recommended operation, you should consult a plastic surgeon in advance, if possible, and arrange to have him on hand during the operation so that he can influence the operating surgeon to take account of the need for satisfactory cosmetic repair. Similar considerations should be taken into account by men and women when the decision pertains to other kinds of surgery.

In order to feel really secure about any vital decision one might ideally consult a fairly large number of experts, let them debate the issues, and then take a vote, which would give you the benefit of the consensus of their collective wisdom. But to be realistic about it, you will usually have to be content merely to get a second opinion. (Lawyers, investment counselors, and most other professionals usually don't like the idea, but many doctors accept and even recommend it when the consequences of the decision can be very serious.)

If the two experts you consult disagree, it is important to find out their reasons for each of the different recommendations. As Bertrand Russell once said, when experts do not agree, no position on the issue can be regarded as certain by nonexperts. Further questioning of experts may supply you with valuable factual information and may help you decide which one to follow. Perhaps it will make you realize that despite the cost and trouble you had better consult a third expert.

If the second expert agrees with the first one, obviously you can feel much more secure that you are on the right track, provided, of course, that their judgments are independent of each other. With this requirement of independent judgments in mind, it is not a good idea to allow the first expert to choose the second expert for you or even to know who the other one is until after you have obtained his or her independent opinion. Professional men and women, for all their training in objectivity and ethical conduct, are inclined to defer to the judgment of whichever colleague is in charge of the case, to present a united front, in order to avoid hassles and rivalries that could affect their own standing among fellow professionals.

Whether you consult only one expert or several, you can supplement what you are told by reading what leading experts have to say in up-to-date books and magazine articles bearing on your problem. Libraries are excellent resources not just for schoolchildren, scholars, and senior citizens but also for all other literate people if they want to be effective decision makers. At any library there is usually at least one knowledgeable librarian who is very good at answering any question that takes the form of "Where can I find information about such and such?" If asked to do so, good librarians can give expert bibliographic recommendations. They can direct you to the appropriate textbooks, handbooks, encyclopedias, and journal articles by leading authorities on the issue you are struggling with. Librarians are probably the world's most underutilized experts.

Should nonprofessionals be consulted?

When you want to purchase an automobile or any other expensive piece of equipment, your main consultants are most often salespeople, whose vested interest in the deal will, of course, make you want to check carefully the supposedly expert advice they supply. In such instances, it is especially valuable to supplement whatever information they give you by reading sources such as *Consumer Reports* on the advantages and disadvantages of alternative brands, based on objective survey data. In dealing with salespeople or anyone else who stands to make money if his or her advice is followed, it is obviously prudent to be highly skeptical. As Herman Melville said, "Though man loves his fellow, yet man is a money-making animal, which propensity too often interferes with his benevolence."

Whether you are dealing with a high-pressure salesman or a trustworthy professional expert, another way to supplement the face-to-face consultations is to obtain nonprofessional comments and advice from relatives, friends, and acquaintances, some of whom may turn out to have valuable expertise that meets your needs. What they say must, of course, be carefully appraised. Much of it may be worthless, but occasionally it may contain golden nuggets—important bits of useful information that your professional experts fail to mention or do not know about.

When the decision requires expert medical advice, it is unlikely that any of your friends or relatives will come up with an alternative course of action better than the treatment recommended by your physician, but they may nevertheless call your attention to new considerations you should think about. What they talk about may stimulate you to raise some important questions to ask the medical expert you are consulting. The same holds for any other type of decision that requires professional advice.

Here is an illustrative example of the value of listening to what relatives have to say, even those who may be grossly ill informed about the whole issue. Mrs. Branford, a middle-aged widow, mentioned in conversation with her very elderly Aunt Mary that she was thinking about investing some recently inherited funds in a deferred annuity policy. The purposes of this investment would be to provide her with retirement income if she were to need it in her old age and, even more important, to serve as an inheritance for her children if she died before using all the original funds and the accumulated interest. Aunt Mary, who knew practically nothing about financial affairs, immediately became very agitated. "Oh, don't you dare do that," she said. "I knew someone years ago who had lots of money in an annuity, but when she died her children got practically none of it. The government took most of it for taxes." Foolish old Aunt Mary's advice on such complicated matters could hardly be taken seriously.

Mrs. Branford realized that she could not rely on Aunt Mary's advice, but in the next session with her financial counselor in the investment company that handled the annuity, she raised the question about inheritance taxes. The counselor gave the casual opinion that the inheritance taxes would be the same as for any other investment. Remembering Aunt Mary's intense agitation, Mrs. Branford asked to see a published statement. Slightly annoyed, the counselor dug through his files and finally came up with an official answer. With considerable chagrin he read the fine print. It said, in effect, that the funds remaining in the annuity would be subject to an extraordinarily high inheritance tax because the tax base would take account of anticipated accumulated interest for the entire lifetime of each beneficiary. And so it turned out that although in her ignorance Aunt Mary had greatly exaggerated the danger, she was basically right after all—right enough for Mrs. Branford to change her mind about the desirability of investing in the annuity. For all her scatter-brained misconceptions, Aunt Mary knew something important that the financial expert did *not* know until Mrs. Branford insisted that he track down the definitive information.

We do not recommend doing exactly what your own Aunt Mary tells you, but we do recommend taking seriously the new questions that come to your mind as a result of discussing your impending decision with her or with any other relative or friend who takes a sincere interest in your welfare.

Sometimes a relative or friend can do more than just raise new questions about the consequences of a course of action you are about to take. Here is an example of a somewhat rarer type of advice from a close friend that provided the basis for selecting a better alternative than the one recommended by expert legal consultants. A fifteen-year-old boy, while driving on an icy day, was hit by another car that slowly skidded into the front of his car and caused a small dent in the fender, with no damage whatsoever to the other car. The other driver admitted he was at fault and offered twenty-five dollars to cover repairs, but the boy did the proper thing: he refused the money and reported the accident to both the police and his father's insurance company. Months later the boy's father was informed by his insurance company that the other party was bringing suit for hundreds of thousands of dollars, claiming that it was a serious accident, that the boy was at fault, and that the driver of the other car was now suffering a permanent disability as a result of it. The insurance company's lawyer said that it was obviously a fake case but there was some danger that in such a case a jury might side with the middle-aged man rather than a boy in high school. Then the lawyer added a double whammy: the insurance company would not handle this case because the boy had only a learner's permit and was driving illegally since he was not accompanied by a licensed driver.

The boy's father consulted his own lawyer, who agreed that the insurance company was not liable and advised trying to make a settlement out of court with the man who was bringing suit, even though the man was lying. When the high school boy told his best friend about it, the friend took his own learner's permit out of his wallet and said, "Look here, it says that if you are a learner you can drive only if accompanied by an adult driver except when the learner is instructed by a parent to carry out an errand. The insurance company will have to take care of your case because you were on an errand for your parents." The boy relayed his friend's solution of the problem to his father's lawyer, who looked more carefully into the legal regulations concerning a learner's permit than he had the first time, and he, in turn, urged the lawyer at the insurance company to do the same. Both agreed that the high school student who caused them to reverse their original judgment about the case ought to be encouraged to become a lawyer.

We could cite numerous other examples, similar to this one, of laymen correcting errors by professional experts. We do not mean to imply that when a decision hinges on the advice of experts—as when you become involved in a legal, financial, or medical decision—you should reject what the experts say and consult nonexperts instead, nor do we recommend accepting without critical inquiry the alleged facts and persuasive arguments presented by anyone you know, even if you believe that their intention is to be genuinely helpful and honest. Our point is that after consulting the best experts you can find, it is still worthwhile to talk the problem over with relatives and friends, even though they may know very little about such matters as compared to the professional experts. Why bother? Because one or another of them may alert you to look into important considerations that were overlooked by the professional experts.

Getting the most from experts

When one goes to an expert for counseling or consultation—a physician, lawyer, financial adviser, marriage counselor, career counselor, or whatever—the expert is typically regarded as the interviewer and the client as the interviewee. Those labels contain a grain of truth because the only way a consultant can find out about a client's problems and objectives is to ask appropriate questions.

But those labels, implying as they do that only the consultant will be asking the questions, are misleading and even pernicious. We say pernicious because the labels may inhibit the client from asking questions in order to obtain essential information from the expert.

As a matter of fact, the most productive conversations between a consultant and a client are likely to be those in which both parties take turns in the role of the interviewer. At the beginning of the session, consultants can be expected to take the lead in obtaining the information they need to fulfill their function. But long before the session is over, it is necessary for the roles to be reversed, with the client interviewing the consultant on precisely those issues about which the client wants facts, explanations, suggestions, and judgments.

As interviewers, clients are often inefficient. They fail to get the information they want because they don't ask the right questions in the right way at the right time. Studies of medical consultation, for example, show that a high percentage of patients—sometimes the majority of them—come away from sessions with their physicians without any clear understanding of what was said about their diagnosis or what was prescribed for them. Although few such studies have as yet been carried out with other professional experts, it seems likely that the same kinds of confusion, misunderstanding, and failure to fill in informational gaps occur fairly often in all types of consultations.

Clients should be able to increase their effectiveness as interviewers by taking account of what is known about the art and science of interviewing, as developed by psychologists, sociologists, psychiatrists, and other behavioral scientists. In order to do so, of course, they must change their views about how consultations are conducted. And they must be prepared to take on a much more active role, with due regard for the feelings of the expert, who may not like being in the role of interviewee. Like John Donne, they have to "observe the physician with the same diligence as he the disease."

What we are proposing may sound like an innocuous little suggestion that is nothing more than common sense. But we think it is a matter of *un*common sense that, if practiced by large numbers of people, would revolutionize the way physicians, lawyers, financial advisers, and all sorts of other counselors deal with clients. Some professionals might even regard our suggestion as subversive because it could undermine their power to keep all their consultations short and completely under their control. Other professionals, however, in many different fields, are already beginning to be swayed by the winds of change, particularly as a result of two recent trends. One is the rapidly spreading conception of clients as consumers, with rights that must be respected by everyone who offers professional services and that are reinforced by new legal statutes. Newly formulated ethical standards of accountability embodied in the codes of professional associations, such as the American Medical Association and the American Psychological Association, also reflect a recognition of clients' rights. The other trend is the emerging new concept of decision counseling. The term "decision counseling" refers to the collaboration of consultant and client in diagnosing and improving the quality of the client's decisions. This type of counseling can be quite nondirective: the counselor refrains from giving advice about which course of action is best. Instead, he or she tries to help clients make the fullest possible use of their own resources and reach decisions consistent with their own values. The counselor may be somewhat directive, however, in suggesting where to go for pertinent information, how to take account of knowledge about alternative courses of action, how to find out if deadlines are real or can be negotiated, what risks might require preparing contingency plans, and the like. In this type of decision counseling, each session can be something like a conference in the business world between an executive and an expert consultant in which both take turns being in control as interviewer. Of course the client must realize that the expert consultant deserves to be treated with respect, as someone who has superior knowledge and skill in his or her own specialty.

Even though the time may be ripe for changing the way professional consultations are conducted, anyone who follows our suggestion should be prepared to meet with plenty of opposition from traditionalistic professionals. To be an effective trail blazer, in the vanguard of a new consumer movement that increases the power of those obtaining professional services, one must be prepared to deal tactfully with professional experts who are surprised, disconcerted, or annoyed by unconventional efforts to reverse the roles of interviewer and interviewee. This makes it all the more important to become aware of relevant knowledge about the art and science of interviewing.

Most people enter a consultant's office believing that the consultation will be directed entirely by the consultant. They leave feeling unsure about what the consultant has told them and regretful about not having obtained answers to important questions that they had been hoping to have answered but did not ask. The professional expert, after asking questions about the person's problems, typically expresses a few judgments and gives a prescription or recommendation about what to do and then asks the client if he or she has any questions. Being unprepared to take on the role of the interviewer, the person seeking help seldom uses this opportunity for anything more than asking one or two meek little queries that skirt around the edges of the really big questions. The client or patient is likely to think it would be presumptuous to say, "Yes, I *do* have a number of questions," and to proceed to ask questions about as yet unmentioned topics to fill in all the important informational gaps that the consultant might have the expertise to answer. Clients are especially inhibited about asking for amplification of all those apparently crucial statements already made by the consultant whose meaning or implications remain unclear. Many patients feel socially embarrassed trying to interview an imposing physician when they feel that they are expected to be nothing more than a receptive listener who is supposed to do exactly what the doctor orders.

At a somewhat deeper psychological level, some patients might prefer to be passively compliant at a time of trouble, to put themselves into the hands of a powerful expert who conveys, by his manner if not by his words, "Just leave everything to me and you won't need to worry any more about your problem." In extreme crises this attitude may help a person to overcome a state of temporary emotional shock or depression, but it is not conducive to working out good solutions to personal problems.

Some patients do leave it all up to the doctor and end up feeling bitterly disappointed about being left with their original problem or even suffering from new complications. Sometimes they become resentful, and switch to another doctor, but then go through the same process all over again.

We believe that both participants in a consultation will be better off if the client or patient occasionally has the opportunity to be in control of the conservation. We have already stated what the client or patient has to gain. But would the professional consultant also be better off? Studies of physicians, including general practitioners and a variety of medical specialists, indicate that one of their greatest sources of dissatisfaction is that their patients frequently fail to do what they recommend. Many patients never even go to a drug store to fill the doctor's prescription. Among those who do, many do not take the medicine regularly or not in the doses the doctor has prescribed. Sometimes physicians avoid making medical recommendations because they know that their recommendations are likely to be disregarded. Several studies indicate, for example, that patients with high blood pressure who are heavy smokers or overweight are seldom advised by their physicians to stop smoking or to get their weight down to decrease the risk of heart attacks. Why? Because such patients are notoriously resistant to medical recommendations, and physicians know it.

If patients were to take on a more active role as decision makers who are conferring with an expert adviser—modeled after the way many successful executives confer with their expert advisers when making important policy decisions—physicians might fulfill their primary functions better by eliciting more adherence to the treatments they prescribe. The same might hold true for lawyers, or any other type of counselor. We envisage a much freer relationship of give-and-take between expert adviser and client to replace the inefficient domination of the professional expert and the passive–compliant stance of the client. The latter results only in superficial deference and seemingly prompt acceptance coupled with smoldering resistance just below the surface and, in extreme instances, subsequent resentment that makes the client all too ready to start a malpractice suit. Experts might also benefit by becoming more aware of the real needs of their clients, correcting some of their own blind spots that come from focusing too narrowly on the technical problems involved in their cases. Left to their own inclinations, as an acute observer has suggested, too many experts are likely to know more and more about less and less.

Rules for effective interviewing

To be successful as an interviewer of physicians and other experts you consult, it is essential not only to be tactful about asking questions but also to convey an attitude of being properly respectful of the expert's skill, knowledge, and social status. As we have already suggested, if you want to follow our recommendation you should become especially skilled in dealing with authority figures who do not want to be interviewed because you will be functioning as a change agent who is breaking down the traditional ways in which professional consultations have been conducted. Some professionals may be quite responsive if you start off explaining in a sincere and straightforward way that you have some important questions you would like to have answered, but others will try to cut off any further questions after you have asked only one or two. Consequently, if you decide to try to achieve the proposed new type of client–consultant relationship, you should expect to terminate some of your interviews quite rapidly—or sometimes not even start an interview—if you meet too much opposition, in order to avoid antagonizing the surgeon, the attorney, or any other professional.

Your success in obtaining the cooperation of the experts you consult will depend partly on how well *prepared* you are to conduct an effective interview, with due regard for reluctance on the part of the expert to answer your questions. You can use the interviewing techniques taught to graduate students in the behavioral sciences to enable them to avoid or minimize the psychological obstacles that prevent interviewers from obtaining and reporting valid answers. One main obstacle has already been mentioned: reluctance on the part of the interviewee to answer the interviewer's questions. This typically arises from suspicions about the purpose, concern about being evaluated by the interviewer, or the interviewee's sense of propriety. A second type of difficulty that arises, even though the interviewee may be quite willing to answer all the questions, has to do with eliciting biased answers that the respondent thinks the interviewer wants to hear. A third type of obstacle to obtaining valid data from interviews has to do with the memory lapses of the interviewer if he or she does not keep careful notes.

Most of the main rules that trained interviewers follow are designed to counteract these three sources of error. The rules apply not just to interviewing professional experts, such as physicians and lawyers, but also to interviewing friends and acquaintances who may have bits of expert knowledge about one or another of the choices that a person is trying to make.

Why do we need to bother to say anything more than the familiar platitudes about asking understandable, noninsulting, unbiased questions? One reason is that many people, including social scientists who are professional askers of questions, keep forgetting those basic requirements and overlook some of the more subtle ways in which the requirements need to be applied in special circumstances. Another reason is that most people have a lot to learn about how to apply the familiar platitudes when it comes to asking completely understandable and unbiased questions. Their skill as effective interviewers might be increased by learning some of the "tricks of the trade" from behavioral scientists who are specialists in interviewing. A third reason is that some of the rules developed for effective interviewing in social science research are *not* platitudes; they involve overcoming covert psychological resistance that most people know little about.

In the sections that follow, we shall apply some of the widely accepted rules of effective interviewing to the specific problems a client is likely to encounter when he or she tries to interview a physician or any other professional expert.

Building rapport

Textbook discussions of interviewing always emphasize the importance of establishing good rapport with the interviewee so that he or she will answer all the questions fully and honestly. A few general pointers are usually given for establishing and maintaining good rapport with anyone who is going to be interviewed. One is to show obvious interest in what the person is saying. This involves frequently looking at the interviewee, maintaining a facial expression that conveys friendly understanding of what the person is saying and nodding one's head to encourage the person to keep on talking. These nonverbal cues are at least as important, if not more so, as the verbal statements (saying something positive like "I understand" or "That's something I hadn't realized before") to show that you are following closely and appreciate what the other person is saying.

Another obvious thing to be kept in mind for the sake of maintaining good rapport involves the wording of the questions. Care must be taken to avoid any wording that implies a lack of respect for the person being interviewed or lack of confidence in his or her integrity. Somewhat less obvious is the third pointer: to order the questions in such a way that the least demanding and least controversial ones are asked first and the most challenging ones are saved for the end. This usually requires preparation in advance, at least to the extent of deciding what would be the best questions to start off with from the standpoint of getting the expert to feel at ease. For the more delicate issues that are to be withheld until later in the interview it is probably worthwhile to work out the wording in advance. If you improvise, your wording may not be as diplomatic as you wanted, and you could offend or annoy the expert.

People usually don't spend time preparing questions when they are going to have a session with an expert adviser. But if one is going to take on the role of interviewer and to carry out that role effectively, it is essential to do what most professional interviewers in the behavioral sciences do—to work out and write down the wording and the sequence of the most important questions in advance with due regard for maintaining rapport, as well as for avoiding biased or leading questions. One cannot expect to use a series of questions exactly as written during an actual session with an expert consultant, but orderly notes may be helpful reminders. After asking a number of questions, it may be a good idea to glance at your notes, explaining that you are doing so because you want to be sure to cover everything you had planned to discuss. Most professional consultants, except those under extreme time pressure, will be willing to wait half a minute while you look over your written questions. After all, it is a sign of your high regard for the expert that you took the time and trouble to prepare notes about what you wanted to discuss. The same consideration pertains to taking notes during the meeting, which we shall discuss shortly.

If you have an important question in mind that you suspect might be distasteful or antagonizing to the expert, you should make a special effort to word it carefully and perhaps somewhat apologetically. For example, if you have heard from a friend that a treatment being prescribed by your doctor is no longer being used because it is considered by most physicians to have too many harmful side effects, you may want to start off explaining that you heard something puzzling from a friend that you realize may be in error but you would like to know more about it. It is probably best to save any such question until near the end of the interview. That way, if it does create some antagonistic feelings, despite your best efforts to word the question tactfully, it will not affect the expert's answers to other important questions.

Avoiding biased questions

Even if you already have tentatively chosen what you think is the best course of action and are merely talking to one last expert to get a last-minute check, you should not tell the expert at the beginning of the session what seems to be the best thing to do and then ask if he or she agrees with your choice. It is much better to start by telling the expert about your problem and its main complications in order to see what he or she says about it. If the consultant knows that you have seen other experts (for example, if it is a medical consultation arranged by your regular physician with a specialist), it may be best to state what you understand are the main alternatives and to ask the expert for his or her judgment of each. In stating the alternatives, it is important to avoid loading the question by saying something favorable about the one you are inclined to choose or by dwelling on it more than on the others.

For many decades one of the best-known rules given to people being trained to be good interviewers is *to avoid leading questions*. Recently, some qualifications have been added to this rule on the grounds that sometimes it can be useful to ask leading questions even though most of the time such questions are likely to have unfavorable effects.

What are the unfavorable effects? One obvious one, well known to audiences who watch courtroom dramas on television or in the movies, is that when people have to answer yes or no to a leading question about what they did or what they observed or what they believe, their answers can be grossly misleading because they are not permitted to give the whole story. A more subtle unfavorable effect is referred to by psychologists as "demand characteristics." People tend to respond to the social pressure being exerted when someone asks a question in a way that conveys the answer that is expected. For example, if a patient says, after a physical examination for cancer, "Nothing is seriously wrong with me, is there, doctor?" the physician surmises that the patient does not want to know the full truth and is likely to modify his or her answer accordingly.

The main point about the rule of avoiding leading questions is that such questions tend to elicit biased answers, sometimes without either the interviewer or the interviewee realizing it. To put the rule in positive form: always try to word questions in a way that encourages the interviewee to tell the whole truth as he or she sees it.

Preventing misunderstandings

Leading questions can, however, be useful in certain circumstances that occasionally arise during an interview. The most usual circumstance is when you have obtained a somewhat unclear answer to an important question, even though you have reworded it several times in an unbiased way. In such circumstances you might resort to a leading question in the following form: "If I understand you correctly, you are saying (such and such). Is that what you mean?"

This brings us to the general problem of what to do when you are not sure that you understand the interviewee's answers to crucial questions. One rule advocated by behavioral scientists is to reformulate the answer in your own words and then ask if you got it right. That is essentially what we have just been talking about as an exception to the rule about avoiding leading questions. But before resorting to that form of leading question, there are two less risky ways to handle the problem. First, you can repeat the question in a slightly different wording by prefixing it with "Could you tell me a little more about . . . ?" If that doesn't obtain the clarification you are looking for, you could try telling the expert frankly that you are not sure you understand what was just said and ask that he or she elaborate on it. Then, if that still doesn't work, the next tactic would be to reformulate what you think is the answer and to check on it by asking a leading question. If the expert tells you that that is not what he or she meant, but you still are not sure what the answer is, there is a last resort that is recommended by some experienced interviewers. That final tactic is to reformulate the answer in a leading question that the interviewer feels quite sure is incorrect. If the misinterpretation is outrageous, the interviewee may make a real effort to explain clearly. When a reformulation is only slightly wrong, especially on technical matters about which laymen are not expected to understand very much, an expert may not feel it is worth the trouble to correct it; however, if it is altogether wrong, the expert may worry about being grossly misinterpreted and become mobilized to give understandable corrections.

Professionals sometimes use technical terms freely without realizing that their clients don't comprehend what they are talking about. There is a strong tendency among clients to respond by nodding their heads and acting as though they understand perfectly everything that is being said. Although this may seem like the polite thing to do, it is obviously a disservice not only to oneself but also to the professional adviser, who is being misled into thinking that his or her expert judgments and recommendations are fully comprehended. It takes a certain amount of social courage to tell the expert that you are not sure you understand what is being said and to ask if he or she could explain it in nontechnical language. Most experts will respond favorably to a frank statement of this kind.

Much more difficult to manage, however, are those rarer instances of a professional who deliberately tries to avoid explaining the reasons for his or her recommendations by using technical language to do a "snow job." One of us encountered an attorney who appeared to be doing just that. When asked to explain the reason for his recommendation in nontechnical terms, he responded that it would take too long to go into it, and anyhow the legal issues were much too complicated for a layman to understand. In effect, what he was saying was "The mysteries of the law can be comprehended only by lawyers, so simply do exactly what I tell you to do; leave the decision entirely to me."

We have encountered experts in other professions who do much the same thing. It may make their professional work much easier in some ways and certainly less time-consuming. But how satisfied are their clients likely to be? In any case, if you are unfortunate enough to run into a professional expert of this kind, it will take considerable skill to get him to open up the way he should. If you are not already committed to continue, you may be best off to switch to another expert. If you are committed, you may find that the only way you can obtain essential information is to resort to a confrontation in which you patiently explain that you want the information in order to make the best possible decision. If necessary, the professional might be reminded that nowadays it is generally recognized that clients have a right to expect their professional advisers to explain the reasons for their recommendations. If the confrontation is carried out well, without condemnation or rancor, you may succeed not only in getting the information you want, but also in initiating a change in the professional adviser's conception of his or her role, from which subsequent clients might also benefit.

Sometimes the issues involved are indeed very complicated. If you want to have profitable sessions with your attorney, financial counselor, building contractor or some other kind of expert you are well advised to do your homework. For instance, you could stop off at your local library and tell the librarian what kind of technical problem you are interested in and ask for a book for laymen that presents the issues. It is reasonable to assume that any technical problem that arises in your conferences with a specialist in any professional field has been discussed in a good book that you will be able to understand, written by an expert who knows how to communicate to nonspecialists. There are literally hundreds of such books published every year and an even larger number of articles appear in popular magazines. By reading up on the problem, you can be in a much better position to obtain the full value of the time you spend with an expert. You will also be in a slightly better position to judge how well informed the consultant is.

Incidentally, when executives or business operators make a major decision affecting the future of their organization, they usually do a great deal of preparatory work before consulting an appropriate legal or financial expert. Then, when they arrange for a professional consultation, they are well primed. As a result, they can present the problem in a coherent way and, after answering the expert's questions, go through all the main questions they want answered. In a relatively efficient way, they obtain the information and advice they need about the alternative courses of action that are open to them. But, strangely enough, despite considerable practice in their business affairs, they are likely to be just as inefficient as everyone else when it comes to using experts in their personal affairs.

One final point about preventing misunderstandings. It is essential to avoid *double-barreled* questions, that is, questions that combine two separate issues and require two separate answers. Here is a typical example of a double-barreled question that a worried patient might ask a physician: "Doctor, could this growth become cancerous and, if so, would it be a good idea to have it operated on right away?" A single answer like "No, forget it" would not necessarily be answering both questions. For example, a physician who says no to this double-barreled question might feel that there is no need for an operation right away because another treatment would be better to try first, but he might know that the growth could become cancerous. If the double-barreled question were asked as two separate questions, the patient would have a better chance of obtaining the full information being sought about both questions. (Whether the patient really wants to know both answers is a separate issue.) In general, the main trouble with double-barreled questions is that the interviewee will typically focus on only one of the two questions and fail to answer the other question. So it is best not to use any compound questions but, rather, to ask a separate question for each separate issue.

Encouraging experts to give full answers

Many experts, especially among physicians, are unused to explaining their ideas to their clients. They believe that their job is to *do* whatever is necessary. Or they simply tell the client what to do without giving much of an explanation. Sometimes physicians may deliberately avoid saying very much because they want to see how much information each patient really would like to have. They may be quite right to wait because a patient may already be too upset to take any more bad news.

If you feel that you are ready and determined to obtain more information, asking the questions you have prepared in advance may be sufficient to get a laconic expert to start talking. But sometimes asking the questions is not sufficient; many of the expert's answers may be too brief for your purposes. To elicit full answers to crucial questions on your prepared list, it is useful to give clear-cut encouragement each time the expert gives a full response to one of your questions. Earlier we mentioned that phrases like "I understand," "I see," "I hadn't realized that before," "That's very important for me to know" help demonstrate your interest in what the expert says. By getting responses of this kind, the interviewee is encouraged to continue talking, to amplify his or her response to your questions. We have also spoken about nonverbal expressions of interest—smiling, nodding your head, looking at the interviewee—which sometimes have more powerful effects than verbal expressions.

One problem about expressing interest, whether verbally or nonverbally, is that you may inadvertently reinforce one particular opinion or position on the issue, which might bias the rest of the interviewee's statements. It is important, therefore, to avoid *selective* encouragement by showing equal interest in all the different kinds of information the expert gives, especially when he or she is talking about the pros and cons for each alternative. The best policy is to try to express a high degree of interest in *everything* the interviewee says.

Overcoming evasiveness

Sometimes you may notice that one of your questions unexpectedly seems to be evaded by the expert. To avoid damaging rapport, it is generally best not to repeat your question or immediately try to reword it. It may be that the topic itself is distasteful to the expert for some reason. If the question is extremely important to you, it may be best to wait until the end of the interview to ask it again and to do so in an apologetic manner. (For example, "There is something that is not quite clear to me, and I wonder if you could perhaps say a little more about. . . .")

Once in a great while, you may encounter an expert who is being evasive in response to practically all the important questions you are asking. If the expert happens to be the surgeon who is going to operate on you or the lawyer who is going to defend you in court, you might well decide to terminate the interview rather than to push for satisfactory answers at the risk of antagonizing the expert. But suppose that the main reason for consulting the expert is to obtain advice or information and that you feel that the expert is withholding information or not being sufficiently frank, so that the entire session threatens to be a total loss. If so, you may decide to adopt a tactic that social survey interviewers use in comparable circumstances. The tactic consists of resorting to a mild confrontation that conveys to the interviewee the fact that the interviewer is aware of the evasions but still expects to obtain genuine answers. For example, after a series of empty answers, the interviewer might say something like this: "I'm sorry to have to say this, but, frankly, your answers are not giving me as much information as I had expected. I would appreciate it if you could be more specific and give me the benefit of your knowledge about these matters." Or, if the interviewee seems to be dancing around the issues without revealing what he really thinks, the interviewer might say something like this: "Maybe I'm wrong, but I have a feeling that you are not being completely frank with me. I hope you will tell me exactly what you think because your judgment about these matters is really very important to me." Often this type of polite confrontation is sufficient to overcome whatever source of reticence may have been inhibiting the interviewee from saying what he or she knows or thinks. But, of course, any such confrontation runs the risk of annoying the interviewee and making him or her even more uncommunicative. Consequently, this tactic should be used only when there is nothing to lose.

Relying on notes rather than memory

When behavioral scientists are being trained in interviewing, they are taught all about the vagaries of memory. Many of the most important points that come out during an interview are likely to be lost if the interviewer does not record the details of each interview. For one thing, the human mind is quite limited as far as memory span is concerned. A day after an interview, only a few general ideas are likely to be left. Much relevant information about pros and cons for alternative courses of action is likely to be forgotten.

Worse yet, memory often operates in a highly selective and biased way. To some extent all of us tend to retain information that is in agreement with our initial preferences and to forget conflicting or emotionally disturbing ideas. Partly this is because we do not spontaneously think about or mentally rehearse unwelcome information. In any case, the best corrective is to rely on the notes you wrote down in order to retain the most important new information you obtained, rather than to rely upon your memory.

Usually it is not feasible (or desirable from the standpoint of rapport) to take detailed notes during an interview with an expert consultant. But you can follow the standard rule given to trainees in interviewing for such situations, that is, to set aside a half hour or so immediately after the interview in order to write down all the important points you can remember while they are still fresh in your memory.

After dredging your memory for as much information as possible, you may find that your notes are somewhat disorganized and may be difficult to use on subsequent occasions. So it may pay to spend some additional time reorganizing your notes in usable form. For this purpose, the outline provided by the balance-sheet procedure (see pages 56–74) could be useful for organizing the new information about the pros and cons of each alternative.

Sample questions for dealing with special problems

As a supplement to our general guidelines for effective interviewing, the following sample questions are provided to suggest how to deal with some of the special problems that are likely to arise when one interviews an expert.

When you are uncertain about professional fees.   It is especially important to ask any professional you consult about his or her fees, especially if there is some likelihood that you will have a series of consultations (for example, with a physician who is prepared to treat your illness or a lawyer who is prepared to handle your case). If the professional has not volunteered any information about fees and is talking as though he or she expects you to return for more consultations, it would be appropriate to ask a simple question such as the following:

- "Could you tell me about your fees?"

If the professional does not make it clear exactly what his or her charge is for each session or for the entire series of sessions that he or she has in mind for you, you could ask such questions as the following:

- "Do you charge a standard fee for each consultation?"
- "Could you estimate at least roughly the total cost I should expect to pay?"
- "Are there any complications that might arise that could make the total cost much higher?"

If it is obvious to you that you cannot afford the cost of the series of consultations or treatments the professional has in mind, it is best to say so immediately, because some professionals adjust their fees to the client's income. If you want to continue with this particular professional, you might say something like this, for example:

- "That fee is a real problem for me. I can't possibly afford it."
- "My income is only ____ a month and I have no savings and no way of borrowing. Do you ever lower your standard fee for people who can't afford it?"

When the expert's judgments or recommendations are not clear. When an expert says something that sounds very important but you are not sure you know exactly what he or she means, it is essential to use follow-up questions to obtain further clarification and amplification. Here are typical follow-up questions that social scientists use when they are not certain about what an interviewee is saying:

- "I'm not sure I understand what you just said. Could you explain it a bit more?"
- "How do you mean that?"
- "Could you give me an example to illustrate what you are saying?"
- "What exactly is it that you are in favor of doing?"

Another tactic to avoid misunderstanding an expert's advice is to summarize it and ask for confirmation. Tell the expert you want to make sure you understand it correctly, then restate it in your own words, and ask,

- "Is my understanding of what you said substantially correct?"

If the expert agrees, you could add,

- "Did I leave out anything important?"

When the expert does not state the grounds for his or her conclusions.   Experts are inclined to state their opinions forcefully, to make them sound as though they are based on solid evidence and as though everyone else in their field agrees. But if you ask the basis for their judgments, many experts will readily acknowledge that they are merely stating their personal assumptions, that the evidence is not clear-cut or too weak to provide the basis for a really definitive conclusion, and that other well-qualified experts might disagree with their personal judgment. But, again, the client has to ask the right questions in the right way to get that kind of information.

Depending on the specific circumstances, some of the following questions may serve the purpose of eliciting relevant comments from the expert about the grounds for his or her judgments or recommendations:

- "Could you explain to me why you take that position?"
- "How definite do you feel about that?"
- "I'm interested in learning your reasons for making that recommendation."

When the expert says nothing about alternative courses of action.   Often a professional will recommend what he or she judges to be the *best* thing to do without saying anything about other good alternatives. Realizing that other experts might select a different alternative as better for your particular circumstances, you may want to find out what the main choices are. Without antagonizing the professional, you should be able to obtain more information about the additional alternatives he or she has been silently considering.

Questions along the following lines may be helpful for this purpose:

- "I realize that you are recommending what you judge to be the best possible thing for me to do. But I would like to know something about the alternatives for a case like mine. Are there any alternatives that you have in mind as possibilities?"

If this type of question does not elicit any definite alternatives, you might resort to a question like this one:

- "I have heard that even the top experts are not always in agreement about what they regard as the best possible thing to do for a problem like mine. Do you think other experts would suggest some other alternatives?"

When you want to hear more pros and cons of the leading alternatives. Professionals frequently talk about the course of action they recommend and the alternatives to it without saying very much about the pros and cons to be considered in making a choice. It may be necessary, therefore, for the client to ask a specific question to elicit the information needed for making a well-informed choice:

- "Could you tell me about the main pros and cons of that course of action as compared to the other possible alternatives you have mentioned?"

If you think that you have not yet been given full information about the pros and cons of the leading alternatives, you may want to ask some detailed questions:

- "Are there any other advantages to that course of action?"
- "Any other disadvantages that I ought to know about?"
- "How about that other alternative you mentioned—what are its advantages?"
- "What are its disadvantages?"

When the expert still says too little. When the expert gives brief answers, restricted to "Yes" and "No," it is extremely important to word questions in a much fuller way than if the expert is more expansive. One essential way to avoid being misled by yes and no answers is to state each question with an alternative answer. For example, if you ask, "Do you favor this course of action?" a tight-mouthed expert who says "No" may be answering accurately but may not mean that he is opposed to it. He may be neutral or merely feel too uncertain about its advantages to endorse it, even though he has no particular objections to it. A better way to word the question would be to include both the positive and the negative answer in the wording of the question:

- "Do you favor or oppose this course of action?"

The expert who feels neutral is much more likely to answer this by saying "Neither" than to give an answer that sounds like he has a definite position. In general, when questions are worded in this more balanced way, the answers are less likely to be misleading.

On complicated issues that require more than a terse answer from a tight-lipped expert, it may be necessary to make a brief introductory statement, laying out the alternatives you are considering before asking your most important question. For example:

- "Some knowledgeable people I've talked to say that the best way to deal with this problem is ____. Others recommend ____. Still another way to deal with it that I've heard about is ____. What's your opinion of each of these alternatives?"

When the expert talks too much. Some experts may be capable of giving excellent information and advice but spend all their time talking about the ramifications of the first idea that comes up or give elaborate explanations of minor details. Their clients have trouble getting the answers to the most essential questions. In such a case, a client may find it helpful to structure the interview in the way that social scientists do when they carry out interview studies with overtalkative respondents. One useful tactic is to say quite frankly,

- "I have a number of other important questions I would like to ask and I want to be sure we have time for all of them. One of the questions is . . ."

If the interviewee continues to give very long answers that elaborate unnecessarily on details, it may be necessary to resort to the extreme tactic of interrupting when he or she pauses to breathe, by saying something like this:

- "You've given me the main information I had hoped to get in answer to that question, so could we go on to my next question, which is . . ."

We hope that these sample questions will be useful in framing questions to ask your expert. If you do use them, be sure to reword each one to fit your own style and your own interview context. If you don't, the question will stick out like a sore thumb and the expert will be puzzled about what is going on. Take the content of the question and the respectful attitude in our version and reword it to fit your style and your language.

All of the suggestions we have derived from the work of behavioral scientists on effective interviewing have been discussed only in terms of consulting an expert for information and advice about personal decisions. But the rules for effective interviewing also apply when executives in a business or government organization consult expert advisers. They also apply to situations in which you are seeking information from someone who does not have an "official" expert role. For instance, when college students are considering career choices, the people in the careers they are interested in are unofficial experts on what it is like.

Young people of college age typically do not know about the drawbacks and frustrations of the careers they select at the time they make their choice. Almost anyone in a given occupation or profession could be a valuable informant, especially with regard to the nonobvious pros and cons—the sources of personal satisfaction and the unexpected disappointments and drawbacks. Surveys on job satisfaction regularly show that large numbers of people in all sorts of occupations are dissatisfied about features of their work that they did not know about before making their career choice. Those people could be regarded as experts on what can go wrong, and they could inform the uninitiated about the undesirable features of their line of work.

But it often requires a good interviewer to get these seasoned career experts to open up, to go beyond stereotyped comments, to reveal their personal discontents. One may also have to be a very competent interviewer to get seasoned veterans in an occupation to tell what they really like about their work, what "kicks" they get out of it, what helps them to keep going day after day despite the discontents. The important point is that it usually takes skillful interviewing to get anyone who can supply expert information to give candid answers to your questions.

9
Participating in Group Decisions

Most of us belong to a number of different groups that make decisions. There are groups at work (sections, departments, committees, work crews, task forces) and at home (families and friends). Some of us are also involved in additional groups—clubs, churches, and other organizations. All these groups have to decide from time to time how best to achieve their goals and how to deal with whatever crises arise.

The stages of decision making (Chapters 1–7) apply just as much to group decisions as they do to decisions made by individuals. We have used examples from both individual and group decisions to show that there is no essential distinction between the two. However, groups encounter difficulties that individuals don't. This chapter specifically deals with the problems of groups making decisions.

Advantages of groups

Are decisions of better quality when made by an entire group rather than by the best-qualified member in the group? Folk wisdom gives contradictory answers: "Too many cooks spoil the broth" but "Two heads are better than one."; "If you would have a thing well done, do it yourself" but "Jack of all trades, master of none." Social science research gives an equally confusing set of contradictory answers. Group decisions have been found to have great advantages over individual decisions under certain conditions, but

177

under other conditions there are serious disadvantages. The trick, then, is to set up the right conditions so that the advantages will outweigh the disadvantages.

What are the right conditions? Some are obvious. Two or more heads can be much better than one when the decision-making task requires a pooling of different skills and resources. One doesn't need to worry about having too many cooks when the task is to brew some fresh ideas to get rid of a stagnating problem or if the decision has complicated ramifications requiring a division of labor. If you and your neighbors want to work out a detailed plan for protecting people in your neighborhood from a health hazard, group meetings provide an opportunity for you and the others to be informed by the physician who lives down the street about the medical aspects of the problem; the lawyer who lives next door can brief all of you on the legal aspects; the mayor's aide who lives around the corner can make shrewd recommendations about how you could deal collectively with anticipated political opposition to your plan when it comes up for approval at town hall. On each aspect a different member may be better informed than the others and that person can pass along his or her knowledge.

Another reason you might be far better off working out a plan jointly with your neighbors, rather than trying to do it entirely by yourself before presenting it to them, is that all the participants are likely to become much more committed to the decision and to implement it more energetically if they were in on it from the start. From your own experience in groups you can probably recall a vivid example of members inspiring each other to keep up the good work when the going gets rough or discouraging. At such times three is not a crowd; the more the merrier.

Somewhat less obvious is the opportunity group discussion provides for testing new ideas and for correcting commonly held misjudgments. (Later in this chapter we shall indicate what you can do if you ever find yourself in a leadership role to promote an openminded atmosphere within your group.) Under the guidance of an effective leader the members are more inclined to stop and think rather than to jump prematurely to conclusions. At each step in the decision-making sequence either the leader or someone else in the group can suggest a better way to proceed or call attention to the best available evidence to settle the issue. At a time when it is easy for everyone to fall into a typical psychological trap, such as group-think (see page 188), anyone can correct the group's collective misjudgment by introducing pertinent factual evidence. Each member who is an expert in some area can call attention to certain erroneous assumptions or unwarranted inferences in that area, thereby fulfilling some of the same functions of the expert who is consulted by an individual decision maker. Unfortunately, all these potential advantages of group decision making are unlikely to materialize unless the specific conditions that foster constructive group work are present.

It is not uncommon for executives at all levels of business and government to be so impressed by the potential advantages of group decision making that they become committee-happy. Indiscriminately, they resort to setting up a committee every time a new policy decision needs to be made. All too often they fail to avert the potential disadvantages of group decision making. At a time when it would be much more expedient to give sole responsibility for the decision to one well-qualified person on the staff, they assign an entire group to grapple with the problem.

It is essential to be aware of potential disadvantages in order to exercise good judgment about when to turn over a problem to a group and when to leave it up to just one person. Further, if you want to figure out how to increase the effectiveness of any decision-making group in which you participate, you need to know a great deal about when, how, and why each of the disadvantages arises. The main purpose of this chapter is to highlight the theories and findings from recent research that bears on preventing the potential disadvantages of group decision making.

Disadvantages of groups

Perhaps the best-known disadvantage of group decision making is the extraordinary amount of time it takes. Research studies show that even when problem-solving groups are clearly superior to individuals with regard to arriving at correct solutions with the fewest number of errors, the groups generally take longer than individuals do. And everyone knows from personal experience that group discussions offer numerous opportunities for being distracted from the work tasks at hand. These derailments can cost so much time that it may be much more efficient to have the very same people work independently after dividing up the tasks among them. Obviously, for minor decisions that are not expected to have serious consequences, it is not likely to be cost-effective to turn the decision-making tasks over to a group.

There are other disadvantages that are far more serious than the added time required. For example, the pooled judgments of a group tend to be *worse* than those of the best-qualified member when most other members are *not competent* to judge the issue. Group judgments tend to be superior only when most members are highly competent. Even when all the members are competent, group members sometimes confuse each other and disrupt each other's trains of thought when the group is asked to work on a complicated problem for which no clear-cut right answer can be expected. For such problems, group decisions again can turn out to be worse than individual decisions made by the best-qualified member. Other serious drawbacks to group decision making have to do with the unfavorable effects of *conformity pressures* that typically arise when people talk together in a group.

A case study of conformity pressures

Here is an extreme example of people in a social club influencing each other to maintain a business-as-usual attitude by collectively treating a serious challenge as a joking matter. In 1950, a local mining engineer issued an urgent warning that the mining town of Pitcher, Oklahoma, might cave in at any moment because it had been accidentally undermined. The warning happened to be given shortly before a meeting of the local Lions Club was scheduled, which was attended by many of the town's leading citizens. Those men knew that the town's mining engineer was a trustworthy expert and probably all of them had themselves seen worrisome signs that bore out the engineer's dire assertions about the town's precarious state. At the Lions Club meeting it was the main topic of conversation. But instead of talking about evacuation plans and other emergency measures that might be taken, the members displayed to each other their apparent lack of concern, laughing the whole thing off. One joker arrived wearing a parachute, which elicited an outburst of hilarity. The men left the meeting believing that practically everyone in the group agreed that "it can't really happen here." The virile stance of those Lions who roared at the sight of the parachute undoubtedly conveyed the norm that "only a sissy would worry about such a warning." Right up until the moment when disaster struck a few days later, all the men continued business as usual. Some of those apparently fearless Lions who had joined in the laughter were killed, along with others in their unprotected families. Chances are that if they had not attended the Lions Club meeting, many of them would have taken sensible protective action.

In this example, group pressures appear to have had an extremely inhibiting effect on accepting an impressive warning. Conformity can also have an inhibiting effect even when all the members accept a challenge and agree that something needs to be done about it. Members often censor their own ideas out of fear at being ridiculed or criticized by others in the group, especially when their ideas are somewhat novel or unorthodox and deviate from traditional ways of thinking. Instead of trying to come up with the best possible solution and giving cogent arguments for it to the group, the member curtails his independent thinking because he is also striving to live up to the expectations of the other members and to stay in their good graces. Some specialists in group psychology judge this source of inhibition to be so pervasive that they recommend limiting group meetings solely to evaluating and comparing alternatives (Stage 3) after individuals have worked independently on generating alternatives (Stage 2). Other social psychologists believe that placing such drastic limitations on group decision making is unnecessary if full account is taken of the conditions under which unfavorable conformity pressures and other disadvantages are most likely to interfere with the advantages. That is the position we recommend. In the sections that follow, as we discuss in more detail the major disadvantages of relying on groups to make important decisions, we shall indicate how these drawbacks might be avoided or at least partially counteracted so as to allow the advantages to predominate. Our main recommendations for preventing interference from conformity pressures will be presented in the final section on effective leadership. There we specify what a leader can do to increase the chances that the members of a group for which he or she is responsible will function well at making decisions collaboratively.

Internal warfare

Excessive conformity is not the worst source of defective decision making in groups. The poorest decisions are made when the members are engaged in a power struggle and cannot agree on fundamental objectives. Such groups either cannot accomplish anything at all or arrive at ill-contrived compromises that fail to meet anyone's main objectives. We have seen a social welfare agency so split by power struggles and professional jealousies among the program directors on the agency's executive committee that the conflict came close to erupting in court in the form of libel suits. At one point the agency was faced with budget cuts by the city government that threatened to cut down drastically on the services offered by all the programs within the agency. Rather than deciding to work together on a plan for preserving their most essential operations, the administrators in charge of the various programs rejected each other's proposals without even listening to the main arguments, which could not be heard because of frequent outbursts of name calling. The only decision on which they could agree was to postpone until a later date the question of whether they should start working together. Before that later date arrived, the mayor resolved the issue by preemptorily withdrawing all funds as an expression of his lack of confidence in the agency, which abolished all their programs. The power struggle to which the members of the agency's executive committee had devoted all their energy ended up with everyone losing.

There is little we can say that would be very helpful in getting a chronically bickering group to make good decisions. Group decision making requires at least some minimum degree of mutual respect, cooperation, and willingness among the members to relinquish personal goals in favor of shared goals. When these attributes are lacking, the leader of a policy-making group may be well advised to disband the combative group, if that is within his or her power, and appoint a new set of advisers. In doing so, the leader should select well-qualified people who can work together toward common goals that are in the best interests of the organization. Otherwise, internal warfare is likely to continue.

However, before giving up hope and quitting a group that is getting nowhere because of internal warfare, you may try using the *linking-pin* concept. Persons who have dual affiliation with two or more groups that have conflicting objectives can serve a linking-pin function by offering satisfactory solutions to disputes—solutions that link the clashing groups together via shared commitments, enabling them to work together without undue friction. Even though the term may be completely unfamiliar, practically everyone knows something about the linking-pin role from vivid experiences at home during family quarrels. Often a parent fulfills this role by offering compromises that are just barely acceptable to both sides during heated arguments. Many a mother or father helps contending members of the family to live together without constant outbursts of resentment and recriminations.

Within the executive committee of the ill-fated social agency there was one program director who could have functioned in the linking-pin role. His regular work duties often brought him in collaborative contact with the social workers in two other programs whose directors were on opposite sides of the main fights that were going on in the executive committee meetings. But this particular man was ineffectual, partly because he was unskilled at negotiating agreements, and partly because no one else at the committee meetings came to his support. In the hubbub of the combative meetings, the participants never even heard the sound persuasive arguments he was prepared to give, which might have convinced them to take concerted action to preserve the life of the agency.

One simple way to apply the linking-pin concept at a stymied meeting is to start off by urging the group to adopt the rule that everyone present will be given a fair chance to speak his or her piece. Then you can express your interest in or agreement with the suggestions offered by those participants who are in linking-pin roles. In addition to helping anyone in that role to be heard and taken seriously, you could also try taking on the role yourself. Even if you do not have dual membership in the contending groups you may be able to look at the big issues from the standpoint of the common goals that both sides share.

Within a group that is corroded and torn apart by the abrasive actions of antagonistic subgroups, it will do little good to take on a linking pin role unless you are prepared to step in as a competent negotiator. In the next chapter, which is devoted to the art of successful negotiating, we shall present a set of recommended rules derived mainly from observations of settlements of labor and management disputes that can be applied by persons acting as linking-pins at any kind of group meeting plagued by internal warfare.

It is easy to tell when a group is functioning as poorly as the executive committee we have just described. Anyone could notice from a few minutes' observation that the members were not helping each other to explore alternatives, to obtain relevant information about consequences, or to meet any of the other criteria of effective decision making. Part of the problem in such cases has to do with the *lack of cohesiveness* of the group, that is, the absence of bonds of friendship, mutual respect, loyalty, and esprit de corps.

Poor decisions seem to be more likely when groups are at either end of the cohesiveness continuum. Those suffering from divisiveness do badly, as we have just seen, but surprisingly, so do some groups with high esprit de corps which *seem* to be functioning the best. At either extreme, groups make decisions in which important alternatives are not considered and dangers are ignored. In highly cohesive groups whose members cooperate beautifully, an insidious form of conformity can arise, which undermines the effectiveness of the group.

Comparison of an ineffective with an effective group

Some cohesive groups do well at decision making; others do not. By comparing two cohesive groups, one ineffective and the other effective, we can learn something about additional factors that make a difference. Although few readers may ever participate in a group decision involving the particular issue that the two groups were grappling with (which had to do with working out a plan for desegregating elementary schools in a large city), many can expect to find themselves assigned to a work group or appointed to an advisory committee similar in important respects to the ones we are about to describe.

First, a bit of background. In the fall of 1970, a U.S. district judge ruled that the city of San Francisco would be required, within one year, to comply with the Supreme Court's ruling to end segregation of black and white students in elementary schools. The Board of Education and the top officials in the school system knew that any plan they put forward to redistribute some 50,000 school children in San Francisco would be politically explosive. Only two years earlier, when a plan for cross-town busing of school children was announced, violence had flared up. Militant blacks and white liberals clashed with white segregationists, thousands of whom had turned out at mass protest meetings. As bureaucrats so often do when confronted with a no-win type of choice, those in the San Francisco school system passed the buck. They appointed a group of professionals within the system to prepare a detailed desegregation plan to meet the legal requirements imposed on the city. They also appointed a large number of men and women representing different ethnic and neighborhood groups in the community to serve as a Citizens Advisory Committee. The advice of this huge, unwieldy committee was supposed somehow to make the professional group's desegregation plan more acceptable to the people of San Francisco.

After a few unruly meetings of this committee, the vast majority of appointees dropped out. Soon the active members consisted mainly of a small group of white, well-educated housewives who wanted to improve race relations within their city. The members called themselves the Round-the-Clock Group because of the huge amount of time they put in as the deadline approached for submitting the desegregation plan. Unexpectedly, this small group ended up being the effective policy makers. When the group discovered that the professional group had developed an extensive cross-town busing plan that would be unacceptable to large numbers of parents and that their warnings about the need for modifying that plan were being totally ignored, they worked hard at developing their own plan. Their forecasts about the unacceptability of the professional group's plan turned out to be correct and it was their own plan that was adopted by the San Francisco Board of Education and approved by the U.S. district judge.

Why did the small group of originally powerless women, whose role was to supply some window dressing, end up becoming the real policy makers? Why did the professional group to whom the power was delegated fail? In order to understand the paradoxical outcome it is necessary to examine the procedures the two groups used in arriving at their respective plans, one of which was promptly rejected and the other enthusiastically accepted.

The ill-starred professional group, which included data processing specialists and educational consultants from the California Department of Education, knew right from the beginning that they were in for trouble because any busing plan to meet the legal requirements would undoubtedly elicit a barrage of public abuse. They also felt hamstrung because of a shortage of dependable statistical information about how many black and white children lived in each school district and how many were likely to move by next year. The members decided to support a busing schedule worked out by a computer specialist, who became the leader of the group. This leader seemed well-qualified because he had more technical knowledge than any of the others and besides he was well trained in rational decision-making methods. In fact, the computer specialist constantly reminded the group that the proper way to proceed was to define carefully the criteria that would have to be met by the best possible plan, then collect the relevant facts, examine each feasible alternative, and finally choose the one that would come closest to meeting the criteria. These procedures are very similar to Stages 2, 3, and 4 of decision making that we have been recommending throughout this book. In this case, however, the group failed badly in their attempts to follow these sound procedures. First of all, they allowed the computer specialist to dominate the discussion of what criteria should be met. Although sophisticated about data analysis, he was completely naive about administrative and political problems of the school system. So when it came to defining the objectives of a good desegregation plan (an essential criterion of effective decision making) the group left out the problem of preventing or counteracting the white backlash that might be mobilized.

In addition to the huge error of omission in listing the objectives, the members of the professional group were also defective in searching for and appraising relevant information (Stage 3). They were repeatedly warned by the Citizens Advisory Committee that the computer-based plan, which required busing huge numbers of children over large distances all over the city, would meet with strong public resistance. But, instead of checking to see if these dire forecasts were sound, the professionals loyally stuck to the "rational" plan worked out by their leader and promptly dismissed the committee as parochial, stupid, and irrational.

Although the professionals prided themselves on using the rational decision-making procedures advocated by the computer specialist, they were actually covering up their own feelings of hopelessness about figuring out a satisfactory solution and their passive reliance on the leader. The irrationality they attributed to those who warned them that the extensive busing plan would not be feasible was essentially a rationalization to bolster their uncritical compliance with what the leader wanted. If they had taken the warnings seriously they might have corrected the errors resulting from their leader's blindspots and worked out a modified busing schedule that met all the essential criteria. As a result of their clinging to the leader's solution, the plan they endorsed was promptly rejected.

Unlike the professionals, the members of the Round-the-Clock Group were optimistic about working out a good solution. They set themselves the task of working out a plan that would require a minimal amount of cross-town busing, to prevent public opposition from mobilizing, but which would nevertheless meet the other essential legal and practical requirements. With great enthusiasm they collected data on the ethnic composition of each neighborhood of the city and picked up whatever information they could about the attitudes of the people living there. While collecting and weighing the information, they began solving some of the technical problems of redistributing the school population, which contributed to their sense of mastery. As they spent more and more time carrying out their homework assignments and attending the meetings they became more and more committed to developing a plan that would be acceptable to all interested parties within the community. With increasing self-confidence and high morale they carried out the essential steps in each stage of effective decision making, some of which had been omitted by the group of professionals who ended up with an unacceptable plan.

In both groups the members had a high degree of respect for each other, shared a sense of loyalty to the group, and worked well together. The fact that one of the groups succeeded in developing an acceptable plan shows that despite all the messy complications at that particular time and place, a good job could be done. From the details we have presented one can see why the group that had the best qualified people from the standpoint of technical competence did such a poor job.

The answer, as we have already suggested, has to do partly with overconformity, which results in a failure of the group members to counteract the leader's all-too-human weaknesses. Nobody is perfect; it is always necessary to correct some of the leader's conceptions or biases and to fill in some gaps in his or her knowledge. When the members of a group are keenly aware of the difficulties of meeting the requirements for a decision and have little hope of finding a satisfactory solution, they are likely to do just what the group of professionals did—they reduce the stress of their decisional conflict by collectively bolstering whatever plan the leader suggests. Here we have an example of a pattern that is referred to as groupthink, which is a dysfunctional malady of cohesive groups that involves a collective form of defensive avoidance.

Groupthink

Groupthink occurs in a wide variety of situations. It can occur in large as well as very small groups. Couples frequently fall into the groupthink trap. In the last few years many couples have tired of the rat race of city life and have moved "back to nature." Some of them have been successful in becoming farmers or artisans in rural areas. But all too many have failed to find the life they expected. They underestimated the effort required, overestimated the money they would be able to earn, and misjudged the way they would feel away from the attractions that cities have to offer. Many of the cases that end in disillusionment begin with the groupthink pattern of decision making. Each spouse has some reservations about the move but each thinks the other knows everything that needs to be known about what they are planning to do and is fully committed without reservation to the plans they are making. Furthermore, they are likely to stimulate each other's enthusiasm for the project with a shared sense that "we are a great team and are bound to succeed." Therefore neither mentions their reservations to the other.

The decision is made without taking into account the drawbacks that they individually anticipate. They don't make contingency plans to overcome the obvious problems that might arise. When the setbacks inevitably occur, the lack of preparation makes them worse. Soon the enthusiasm for the natural life turns into recriminations about who is responsible for getting them into such a mess.

The most thoroughly analyzed case of groupthink occurred at the highest levels of government policy making. The planning of the notorious Bay of Pigs invasion of Cuba is a classic case showing all the different aspects of the groupthink pattern of decision making. When John F. Kennedy became president in 1961 he was informed of a plan to invade Cuba that had been developed during the Eisenhower administration. Kennedy and his advisers had to decide whether to go ahead with it. Since it seemed to be an excellent plan, they approved it, and on April 17, 1961, the Bay of Pigs invasion was launched. Instead of the success that Kennedy anticipated, the invasion turned out to be a perfect failure. *Every* major aspect of the invasion plan was seriously flawed. The Bay of Pigs invasion stands as one of the major fiascos in American history.

The invasion plan involved a number of key assumptions. The first assumption was that, whatever happened, the U.S. involvement would not be known. The invasion would be blamed on Cuban dissident groups acting independently. But with thousands of people involved, there was actually no hope of keeping U.S. involvement secret. The second assumption was that the Cuban air force could be destroyed by a surprise attack using a few old planes. In fact, the Cubans were well prepared, and when the invasion came they won control of the air space. The third assumption was that the Cuban exiles who were to be the invasion forces had the high morale necessary to carry out the invasion alone. In fact, the CIA had put down a revolt within the brigade only a month before the invasion. The fourth assumption was that the weak, ill-equipped, and poorly trained Cuban army would be no match for the invading brigade. In fact, the 1,400 invaders were immediately surrounded by 20,000 well-equipped and very effective Cuban soldiers. The fifth assumption was that the invasion would touch off a revolt against Castro within Cuba. But the experts on Cuba within the CIA, none of whom was consulted, knew this assumption was false before the invasion. The sixth assumption was that if anything went wrong, the invaders could fade away into the mountains and become guerrillas. This might have worked for an earlier plan with a different landing site, but the Bay of Pigs was separated from the mountains by eighty miles of impenetrable swamps and jungle. The sixth assumption could have been corrected if anyone in the group had taken the trouble to look at a detailed map of Cuba.

With a little bit of effort Kennedy's decision-making group could have found out that every one of their assumptions was false. But they did not take the time or trouble to check them out, even though they spent a great deal of time discussing the invasion plan at a series of meetings in the White House. As one inside observer put it, there was an enormous gap between their expectations and the realities they should have anticipated as a result of "a shocking number of errors in the whole decision-making process." And yet the group that approved of the Bay of Pigs invasion plan included men who were well qualified to make vital policy decisions. The president and his advisers were shrewd thinkers, with well-deserved reputations as men of sound judgment, capable of critical evaluation and rational analysis. Why did they fail so badly? The answer seems to be that they fell victim to groupthink.

Symptoms of groupthink

The three main types of symptoms of groupthink are all well illustrated by the way President John F. Kennedy and his group worked on the Bay of Pigs invasion plan. The first involves extreme overestimations of the worth of the group. The members believe that their group is "special." They believe that they have the magic touch that makes them invulnerable—whatever they do, whether very risky or very conservative, will succeed. They are also likely to believe in their own inherent morality—whatever they do is morally right. President Kennedy's group showed these characteristics at the time of the Bay of Pigs decision. In the first exciting months of the New Frontier, the magic of Camelot had not yet dimmed. Similarly, the group of professionals in the San Francisco school system believed that the computer expert and the superb technology at his command was supplying them with the only completely rational plan for desegregation of the schools.

The second type of symptom is an abundance of rationalizations rather than sound reasons. The shared rationalizations are frequently used to dismiss warning signs of the dangers they face. Rationalizations often take the form of stereotyped views of the opponents as too weak or too stupid to be a strong threat. Kennedy's group showed this type of symptom in their misjudgments of the capabilities of Fidel Castro and the Cuban armed forces. The group of professionals in the San Francisco school system dismissed the dire forecasts of public resistance to their extensive cross-town busing plan with rationalizations about the ignorance and irrationality of their opposition and of the housewives who gave them the warnings.

The third type of symptom is self-imposed censorship within the group to ward off challenges to the assumptions and beliefs supporting the first two symptoms. Each member feels that it would be disloyal to raise questions when all the others seem to agree about what should be done. The group atmosphere discourages anyone from expressing a dissenting opinion. If any member argues against one of the group's assumptions, the others exert direct pressure, making it clear that this type of dissent is contrary to what is expected of loyal members. The members begin to censor their own doubts and reservations. Some appoint themselves as mindguards to actively discourage certain members from bothering other members with challenging evidence or arguments. This censorship can lead to an illusion of unanimity. Although each member may have some unexpressed reservations, each believes that everyone else agrees.

All of these symptoms occurred in John F. Kennedy's inner circle of advisers during the planning of the Bay of Pigs invasion. Various individuals apparently had reservations about each of the key assumptions that turned out to be disastrously wrong, but no one realized the extent to which other members of the group had similar reservations. If everyone had known what the others were thinking, the group would have been much more likely to realize the flaws in time to change the ill-conceived plan. The same probably can be said about the professionals who worked out the unacceptable plan for desegregating the schools in San Francisco.

The symptoms of groupthink are not uncommon among experienced decision makers in high places. Other historic fiascos during the twentieth century have been traced in part to defective decisions on the part of government leaders who received social support from their in-group of advisers. One such fiasco was the failure to be prepared for the attack on Pearl Harbor in 1941. Another was the escalation of the war against North Korea, which led to an unwanted war with Communist China during President Harry Truman's administration. A third was the escalation of the Vietnam war by President Lyndon B. Johnson and his close advisers, known as the Tuesday lunch group. Symptoms of groupthink have also been observed in the White House tapes of President Richard M. Nixon's meetings with his closest aides when they made their series of decisions to cover up the Watergate break-in.

Some disastrous decisions made by policy-making groups in industrial firms might also be attributed partly to groupthink, although such cases have not yet been fully analyzed. One likely example is the Ford Motor Company's decision in 1956 to manufacture the Edsel, a big car loaded with costly extras, at a time when the market was shifting to low-priced compacts. This defective decision resulted in a loss to the firm of more than 300 million dollars. Another possible example is the decision in 1961 by the German manufacturer of Thalidomide, a tranquilizer, to ignore alarming medical evidence about dangerous side effects and to advertise their drug as safe enough for use by pregnant women. This unwarranted decision resulted in the birth of about 7,000 deformed babies. Criminal charges were brought against the firm's directors, and the lawsuits by parents of "Thalidomide babies" cost the firm many millions of dollars.

A more recent example of a fiasco in which groupthink may have played a role was the disaster in 1972 that resulted from the decision by the Buffalo Mining Company in West Virginia to ignore warnings about the unsafety of their massive piles of coalwaste refuse that were damming a stream in Buffalo Creek. Their own dam inspectors as well as their insurance underwriters and numerous engineers repeatedly warned the company that this dam might burst at any moment and was a grave threat to all the small communities downstream. After each warning the company executives decided to do nothing and to continue the dangerous, old Appalachian practice of heaping slag to dam up the creek. On the morning of February 26, 1972, the dam broke, just as the experts predicted it would, creating one of the worst man-made disasters in American history. Over 125 people were killed, thousands were made homeless, and property damage came to more than 50 million dollars. In 1976 the company was ordered by a court to pay 26 million dollars in damages to the survivors.

Groupthink is most likely to occur in any cohesive decision-making group—whether a social club, a team of technicians, partners in a business firm, or a policy-making committee—if the discussions are so insulated that the members hardly every have a chance to talk about the decision with people outside the group who know a great deal about the issues that are being considered. When the members are insulated in this way, they receive only brief summaries of warnings from outsiders; they look inward rather than outward for information relevant to the decision. Directive leadership makes the situation worse by indicating which choice should be bolstered by the group. Groupthink often occurs during crises when the group does not have standard operating procedures for promoting critical thinking. The pressure discourages the members from thinking that a better solution is possible and increases their tendency to support the one choice apparently favored by the others. All of these aspects of the situation function to increase the likelihood of groupthink and to decrease the open-minded consideration necessary for effective decision making. Figure 4 summarizes the main conditions under which groupthink is most likely to replace critical thinking in any decision-making group.

Preventing groupthink

There is one sure way to prevent groupthink: eliminate the group and have all decisions made by single individuals. Unfortunately, this procedure is apt to replace groupthink with even worse decision making by an individual. For crucial decisions, as we have already noted, a group is potentially much better at problem solving than any individual, but we need some way to insure that the advantages are not lost by slipping into groupthink. The opposite of the groupthink situation exists when there are several alternatives seriously advocated by different members of a cohesive group. A multiple advocacy system in which the pros and cons of different alternatives

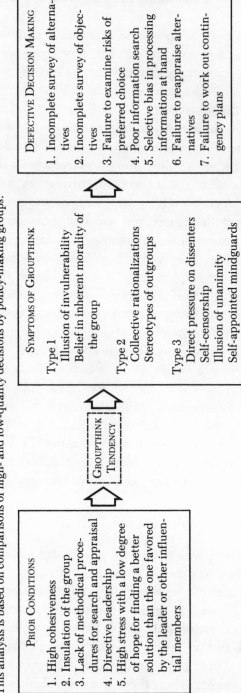

FIGURE 4   Analysis of the groupthink process.

This analysis is based on comparisons of high- and low-quality decisions by policy-making groups.

PRIOR CONDITIONS

1. High cohesiveness
2. Insulation of the group
3. Lack of methodical procedures for search and appraisal
4. Directive leadership
5. High stress with a low degree of hope for finding a better solution than the one favored by the leader or other influential members

GROUPTHINK TENDENCY

SYMPTOMS OF GROUPTHINK

Type 1
Illusion of invulnerability
Belief in inherent morality of the group

Type 2
Collective rationalizations
Stereotypes of outgroups

Type 3
Direct pressure on dissenters
Self-censorship
Illusion of unanimity
Self-appointed mindguards

DEFECTIVE DECISION MAKING

1. Incomplete survey of alternatives
2. Incomplete survey of objectives
3. Failure to examine risks of preferred choice
4. Poor information search
5. Selective bias in processing information at hand
6. Failure to reappraise alternatives
7. Failure to work out contingency plans

are debated within the cohesive group helps insure that they are adequately considered. Much of our advice about avoiding groupthink boils down to advice about how to set up and maintain a multiple-advocacy system.

Prevention of groupthink, like many other ills, is much easier than curing it. Once groupthink sets in, censorship within the group will block the recognition of the fact that groupthink is occurring and members will resist any efforts to change toward multiple advocacy. Furthermore, in crisis situations when prompt action is required the members of a group are unlikely to take the trouble to institute new procedures just for that crisis, especially since to do so would appear to increase the time and effort required for making the decision. Therefore, we recommend that groups adopt anti-groupthink procedures when they are making important noncrisis decisions and follow the procedures regularly. These standard operating procedures are then more likely to be maintained for those critical decisions in which groupthink might otherwise lead to devastating errors. Standard operating procedures are also useful for avoiding other sources of defective group decision making, such as excessive bickering over territorial rights among representatives of different departments within an organization and fear of being fired by the top boss if one disagrees with his pet ideas.

Effective leadership

Most of our suggestions for preventing groupthink are directed at the leaders of groups. The leaders are the ones who have the power to implement the procedures that will reduce the occurrence of groupthink. But by leaders we don't mean just the people officially in charge of a group. Different leaders often emerge from within the group. And frequently someone who knows something about appropriate procedures can suggest them to the group and thus become the leader for the time being if the group accepts the suggestion.

Establishing the decision-making group

When an organization detects a challenge that indicates the need to make a decision, the first step is to establish the group responsible for making the decision. Sometimes the group is established from scratch. A chief executive may appoint an ad hoc committee or task force to deal with the situation. At other times the leader may turn over the responsibility to an already existing group, such as an executive council or a standing committee. In either case, the leader's major concern is to have the right people in the group, people who can think straight and are willing to speak their minds. If the multiple-advocacy system is to work, the group must have a good mix of relevant viewpoints and expertise. There should be a balance among the factions. If one faction has too much power, it may succeed in enforcing its viewpoint regardless of the merits of the case. Power includes both rank of the participants and their skill in persuasion.

These considerations are important even when the group already exists. The first thing a leader should do is to ask whether other well-qualified people should be invited to join the group for this decision. When outsiders are invited to join the group it is best to treat them as regular members. Sometimes they are given too much power ("You are the expert. Tell us what to do"), more often, too little power ("We are the real decision makers. We'll ask for your views when we want them").

Consider the case of a university president who was trying to decide what to do about summer school. The problems that arose and the reactions of the members were similar to those that occur in all sorts of work groups and committees; they are likely to be encountered by anyone in a position of leadership within an organization, large or small. In this case the initiating challenge was a statement from the University finance office: Summer school was no longer making a profit because enrollment had been declining. Since the school was in a tight financial situation, the decrease in enrollment (and therefore, profit) was a serious problem. Some advisers argued that the summer school budget should be cut in proportion to the decrease in enrollment. The dean of the summer school argued that the summer school budget ought to be increased so that they could introduce new programs and increase publicity and advertising efforts. These measures should make the enrollment go back up and therefore should increase the profit from the summer school part of the university budget. The president decided to set up a special committee to make recommendations about summer school.

Who should be on the committee? The mix included three subgroups. The first consisted of three top people in the university administration who would be involved in implementing the decision. The second subgroup included two powerful faculty members: the chairperson of the faculty senate and the head of the faculty collective bargaining team. They were expected to argue for maintaining academic standards and for maintaining the opportunities for faculty members to earn extra money from summer school teaching.

The third subgroup would represent the client or consumer population of the summer school, the people who either were or might be students in summer school. Finding suitable group members presented several problems. Typical students probably wouldn't have sufficient power to balance the power of the other group members. The group of potential students was poorly identified. If the summer school policies were changed, the university might begin attracting a group of students very different from those who were presently enrolled. Finally the president settled for an articulate summer school student and a community leader with widespread contacts. They rounded out the group quite nicely.

The remaining problem was who to pick as chairperson. Most of the members represented factions of one sort or another. It would be better to have a chairperson who was neutral. Another requirement, of course, was that the person had the skills to run an effective decision-making group. Finally, the chairperson should be someone of sufficient rank and status to be accepted as leader by the members of the group. If the chairperson was not accepted as a legitimate leader by the group, some of the members would be apt to compete for control of the group. The president realized that there was no one available who filled all these requirements. Therefore, as often happens, he appointed himself as chairman of the summer school decision group.

The composition of the group was a proper mixture of well-qualified representatives of each faction. This does not guarantee that such a group will function effectively. A serious danger with the group just described is that it may turn into a territorial competition in which each of the participants is more interested in protecting his or her own area than in furthering the good of the whole university. The president took this danger of internal warfare into consideration when forming the group and tried to select people committed to the university as a whole who had shown in the past that they could work together smoothly. The basic problem of avoiding the disruptive effects of internal struggles for power are the same in business and service organizations.

Getting the group started

The beginning of a group can be crucial. The leader's actions at the opening meeting may determine whether the group will engage in effective decision making or will head down the groupthink path or one of the other paths that lead to fiasco. The leader has two main tasks at the beginning of the group. The first is to state the problem in an objective manner that does not bias the group toward any particular solution. The second is to establish standard operating procedures for the group that promote an atmosphere of open inquiry and help the members to go through all the essential stages of effective decision making.

The best statement of the problem does not seem to be a statement of the problem at all. It consists of a briefing about the challenge that precipitated the need for the decision along with a review of the constraints and considerations that must be taken into account. From this information the group can define the problem for themselves. They can even consider alternative ways of defining the problem.

The importance of describing the situation rather than defining the problem stems from the fact that defining the problem often suggests a particular narrow set of possible solutions. With many problem situations, once the problem is defined the solution follows easily. The hard part is figuring out what the main problem really is and what its ramifications are.

The university president had a choice about how to describe the summer school problem at the first meeting of his decision-making group. He could have said that the problem was "how to increase summer school enrollment." This would have steered the group toward choices like advertising and increasing the number of courses offered. Or he could have said that the problem was "how to increase the profits from summer school so that this year's budget will be balanced." This would have biased the group toward cutting the summer school budget. The best way the leader can present a problem is to describe the situation in as neutral a way as possible. Any description, of course, carries a bias of its own, but a descriptive briefing on the problem given by a leader attempting to be neutral is usually much less biasing to the decision-making group than a sales pitch given by a leader to get the others to adopt his or her own solution.

Promoting open inquiry

After describing the situation, the leader faces the second task of starting the group, establishing procedures that promote an atmosphere of open inquiry along with sound decision-making procedures. There are two aspects to these objectives that impose somewhat contradictory requirements on the group. The first requirement is that the group must encourage the development of new ideas, even when they run counter to the prevailing views of the majority, by suspending the immediate critical reactions that usually occur. When someone in the group makes a suggestion for a new possibility, the leader must get the rest of the group to help the person develop the idea to the point where it is a serious alternative. The second requirement is that the group must be critical of each attractive alternative being considered and thoroughly explore all the flaws it has.

It is hard for any group to be inventive and critical at the same time. This frequently creates difficulties in executive committees and in work teams when the members are planning how to carry out the tasks they have been assigned. When the members are too critical too soon it not only has an inhibiting effect on generating alternatives but also disrupts the cohesiveness of the group. These same difficulties are a common source of family discord when members of the family are trying to make a decision jointly. Here is a typical exchange at a family dinner table:

Mother: The ads haven't helped us any. We'd better contact a real estate agency to find another apartment.

Elder daughter: I've been thinking about what we should do ever since the landlord said he can't renew our lease. I think we should buy a small house out in a suburb, like somewhere near Shady Grove, instead of renting another apartment here in the center of town. We could—

Younger daughter [*interrupting*]: But I don't want to have to leave Central High.

Father: Those houses around Shady Grove are very expensive.

Mother: They don't have a shopping center anywhere near Shady Grove.

Elder daughter: God damn it, every time I make a suggestion in this family you tear it to pieces. You didn't even wait to hear my reasons. To hell with it! You can do whatever you damn please. I'll get a place of my own.

This painful family quarrel might have been averted and the conversation might have been guided into a constructive channel if a bit of good leadership had been exercised. For example, at the point where the younger daughter's interruption prevented the older daughter from continuing to explain her proposal, the mother or father could have said something like this: "Wait a minute. First let's give Nancy a chance to tell us about her idea. Then we can raise questions and see what objections there might be." When the time comes to evaluate the proposal, there is again a need for good leadership to encourage free discussion in an objective but friendly way, so that the person whose proposal is being criticized does not feel personally attacked and realizes that the proposal is being dealt with fairly.

A family, a work team, or an executive committee is likely to work best if the leader gets the group to be supportive first and critical and challenging later. The developers of a group problem-solving method called Synectics have devised a rule, called the "spectrum policy," for encouraging the supportive development of ideas that might lead to a good solution. All ideas have a spectrum of aspects from good to bad. Even the worst ideas have some good points. In Synectics groups the participants are trained to start off by pointing out good points before mentioning drawbacks or disadvantages. During the first phase of the discussion they can mention the negative aspects of an idea only if they can suggest a way around the problem or a modification that reduces the disadvantages. Later on, of course, it is necessary to take account of all the unfavorable aspects of each alternative and to weigh them against the positive aspects.

The spectrum policy, which is similar to brainstorming in that the group members are asked to suspend their critical judgment temporarily, can be useful in decision-making groups even though they aren't using the rest of the Synectics procedures. In the president's summer school committee someone might respond to the leader's request for all sorts of suggestions by blurting out that the university could make summer school enrollment go back up by not charging any tuition. In many groups this suggestion would be met with a sarcastic remark about how that would *really* help the budget. In a group following the spectrum policy, however, the members would try to build upon the idea rather than tear it down. After mentioning the positive aspects (increasing enrollment), someone might suggest that local industries might support free summer school programs for their employees. Another person might build the idea further by suggesting specific kinds of workshops for training executives that the university might want to offer. Someone else might know which companies would be sufficiently interested in this kind of possibility to consider financing it. If the idea were developed like this, it could clearly become a potential contribution to the solution of the summer school problem. At least it would deserve careful evaluation of its feasibility. If the spectrum policy had not been in effect, this alternative might have been lost.

The spectrum policy ought to be adopted during Stage 2, the generation of alternatives. When the group begins serious evaluation of the ideas (Stage 3), the spectrum policy is no longer appropriate. The members must be encouraged to give a deep, critical analysis of each alternative. But even then, if a new idea is suggested, or even a new modification of one of the old alternatives, the spectrum policy should apply long enough for the new idea to be fully developed before it is evaluated critically.

Encouraging critical analysis

Most of what we said in Chapter 4 about evaluating alternatives applies to groups as well as to individuals. The balance sheet is useful for groups as a way of preserving the information brought out in the group and of organizing the information in a way that makes it easier to compare the alternatives. The group leader or someone else in the group can record the balance-sheet entries on large sheets of paper that everyone can see.

The use of scenarios to project the future consequences of alternatives is another technique we described earlier that applies as much to group decisions as it does to individual decisions. By generating "best case" and "worst case" scenarios the group can foresee the potential positive and negative consequences of the leading alternatives.

These techniques for individual decision making can help groups avoid the dangers of groupthink by encouraging them to think critically and systematically about the alternatives they are considering. But they are not always enough to counteract the tendency toward groupthink. President John F. Kennedy's group that approved the Bay of Pigs decision probably would have produced a biased balance sheet that would reflect the group consensus rather than work against it. Their "worst case" scenario would have had the invaders failing to win but still being able to reinforce the anti-Castro guerrillas in the mountains. As long as the policy makers had little interest in seeking information to check on the validity of their assumptions, none of them would discover that the mountains were too far away from the Bay of Pigs for the invaders to reach. Something more is needed to prevent groupthink.

Defenses against groupthink

Individual participants in groupthink situations frequently have doubts that they do not present to their fellow members because each one thinks that he or she is the only person who has any reservations. Self-censorship can be reduced by having periods when everyone takes on the role of critical evaluator. The leader can ask the participants to talk freely about their reservations and what they see as potential problems. At a time when the group seems almost ready to choose what seems to be the best course of action, the leader could introduce a reverse spectrum procedure, this time asking the members to focus entirely on the bad end of the spectrum. When everyone is suggesting drawbacks to the plan formed by the group, the tendency toward self-censorship can be greatly reduced and the important problems that a few people may see can be brought before the entire group.

The leader of the summer school committee narrowly avoided a groupthink solution by using a critical evaluation period. The committee had become stimulated by a report about the success of the summer school program at another university. The other university had increased enrollement by bringing alumni back for "continuing education" programs in their own fields. The programs helped the alumni keep up to date and broaden their expertise. The committee became enthusiastic about this idea. Since their university had several professional schools, the plan should work. It wouldn't cost much to begin the program because the alumni association could provide a mechanism for advertising the program and coordinating enrollment.

The group seemed ready to agree on continuing education as their major recommendation when the leader asked for everyone to take on the role of critical evaluator and to bring up any potential problems that could be foreseen. At first only some minor problems, like insufficient parking space, were mentioned. But then three people brought up points that together suggested that the alumni plan had a good chance of failing at their university. One person reminded them that the other university was in a larger city with many more alumni living nearby. The second person pointed out that the alumni association at their school was very weak and probably wouldn't be effective in helping with the summer school program. A third person called attention to the other university's summer school report, which asserted that the most successful part of the program was in nursing and dentistry. Their university did not include a nursing or dental school. After these three points were raised the enthusiasm of the group dissipated. The members arrived at a realistic evaluation of the continuing education option: it might work if carefully planned and implemented, perhaps as an additional program to be included along with programs for undergraduates, but it was not a panacea for all the problems of the summer school.

Devil's advocates

A well-known technique for insuring that the negative aspects of an attractive alternative are considered is to appoint one or more members of the group to be the devil's advocate. Each person in this role should probe for the weak spots and false assumptions in each of the alternatives. The questions asked by good devil's advocates, like those asked by good lawyers, don't necessarily reflect their personal beliefs. They probe wherever they see a possible weakness. The members of the group must understand this and must not try to inhibit the devil's advocate but must take seriously any of the genuine arguments against their pet ideas. The leader can help by setting up the devil's advocate role with this as a ground rule and by protecting the devil's advocate from snide remarks and other forms of attack during the session. The devil's advocate role should rotate among the members so that no one is stuck with it all the time. Although some group members may not be as good as others in playing devil's advocate, the experience of having taken a turn will help everyone be more tolerant when others are playing the role and less likely to discount the objections they raise.

The devil's advocate procedure probably would have accomplished the same thing as the critical evaluation technique in the summer school committee, provided that it had been used in a genuine way, not as mere tokenism. At some point the questions from the devil's advocate would have brought out the same three criticisms of the plan to start a continuing education program for the alumni. A really clever one who is devilishly good at it might bring up some new objection that no one thought of before. One big difference between the two techniques is that the devil's advocate can supply a critical view throughout an entire group discussion, whereas the critical evaluation technique can be used only at specific times when everyone is asked to work on potential weak points of the plan. The devil's advocate may find the problems earlier, but when the whole group works on critical evaluation they may be able to go deeper to find hidden weaknesses in the plan.

Why not use both techniques? This should provide the advantages of both. But too much critical analysis may interfere with the development of sound ideas. It is little help to avoid groupthink if the price is that the group loses hope and doesn't find a solution at all!

Second-chance meetings

Decision-making groups are frequently disbanded shortly after the third stage when a choice is made among the alternatives considered. The leader or administrator usually takes actions that commit the organization to the decision made by the group. But the process of commitment is only part of what goes on during Stage 4 when individuals make decisions. The other important part is to look at the adequacy of the decision-making process and estimate the riskiness of the decision. If individual decision makers begin to feel uncertain about the decision, they can stop moving toward commitment and return to Stage 3 to weigh the alternatives again. To give decision-making groups an opportunity to have second thoughts about a really crucial decision that could have devastating consequences if miscalculated, it is a good idea for the leader to arrange a "second-chance" meeting. After the group makes its "final" decision the leader can announce another meeting for the following day with instructions that everyone is to think about any uncertainties and reservations he or she may have about the decision.

During the second-chance meeting everyone gets an opportunity to discuss second thoughts. Only then does the group make an explicit commitment to the decision they arrived at the day before. If there is considerable discussion about whether they are ready, they can go back to Stage 3 to reconsider other alternatives.

Decision-making groups sometimes choose actions that are more risky than those that individuals would have selected. Many social-psychological studies during the early 1960s seemed to show that the average person was more prone to take risks after participating in a group discussion than when making a decision on his own. But this so-called risky-shift phenomenon did not stand up very well in research conducted during the late 1960s and 1970s. The accumulated evidence indicates that the effects of group discussion can induce shifts in either the risky or the cautious direction. As each member becomes aware of the dominant point of view of others in the group, his or her own attitudes and choices tend to shift in that direction. The important point here is that those who place a high value on being courageous or willing to take risks shift even more toward risky choices when in a group with like-minded people. One of the factors that may contribute to this phenomenon is the dilution of responsibility in a group. If a group decision turns out badly, each member can deny responsibility by claiming that he or she had some reservations but went along with the rest of the group. The second-chance meeting reduces the possibilities for denial of responsibility by forcing the participants to express their reservations and by making them agree that the group is ready to commit the organization to the decision.

The summer school committee was saved by a second-chance meeting. They had decided after several months of deliberation on a plan to air-condition three entire classroom buildings and to advertise the fact that all summer school classes, large and small, would be held in air-conditioned rooms. The committee had reliable evidence that the lack of air conditioning had been an important source of student dissatisfaction with summer school. An expert consultant hired by the committee conducted a survey and reported that the advertising plan was almost certain to succeed.

At the second-chance meeting two members expressed concern about the size of the outlay required. If the plan didn't succeed, the university would be in even worse financial shape. The resulting financial crisis would probably be so bad that some programs would have to be abolished and many on the faculty would be fired. Other committee members were concerned about the expert's judgment. Advertising is an uncertain art at best, and any predictions about the success of an advertising campaign should be taken with more than a grain of salt. These reservations made the committee see that their choice was riskier than they thought. They decided that they weren't ready to commit themselves to an expensive, risky plan. At another meeting they decided on a modified plan (to air-condition only the largest classrooms) that was much less costly and almost as likely to succeed. At the second-chance meeting for that decision, they decided they were ready for commitment.

In competitive situations

When opponents are involved in decision-making situations, groupthink often includes very unrealistic estimates of the opponent's capabilities and probable actions. The opponents may be stereotyped as evil, weak, and stupid. In the San Francisco school desegregation planning, the professional group grossly underestimated the strength of opponents of extensive cross-town busing. In the Bay of Pigs invasion the planners badly misjudged Cuba's ability to counterattack the invading force; they didn't believe the

Cubans were capable of the effective action they took to repel the invasion.

The tendency toward stereotyping opponents can be reduced by spending time in the group figuring out the most realistic counter-move that their opponents could take for each alternative being considered. By putting themselves in their opponents' shoes they can estimate more realistically the consequences of the alternatives.

Multiple groups

For very important decisions the leader of an organization might find it useful to set up two policy-planning groups rather than one. If groupthink takes over in one of the groups, the contrasting rec-ommendation from the other group might serve as a caution. A new or combined group can explore the reasons for the difference and make a single recommendation. If the two groups agree in their findings, it is less likely that either group has overlooked or ignored any of the important considerations. The decision can be imple-mented with more confidence than if only a single group had worked on it.

The same idea can be used with only one group by dividing it into subgroups for crucial decisions. After the subgroups have reached their conclusions they rejoin to work out any differences that arise.

There are high costs involved in duplicating the decision-making groups. The most obvious cost is that more people will be spending their precious time on it, with some duplication of effort. For cru-cial policy decisions these costs may be worthwhile. But other prob-lems can occur. The members of both groups may feel that the deci-sion isn't really their "baby" and that what they do or leave undone won't matter very much. This may reduce their sense of responsibil-ity and dedication to the decision-making tasks. Thus, both groups may suffer from poor morale. If this occurs, most of the advantages of independent groups will be lost.

In the grip of groupthink

What can you do if you are not a leader and you suddenly realize that the group you are in is in the grip of groupthink? It may be too late to apply the preventive measures discussed so far in this chapter. If you suggest a critical analysis session, most of the criticism will be directed at you for disrupting the group spirit. If you try the devil's advocate role, the other members will react as though you were disloyal. If you tell the others of your diagnosis and point out the symptoms of groupthink, they are likely to resent your psychologizing because they feel you are accusing them of being incompetent.

We cannot be very encouraging about the likelihood of success. The best approach is probably to state your reservations about the group's plan as clearly and logically as you can, without mentioning groupthink at all. Present your evidence in a straightforward manner and avoid being drawn into name calling or other personal attacks. You may succeed in raising enough doubts in enough minds to get support from some of the other members in moving away from groupthink long enough to reconsider the alternatives.

In any group the members are allowed only a limited amount of "idiosyncrasy credit." Each member can argue his or her own pet points up to a certain limit. Beyond that the group stops listening. If you have serious reservations about a plan, you should avoid arguing about minor problems. It would be unfortunate if you argued so hard for wine instead of eggnog for the office party that the rest of the committee would ignore your argument that holding the party after supper in the evening would create hard feelings among employees who lived far away.

The standard operating procedures and the leadership practices we recommend are based on analyses of what went wrong in cases where groupthink or internal warfare or some other source of defective decision making in groups occurred. Our recommendations are our best guesses about what could have prevented those cases in which the advantages of making a decision jointly were outweighed by the disadvantages. They are also consistent with current theoretical and empirical knowledge about groups. But, obviously, you should select from our recommendations only those that make sense to you in your own particular group situation.

10
Negotiating

In this chapter we shall present a number of useful hints from what is currently known about the psychology of effective bargaining. These hints or pointers might help you to be more effective in arriving at a mutually satisfactory agreement with a contending party, whether at home or at work, whenever you need to negotiate.

Much of the relevant research carried out so far deals with formal negotiations between representatives of two groups involved in a dispute—such as a dispute over wages and working conditions between a labor union and the management of a manufacturing company. This research on collective bargaining is directly applicable whenever we are put in the role of representing a group to work out a settlement with representatives of another group that has clashing interests. Most of the important principles of effective bargaining are also applicable to negotiations that take place when two people are trying to settle their personal disagreements. Here we have in mind conciliatory discussions such as those between a dissatisfied employee and a boss or between a husband and a wife who want to stop quarreling.

One common psychological problem among persons who are in conflict with each other is the failure to recognize the need to negotiate. Many people facing crucial choices are unhappy about having to select any of the unsatisfactory alternatives offered to them by their partners or by persons in positions of power. They often do not realize that they might be able to arrive at an acceptable alternative through negotiation.

Consider, for example, the common dilemma of marital partners who often quarrel about whether each is taking on his or her fair share of family responsibilities. If they recognize the need to negotiate and know how to do it well enough to avoid the main pitfalls, those embattled partners sometimes can arrive at an agreement that works out well for both of them. There is no guarantee that they will live together happily ever after, but negotiating their respective grievances can greatly decrease the chances that they will live unhappily apart. One of the main reasons why negotiating often leads to less discord between two persons who live or work together is that each one becomes much more aware of the other's main objectives and priorities, which enables them to function as an effective two-person group of joint decision makers.

An example of successful negotiation between marital partners

Here is a typical example of what can happen in negotiations between husband and wife on the seemingly ever present problem of equitable division of child care and household chores. In this instance, the earlier agreement that Ellen and Phil Comstock had made was not working out at all the way it was supposed to. That was somewhat surprising to them because right from the outset both had acknowledged that they basically shared contemporary views about family life, like those put forth in Dr. Benjamin Spock's guide to child care—that husband and wife have equal rights to a career, that old prejudices about sex roles should not be perpetuated, and that both should give high priority to providing good care for their children. With those considerations in mind, Phil had agreed to take on the main responsibilities at home every other evening, which would give Ellen some of the time she needed in her home studio to pursue her career as a free-lance illustrator.

But in practice Phil was living up to the agreement only on weekends and was quite remiss about it during the rest of the week. He seldom did his full share of the evening kitchen chores after coming home from work. Usually he did prepare dinner with great gusto when it was his turn but he seldom cleaned up afterwards. Most often he said he was too tired right now and would take care of it later. On more than half of those evenings when "later" arrived Phil had already gone to sleep for the night and Ellen was left with the choice of cleaning up the dirty dishes before going to bed or doing so the next morning.

Worse yet, the more crucial part of their agreement was also not being carried out regularly. Phil was supposed to take over the care of their two children after dinner half the time. This arrangement was of great concern to Ellen because she needed to have those evenings free in order to work on her professional projects. During the daytime she had so many errands and household chores that she could seldom eke out more than two or three hours for her professional work while the children were at school. The trouble was that at least once a week and sometimes more often Phil would say that he wanted to go out that night to attend a sports event or to see his friends, even though he was scheduled to take over the children. He always spoke about it as though he was only postponing his obligation and would make up for it later in the week, but he never did so unless Ellen had an unpleasant argument with him.

When they quarreled about the night-time schedule Phil would argue vehemently that he had a right to a little bit of independence and spontaneity in his life, that he couldn't be expected to be tied down working like a dog on his job eight hours every day and then be so tied down at home that he was not free to take a night off when he felt he needed to. Ellen retorted that she was more tied down than he was and that Phil's failure to live up to their earlier agreement was unfair and was interfering with her career.

One night during a rather heated interchange about all of this they became more angry at each other than ever before. Then, after a period of hostile silence they began to talk in a calmer mood about the need to work out a new agreement. They discussed what was going wrong and asked each other the usual provocative type of question: "But why in the world couldn't *you* just do this . . . ?" After a while they began to ask "Wouldn't it help if *we* tried this . . .?" During the discussion, they discovered something they had not fully realized before about each other's priorities. Phil found out that what bothered Ellen most was his undependability about doing his share at home. In order for her to take on assignments she had to commit herself to publishers' deadlines, and it was essential for her to know in advance how many evenings she would be able to work each week. With regard to the kitchen chores, Ellen was annoyed about the same kind of undependability, especially when she was stuck with the dirty dishes at bedtime on nights when Phil said he would do them as scheduled. Ellen made clear to him that the most aggravating problem for her was that she could never count on his living up to their agreement.

Ellen, in turn, realized for the first time that for Phil the main priority was to cut down on the total amount of time he was expected to spend on his obligations at home. In his view his hard work on the job was providing the main financial support for the family, and so it was not fair for him to have to devote most of his time off to fulfilling household obligations, though he wanted to spend some time with the children and was quite willing to participate enough to enable Ellen to pursue her career.

Once each became aware of the other's main priorities, the two of them were able to arrive at a specific compromise solution that met each of their rock-bottom requirements. Instead of the old agreement, a somewhat more complicated schedule was worked out that both of them felt was fair, realistic, and could be lived with. Phil would prepare and clean up lunch and dinner every Saturday and Sunday, even when they had guests for a weekend meal; Ellen would take on those chores the other five days so that Phil could always relax after he came home from work. On the more important matter of taking care of the children after dinner, they made a new arrangement that would guarantee Ellen much more time for her professional work and one free night. On a regular basis, every Monday they would hire a sitter to take over the children all afternoon and evening so that they could go out together that night if they wanted to. On every Wednesday, Friday, and Saturday night it would be Phil's turn to take over. Phil agreed that when he wanted to exercise his freedom to do something on his own it would be limited to one of the other four nights of the week, except for very special circumstances.

As it turned out, Phil seldom invoked the escape clause in their contract and was able to live up to the agreement fairly regularly. Ellen was pleased to have the dependable work periods each week, although she continued to wish that somehow she could get more time to pursue her career and her other interests outside of the home.

In other kinds of disputes, such as those that arise in business organizations, negotiations can lead to similar mutual discoveries of the priorities and of the requirements for a settlement that will not generate new grievances on either side. For example, an employer who is negotiating with employees may learn that currently their main grievances center on their not being permitted to participate in policy decisions about their work loads, safety standards, or prevention of pollution, which could affect their health. The employees, in turn, might find out that the employer is suffering from apparently genuine financial setbacks right now and is mainly concerned about holding the line on wages and other costs. These mutual discoveries can point the way to a settlement that is at least minimally satisfactory to both sides.

Extreme circumstances where negotiating can be beneficial

White-collar crime is big business in America, resulting in over 50 billion dollars in losses each year. Mainly the huge losses are a result of employees stealing valuable merchandise, accountants juggling sales accounts and putting fake names on payrolls, managers falsifying their inventory, and a variety of other illegal activities that usually require the complicity of large numbers of employees. The evidence implies that every year hundreds of thousands of working men and women are put under pressure to participate in collective crimes and coverups. They are urged by their bosses to cheat customers, to steal from the company by participating in pilfering, and to engage in all sorts of other unethical or illegal acts.

When someone on the job is given a strong invitation by a superior to join in the illicit activity or at least to help keep it covered up, the person usually feels that the invitation is something like the Mafia godfather's offer that cannot be refused. Confronted with illegitimate demands from powerful superiors, many people think they have no choice but to give in or to give up the job, with or without informing legal authorities. In these circumstances, however, those who recognize that there is a need to negotiate have a clear-cut third alternative, one that could prove to be far better than the other two because it could influence the boss to withdraw the illegitimate demand without imposing any penalty at all. In a negotiation session with the boss, a harassed employee may be able to argue persuasively that if he did what the boss wants him to do, both of them would probably end up regretting it.

One employee, for example, pointed out to his boss that he regarded the illegal action of falsifying sales receipts as morally repugnant and even if he tried to do exactly what the boss was asking he would probably bungle it so badly that both of them would be caught. One of his main arguments was that even without being caught red-handed, if higher authorities were to conduct an inquiry, he would probably be unable to control his emotions sufficiently to avoid spilling the beans. The boss soon realized that under those circumstances it would be to his own best interests to give up the illegitimate demand entirely. In other instances reported to us no such argument was needed. In each of these instances the employee's services were valued so highly that only one strong argument was sufficient to convince the boss in a negotiating session. The employee merely said, in effect, that the boss's demand was so unacceptable that he would be unable to continue on the job unless the boss relented.

As these examples illustrate, successful negotiations do not always end up with compromises requiring each party to give in to one or more of the other party's demands. Sometimes one party is convinced by the other's arguments and, like the boss in each of the examples just cited, is willing to make a one-sided settlement, just as happens when a lawyer wins a case in a court of law. Even though an employee may firmly resolve right from the outset that a demand for illegal acts by the boss will be *nonnegotiable*, he or she may still find it worthwhile to decide to postpone resigning from the job in order to try negotiating first, to see if the boss can be convinced to stop making any such demand. Of course, if pressures to engage in unacceptable acts are only one of many grievances, along with other concerns about working conditions and wages, the employee might be prepared to work out a joint settlement with the boss that involves some compromises on the other grievances even though he or she will not compromise on the crucial one.

The same third alternative—to negotiate rather than either to give in or to quit the job—usually is a viable one when other sorts of illicit demands are made, such as the sexual harassment so frequently encountered by women whose bosses try to take advantage of opportunities to display their masculine prowess. Relatively few bosses make blatant demands that will give them the reputation around the office of being prime candidates for a casting couch award. But many engage in more polite forms of propositioning. It is not at all rare for older men in positions of power to be dedicated to the proposition. Whether young or old, the boss may sincerely believe that he is not engaging in sexual harassment because he asks pleasantly and flatteringly, without making any references to his power to hire, promote, and fire. But his message may still come down to "Give in or you'll be sorry." Nevertheless, as we have just suggested, some bosses who repeatedly convey such messages can prove to be quite decent about dropping their demands and maintaining a friendly attitude, without any recrimination—*if* the woman decides to open negotiations in order to present her nonnegotiable demand that the boss stop his sexual harassment. She can explain that she is prepared to resign (or to take legal action) if the boss persists in making demands.

Most of the pointers that we can extract from studies of negotiation can be applied to harassments of the kind we have just been talking about as well as to a variety of nonharassment situations where someone with power asks you to do something you would rather not do. The pointers also apply to some of the problems you can expect to encounter if you have the power to make legitimate demands on others—whether as a boss in your office or as a parent in your home. It is now widely recognized that in order to be successful, bosses and powerful leaders of all sorts of groups often are obliged to negotiate with people subordinate to them, to work out acceptable compromises, even though they may have the power to impose their demands. It is considered to be sound administrative practice to set up procedures for enabling subordinates to communicate their grievances to superiors and to negotiate settlements that are fair to both parties. Bosses, leaders, or parents who do not regularly engage in negotiations with those who are expected to carry out their orders are likely to suffer serious defeats in the long run because their underlings become chronically resentful, and orders may be implemented in a careless manner or subtly sabotaged.

Formal negotiations

Assignments to participate in formal negotiations are given to executives in all sorts of business firms, professional organizations, and government agencies. When executives are unskilled at conducting such negotiations, their poor track record soon becomes apparent, which obviously does not help to advance their careers.

The need for similar skills in formal negotiations could arise in the life of any citizen who belongs to a local political, professional, or social club that is affiliated with a national organization. If national headquarters issues a policy directive that has a bad effect on your local club, you and a few other members might be asked to be representatives to negotiate with officers of the national organization to work out a mutually acceptable change of the policy. For example, in one prestigious local club we know about, which was supposed to be devoted to civic improvement projects that would benefit the entire community, the leading members in that city objected to the national organization's directives to give priority to prominent professional people for membership, which had the effect in practice of undercutting the organization's nondiscrimination policy. The local members felt that the guidelines issued by national headquarters constrained them to limiting new members mainly to upper-middle-class men. In negotiating sessions with the national board of directors, the representatives of the local branch were able to win them over sufficiently to agree that they would issue new guidelines. The new version would state that any outstanding citizen in the community could be invited to become a member irrespective of occupation. The representatives of the local branch had wanted a much stronger statement than that, but in consultation with local members, they decided that it was basically satisfactory because it was a big step in the direction they wanted the organization to go. They planned to wait a year or so before reopening negotiations for their full set of demands, which included giving priority to inviting for membership those leading citizens who would make the membership more representative of all sectors of the local community.

Similar formal negotiations sometimes result in settlements of larger disputes involving a wide variety of policy issues, especially within business organizations. For example, if two departments or two factions within the same department are constantly quarreling about priorities, the chief executive might put the contenders together into a problem-solving group, "to crack their heads together," to get them to work out an acceptable settlement. Even when there are no open disputes, representatives from different departments or sections of a business organization (representing, let us say, production, promotion, sales, and personnel) are likely to have a number of longstanding disagreements, despite sharing many common objectives, because certain of their other objectives clash. In a sense, practically every policy-making group is made up of persons who have some conflicting goals whenever the group includes representatives from different sections of the organization. Insofar as the objectives of the various representatives are not completely the same, the policy-making process requires negotiations in order to work out policy solutions that are basically satisfactory to all concerned.

Formal negotiations may help to prevent some of the worst consequences of internal warfare within a decision-making group because the designated representatives are usually governed by traditional rules and sometimes by law, as in the case of certain kinds of collective bargaining in labor–management disputes. As a result, formal negotiations usually have more orderly procedures and more decorum than informal ones, as when two business partners try to settle a disagreement about whether to take advantage of an opportunity to expand their business. Sometimes the participants in a formal negotiation session start off with just as much furious shouting and table pounding as in informal negotiations by business partners or even by marital partners. But as a result of all the rules governing formal negotiations, the participants are more likely to settle down after a while to the business of working out a satisfactory settlement.

There is another big difference between negotiators who speak only for themselves in person-to-person negotiations and *representatives* of a business firm, a professional organization, a social club, or any other group negotiating with representatives of another group. Whenever the negotiators are engaging in collective bargaining—or "diplomacy" as it is called when the bargainers are representatives of nations—they have to reach a joint agreement that will be acceptable to the parties they represent; in person-to-person negotiations the agreement needs only to be acceptable to each negotiator. Business partners negotiating about whether to expand their business or a husband and a wife negotiating about which house to buy need to satisfy only themselves. Such partners are free to make a binding agreement as soon as the two negotiators arrive at a settlement that is satisfactory to both. If, however, you are a representative of a local organization negotiating with representatives of national headquarters, you will have to worry about whether the other members in your local branch will find the tentative agreement acceptable and you will postpone signing a contract until you have obtained the consent of the people back home. This added complication, as we shall see shortly, often requires each negotiator not only to engage in prolonged bargaining with opponents but also to do some hard bargaining with people on his or her own side.

The main acts of the drama

Negotiation is needed whenever two or more persons who are trying to arrive at a mutually satisfactory decision have conflicting aims. Whether carried out in a formal way at a conference table or in an informal way at a dinner table, it requires discussion in which there is a battle of wits as each contending party attempts to persuade the other to relinquish certain demands or to agree to a compromise. Among the least successful negotiations are those that take the form of simultaneous monologues, with neither contestant hearing what the other is saying. The French have a name for this type of nondiscussion; they call it *un dialogue de sourds*, a dialogue of the deaf. In contrast, negotiations that end up successfully, with an agreement satisfactory to both sides, generally are ones in which the contestants sooner or later exchange information relevant to the issues about which they disagree, while engaging in a great deal of give-and-take haggling.

Few successful negotiators act in a way that lives up to the popular image of the suave, unflappable diplomat. In the worlds of business and of local and domestic politics, successful negotiators usually are not much more tactful, gracious, or deferential in dealing with their opponents than are ordinary couples who are fighting it out at home. They are quite capable of proclaiming wildly exaggerated accusations and illogical arguments in their efforts to propagandize. But no matter how loudly they shout nor how much they "ham it up," there is one important feature that distinguishes the way successful negotiators act in contrast to unsuccessful ones. The successful negotiators generally *listen* to each other at least part of the time. In addition, every once in a while they say something that shows that they understand what their opponents are driving at.

According to social psychologists who have made careful observations of a variety of bargaining situations, negotiators typically have to take three main steps in order to end up as a successful problem-solving group that works out a solution acceptable to both sides. We can regard these steps as the acts of a negotiation drama that has a happy ending. They are broadly applicable to all types of successful negotiation, whether formal or informal. In unsuccessful negotiations, the curtain comes down on the melodrama before the end of the first act.

ACT 1. *Clashing: Laying out the conflicting claims.* Occasionally the first act builds up dramatic tension very slowly, with one of the protagonists announcing at the outset, "I don't see why we need to have any discussion, our disagreements really are only trifling matters. Basically, we are in agreement." Much more often the opening act starts right off with a lot of hot air from the contending parties as they try to show that all the Right is on their own side and that the other side is just plain Wrong. Disagreements are highlighted and exaggerated. That is how it was when Phil and Ellen Comstock had their big quarrel about whether Phil was doing his fair share of taking care of their two children, which was the opening act of their successful negotiation drama. In the first of a series of formal labor–management bargaining sessions, a spokesman for one side will start right off trying to convince the opponents that the differences in requirements for a satisfactory settlement are so enormous that there will be no use talking unless they are willing to make huge concessions. Someone on the other side angrily retorts that the differences are even more irreconcilable than the first speaker claimed and will certainly remain that way unless the first side gives up its completely unreasonable requirements.

Why so much sound and fury that later on may turn out to signify nothing? One obvious function is to lay out all the disparities fully so that the contending parties correct their overoptimistic expectations and learn as early as possible how difficult it is going to be to meet the requirements for an adequate settlement. By the time all the rival claims are on the table, at the end of the first act, each participant will have a pretty good idea of the nature of the problems to be solved and what concessions might have to be made by both sides. Again, that is what happened by the end of the big quarrel between Phil and Ellen Comstock.

During the initial clash, each of the parties to a dispute usually conveys determination not to retreat from just demands for what should rightfully be done (everything in one's own favor, of course). An outsider hearing the contenders heatedly presenting their uncompromising positions is likely to be reminded of the well-known declension of "stubborn": "I am strong-minded, you are obstinate, he is pigheaded." Actually, though, successful negotiators seldom use insulting epithets like "pigheaded" as they vociferously lay out their opposing claims. They are careful not to confuse antagonistic positions on the issues being debated with antagonism toward the person advocating the opposing position. If insulting or humiliating remarks are made during the opening arguments, the next two essential acts in the negotiation drama are not likely to take place.

ACT 2. *Exploring: Finding the openings.*   After the first act of exaggeratedly heroic, unyielding verbal combat, the negotiators begin to relax a bit and get down to the business of sensibly discussing the main differences that pose the various problems to be solved. As they do so, the negotiators also begin to recognize the openings for possible agreements that could conceivably lead to solutions of the problems. Spirited debate goes on and on and on, but instead of continuing to present exaggerated claims and propagandistic attacks that are full of hot air, the protagonists give hardheaded critiques of each others' views and proposals. As specious arguments on both sides are exposed and discredited, the negotiators slowly and painfully learn which issues are genuine, which are the criteria that really will have to be met in order for solutions to be satisfactory to both sides. As successive proposals for reconciling differences are put forth, first by one side and then the other, productive bargaining begins to occur. That is exactly what went on after Phil and Ellen Comstock calmed down following their quarrel and began to discover each other's main priorities.

Even when the endless haggling seems to be getting nowhere, the negotiators gradually see the direction in which they will have to move to get out of the morass of conflicting and seemingly irreconcilable demands. Some segments of a pathway to an acceptable solution begin to emerge. The negotiators start thinking, "We shall undoubtedly have to give in on this and they will have to give in on that." Eventually the negotiators focus on the possible solutions that are most promising among those that already have been mentioned or that are in the back of their minds. Once they know the range in which a settlement can occur, they can proceed to the third and final act of the drama.

Act 3. *Solving: Choosing and checking solutions.* In the third act, the negotiators arrive at a decision by choosing and checking satisfactory solutions to the conflict. As the denouement approaches, the protagonists are no longer acting like provocative antagonists. They talk more and more about wanting an agreement that is fair to both sides, about the need to subordinate individual interests, and about the virtues of being flexible. Now instead of recriminations from one side provoking recriminations from the other, as occurred during the first act and to some extent during the second, concessions from one side invite concessions from the other. A much more cooperative form of bargaining goes on as each point in a possible settlement is discussed ("I am willing to do this if you are willing to do that"). That is the kind of constructive give-and-take that Phil and Ellen Comstock engaged in after they became more fully aware of the main requirements that would have to be met, which resulted in a joint agreement about sharing household and child care responsibilities that both could live with.

When the negotiators are representatives of organizations, they check out and modify the proposed solution not only through discussion with each other but also through consultations back home with leaders and members of their respective organizatons. Then, before submitting the proposal for final ratification by each of the contending organizations, the negotiators prepare a detailed written statement in which they spell out in considerable detail all the various provisions, contingency plans, and implementation plans to which they have tentatively agreed. Preparing and signing this kind of written statement guarantees some degree of mutual commitment to the proposed settlement. It also helps to clear up some of the remaining misunderstandings about exactly what each side is agreeing to, which could prevent an outbreak of subsequent disputes and mutual accusations of untrustworthiness and hostile recriminations ("*You* are the bastards who broke the agreement!" "No, *you* are the bastards . . . !")

During the third act it sometimes happens that for a long time the opposing parties in a negotiating group cannot agree on any one of the alternatives under consideration and then, as a result of continuing to bargain in good faith, they finally get their happy ending: someone comes up with a new compromise involving concessions acceptable to both sides.

In terms of the sequence of stages of active decision making, the first act of a successful negotiation drama involves a rather noisy confrontation with the *challenge*, as each antagonist threatens to use whatever power he or she has to punish the other if the demands being made are not met. The second act is devoted mainly to *surveying the viable alternatives*. The third act involves *evaluating* alternatives, *choosing* the one that both parties agree looks best, and *becoming committed*.

One of the main values of keeping in mind the three-act sequence is that you are less likely to become unduly pessimistic about reaching an acceptable agreement during the opening act if you find yourself embroiled in a quarrel. What at first seems like a heated fight between husband and wife, with all the accompanying fireworks, can actually turn out to be act 1 in a successful negotiation drama, soon giving way to the more reasoned bargaining of acts 2 and 3. The third act of such a drama can continue for many days or even months, until the two contending parties arrive at a solution that they both find acceptable. Because the settlement does not have to be ratified by any outside group, those who participate in informal person-to-person negotiations usually don't end up writing a statement of the agreement that spells out all the provisions. But leaving out that final scene of the third act could ruin the entire drama because the agreement will not last very long if either of the two parties misremembers the major concessions that were promised.

Using the balance sheet to decide whether to negotiate and with whom

If you ever become discontented with your career or with any other aspect of your life, you may be able to find a satisfactory solution to the problem if you can identify someone with the power to alleviate your grievances who is willing to negotiate. It sometimes happens that a person's job or life style is unsatisfactory in a number of ways but the person definitely does not want to change because all the alternatives he or she can think of are much worse. Whenever this is the case, each source of dissatisfaction with the current course of action can be regarded as a challenge that requires a new minor decision about how best to solve that particular problem, which usually requires negotiation.

In Chapter 4 we suggested that the balance-sheet procedure might prove to be a useful tool for a "fractionating" approach to solving such problems. We shall describe and illustrate this special procedure in detail because many people may find that by using it they can find a satisfactory remedy for some, if not all, of the main difficulties that are preventing them from feeling satisfied with a course of action that appears to be better than any other available alternative. Suppose, for example, that you are feeling vaguely dissatisfied with your job and you do not want to change to any of the other jobs you know about because none of them is as good. The first step of the slicing-up procedure is to analyze your overall feeling of discontent in a way that will break it down into specific problems. You might start by asking yourself "What in particular is it about this job that is making me feel dissatisfied?" After thinking about your answers to this question, the next step is to write down a list of the most important problems, each of which can then be treated as a specific challenge for which a solution might be found by constructing a balance sheet of alternative ways of alleviating that particular difficulty.

A young executive's list, for example, included the following:

- Every so often the head of the division gives me a so-called emergency assignment that requires me to work overtime. Sometimes this takes up all my free time during an entire week, disrupting my social life and also disrupting any of the regular assignments that I am working on.
- I hate having to drive to and from my office everyday in rush-hour traffic.
- I have to spend many hours each week on certain dull, routine tasks of tracking down information. I wish I could spend that time on the more important and interesting tasks that I work on most of the time.

Obviously there is not likely to be an easy solution to any of these problems. If there were, the executive, as a reasonably intelligent and socially competent person, would have hit upon the solution a long time ago. The decision counselor he consulted suggested that he take up one problem at a time, as a challenge for which a new decision needs to be worked out. For dealing with the first problem, the young executive, Tom Myerson, was encouraged to try to overcome his long-established attitude that "nothing can be done to get rid of those disrupting emergency assignments" by setting himself the task of preparing a balance sheet in which the first alternative to be listed is "Do absolutely nothing about it," which was his current course of action. Tom's next step, of course, was to generate some alternative courses of action to compare with the unsatisfactory one he was following. At this point some of the methods for stimulating innovative ideas, discussed in Chapter 3, could be applicable. But sometimes, as in Tom Myerson's case, merely posing the following three questions can be sufficient to generate fresh alternatives that are worthy of being weighed in the balance sheet:

- Which person (or persons) has the power to do something to alleviate this problem of mine?

- If that person wanted to use his or her power to help alleviate this problem, what are the specific changes that person could make?
- How could I negotiate to get that person to cooperate with me, to use his or her power to make the desirable changes in order to alleviate this problem?

Incidentally, these same three questions, in slightly modified form, might be used for specific problems pertaining to many other spheres of life besides job dissatisfaction. When the problem involves marital difficulties or defects in a close friendship, the last part of the second question needs to be slightly reworded to "What are the specific changes that would be the best ones for *the two of us* to agree to make?"

Returning now to the example of the dissatisfied young executive who preferred not to change to a different job, Tom Myerson's list of alternatives for the first problem included:

- Explain the problem of emergency assignments to Mr. I (Tom's immediate superior) and ask him to talk over the problem with Mr. C (the chief of the division) to see if those rush assignments could be anticipated sooner.
- Arrange for a conference with Mr. C (the chief of the division) and explain to him the nature of the problem to see if he can avoid giving so many rush assignments.
- Go over the head of Mr. C by arranging for an appointment to explain the problem to Mr. P (the president of the company), who might then instruct Mr. C to avoid giving so many last-minute rush assignments.
- Send a letter to Mr. C (the chief of the division), with a copy to Mr. P (the company's president), stating as diplomatically as possible that if the problem of rush assignments cannot be solved, you will request a transfer to another job in a different division (which is tantament to threatening to resign from your present job in Mr. C's division).

While filling out the balance sheet for each of these alternatives, Tom realized that these four alternatives in the order listed would involve increasing risks of getting into trouble with higher-ups because they required putting more and more pressure on powerful superiors. But he also recognized that if his services were highly valued and the higher-ups wanted him to stay on the job, the incentive for the chief of the division to change would also increase with each successive move from the first to the fourth alternative.

Seeing this all laid out on the balance-sheet grid, with the advantages and disadvantages of each briefly noted, Tom was able to select the alternative he thought would have the best chance of success with the minimum of costs and risks. He noticed, for example, that his balance sheet contained several undesirable consequences if he asked help from Mr. I, his immediate superior (such as being indebted to him for doing him a favor and not knowing whether Mr. I might deliberately or inadvertently sabotage the whole thing by saying something undiplomatic that would make the chief irritated). Studying the array of pluses and minuses in the balance sheet led him to select the second alternative as better than the others. Tom was also able to rank-order the remaining alternatives. As a result, he worked out a detailed course of action involving contingency plans. First, try to negotiate personally with the chief; then, if that fails, move on to the next best alternative, negotiating with the president of the company; finally, if that also fails, resort to an even more risky course of action, the fourth alternative, attempting to elicit concessions by asking in a formal letter to both of the top executives to be transferred to a different division. As it turned out, the initial plan to negotiate with the chief was successful, so there was no need for Tom to escalate to the more risky alternatives.

Avoiding common pitfalls

If Tom's efforts to alleviate his grievance by negotiating with the chief of his division were carried out badly, the attempted cure could prove to be much worse than the disease. The ranks of the unemployed could become greatly swollen and the rate of divorce could go way up if large numbers of people followed our suggestions unskillfully.

Of course it is only on rare occasions that failing to negotiate effectively might result in such a profound loss as a ruined career or a ruined marriage. But very often a person will become involved in less momentous conflicts that require the basic skills of an effective negotiator in order to avoid other losses—especially money. P. G. Wodehouse, in one of his satirical novels, gives this account of a singularly ineffective negotiator:

> "How much do I want, sir?"
> "Yes. Give it a name. We won't haggle."
> He pursed his lips.
> "I'm afraid," he said, having unpursed them, "I couldn't do it as cheap as I'd like, sir . . . I'd have to make it twenty pounds."
> I was relieved. I had been expecting something higher. He, too, seemed to feel that he had erred on the side of moderation, for he immediately added:
> "Or, rather, thirty."
> "Thirty?"
> "Thirty, sir."
> "Let's haggle," I said.
> But when I suggested twenty-five, a nicer looking sort of number than thirty, he shook his grey head regretfully, and he haggled better than me, so that eventually we settled on thirty-five. It wasn't one of my better haggling days.

From studies of successful negotiating, we can extract some pointers that might help everyone to have better haggling days. These pointers are intended not only for person-to-person negotiations that are self-initiated, as in Tom's case, but also for all sorts of other negotiations, including formal ones in which the participants are representatives of opposing groups or organizations. The evidence supporting their efficacy, however, is far from complete and in some instances is merely suggestive. So they should be regarded as reminders of some of the ways to try overcoming common obstacles to successful negotiation, if you judge them to be applicable to the particular circumstances at hand.

Disagree forcefully but not insultingly.

During the first step of any negotiation, it is essential to express disagreement with your opponent without inducing hatred and animosity. Mahatma Gandhi, who had considerable success as the leader of India's nonviolent struggle against the domination of Great Britain, urged negotiators always to treat their enemies with respect, as potential allies in the future. It may require considerable self-control to avoid saying something insulting when your opponents appear to be responding to your well-reasoned firmness by being irrationally pigheaded. Or when you are convinced that they are resorting to cheap propagandistic tricks and blatant lies, whereas you are only exaggerating a little to make your points emphatically. But the chances of working out a satisfactory agreement are better if you can limit your rebuttals to presenting the truth as you see it, discrediting your opponent's arguments but abstaining from discrediting your opponent as a person.

After being insulted or humiliated, an opponent is likely to become even less cooperative than before. The more damage is inflicted on an opponent's self-esteem, the stronger will be that person's need to save face by becoming harsh, inflexible, and aggressively demanding. Retaliatory reactions to even nonobvious slights, such as witty remarks that could be construed as clever put-downs, are especially likely if the person who is the target is deeply worried about his or her competence, or is trying to cover up chronically low self-esteem by acting in a belligerent manner. If you size up an opponent with whom you are negotiating as being that type of person, it is more imperative than ever to provide the opponent with plenty of opportunities for saving face and to abstain from making any personally damaging remarks.

Abstaining is particularly difficult when your opponent has already started hurling insulting accusations, attempting to humiliate you personally. We do not mean to imply that personal and ethnic slurs are to go unchallenged. On the contrary, it may sometimes be essential to convince your opponent the first time he or she does it that you will not tolerate being insulted again. There are ways of putting this important point across without resorting to hurling back insult for insult. Escalating the verbal attacks, which usually results in a complete breakdown of the negotiations, may be far less effective than a simple ultimatum to put a stop to insults—something like, "One more insult like that and I'll leave. If we're going to continue to talk, we're going to have to get down to business on the issues."

Don't give up hope just because your opponents appear to be hope-less cases.

It is very easy to become discouraged and to decide that further discussion is going to be a waste of time on the basis of what your opponents say during the first formal or informal negotiation session. For instance, they may repeatedly and rashly reject one of your most essential requirements or maybe all of your essential requirements. If they are making exorbitant demands on you to give them all sorts of concessions and there is no hope of their being reasonable about granting you the rock-bottom concessions you need, why go on? You might as well walk out on them right now. But wait. Remember that successful negotiation is usually a three-act drama, with the first act sometimes devoted entirely to chaotic sound and fury. And like good actors in a melodrama, some negotiators put on a convincing performance of uncompromising toughness that misrepresents their willingness to make compromises. In well-publicized negotiations where the negotiators are representatives of opposing parties to a dispute, the aggressive performances during the first act and in the accompanying news releases about it may be directed more to the audience back home than to the persons present at the meeting. The folks back home might not believe there was a real fight if they didn't see any bloody noses. There are also other reasons why one can't take a negotiator's opening stance at face value. The important point is that it could be a serious mistake to assume that your opponents will not end up making concessions just because they start off talking as though they won't.

Keep in mind what was said earlier about the first act in successful negotiation dramas: to keep the prospects of an agreement alive during the heated interchanges at the beginning of a negotiating session, the best assumption may be that the main issues will turn out to be negotiable. And remember that cooperation can beget cooperation.

If you can't present your case, insist on calling in a mediator.

Most of us have had the experience of arguing with pigheaded opponents who insist on heckling and shouting whenever we are presenting our firm position. Much as we would prefer to talk quietly, we are forced to shout louder and louder, and still they won't listen to what we are saying. Whenever the opening act of a negotiation drama degenerates into an intolerable shouting match or whenever there is no shouting but the dialogue of the deaf is threatening to go on and on, there is a simple tactic that can help both parties move constructively to act 2. The tactic is to insist on calling in a mediator. That means breaking off the nonproductive session and then starting a new one with someone in the role of mediator, preferably a respected person who is neutral.

One of the main functions of a mediator is to serve as a chairman, to introduce orderly procedures and to see to it that both sides have equal opportunity to present their cases. In a dispute between business partners, for example, a respected lawyer can do wonders to improve the hearing of formerly deaf dialoguers. Most lawyers are trained in orderly procedures for handling disputes and some have had experience dealing with contending parties in a neutral way that enables them to grasp the essential issues. For collective bargaining, as in labor–management disputes, there are professional mediators who are skilled not only at bringing order out of chaos but also at helping the participants to generate compromise solutions acceptable to both sides. For family disputes, a respected friend or professional counselor can sometimes serve a similar function. By introducing formal procedures a mediator can transform a shouting match into a problem-solving group.

Of course anyone who has a very weak case might well prefer not to permit any such transformation. One of the secrets of a famous orator was once discovered when he inadvertently left behind on the podium a typewritten script of his speech. There was a pencil notation in the margin on the last page, where he was summing up his main arguments: "Logic weak here, so yell like hell!" Psychologists studying bargaining have belatedly discovered the same secret. There is some evidence indicating that when orderly procedures are introduced to get people to stop yelling during negotiation sessions, the final settlement is more likely to be in favor of the side with the stronger case.

Make whatever concessions you are willing to make only when the time is ripe.

Why not skip the painful first two acts of the negotiation drama by starting right off with the final act, which concentrates directly on finding a solution? Wouldn't it be a good idea to avoid all the unpleasant belittling and haggling by being completely open and as conciliatory, flexible, and generous as possible from the outset? Well, have you ever tried it? If so, you probably discovered that instead of respecting you all the more for your forthrightness, your opponents ended up regarding you as a villain who was not negotiating in good faith. Inadvertently you were violating powerful norms—rules of the game—that are linked to deep-seated conceptions of social equity. When your opponents reach the point where they are ready to start to make some concessions to you, they expect you to offer something substantial in return. When it becomes apparent that you are being absolutely rigid, not moving one little bit from your initial offer, they see you as simply unwilling to enter into the spirit of give-and-take of genuine negotiation. They assume that, like themselves and all the other players they know, you have been playing the same game they have and that you started off by inflating your demands to well above the level you are willing to settle for. No matter how many times you tell them, they simply won't believe that you were so extremely magnanimous at the beginning that you actually left yourself nothing to trade with.

Very well, then, why not start off the way they expect but at least condense the rest of act 1 and most of act 2 by presenting all the concessions you are prepared to make as soon as both sides have presented their initial position? Here again you would run into misinterpretations of your generous offer based on expectations of give and take. If you are offering a great deal when your opponents are offering little or nothing, they are likely to assume that you are so foolish or have such a weak case that they need not offer much in return. Or else, later on when they think the time has come to move toward closure and they offer a big dramatic concession, they will expect you to do the same. Again, no matter what you say, they simply will not believe that you gave away everything you could before the time was ripe to strike a bargain.

So, when is the time ripe? As usual, there is no simple formula that can readily be applied to give a definitive answer. It is more a matter of trial and error, of making repeated tentative soundings without making any explicit offers. Before judging that the time is ripe for saying "All right, I am prepared to offer this concession," there has to be a great deal of tacit communication back and forth.

Hypothetical instances have to be presented in a tentative way: "Just suppose, for the sake of argument, that I could consider doing what you are asking. What could you consider doing about that?" You have to watch for subtle signs that your opponents at long last are ready to move toward an accommodation. Incidentally, whether you are presenting a hypothetical, tentative, or definitive concession, it is probably a good idea to show that you have the equity principle in mind by indicating that it is conditional on similar concessions being made by the opposition. But exactly when and how to make concessions that will induce your opponents to do the same still remains in the sphere of art rather than science.

When deadlocked, try the salami tactic before resorting to an ultimatum.

Most often there are at least several different issues on which the opposing parties disagree. Negotiators usually attempt to settle a number of them simultaneously by "log rolling"—by working out a package deal containing concessions acceptable to both sides. If one such attempt after another fails, the salami tactic might succeed in breaking the deadlock. You will recall that the salami tactic involves breaking down the dispute into smaller issues that are then dealt with one at a time. This fractionating approach is especially likely to be beneficial when the main issues that cannot be solved involve matters of principle, fundamental ideology, or prestige on one side or the other. By cutting up the big issues into small manageable slices, you may find that your opponents are willing to accept one discrete compromise proposal after another, whereas if you continue to offer a total package they may see so many objectionable ingredients that they will continue to reject it out of hand. The salami tactic can revive hope of arriving at an agreement at a time when the participants are beginning to feel hopeless. After a series of specific proposals are agreed upon, it may be possible to put together a combined package deal that settles at least some, if not all, of the major issues.

When your opponents are unyielding despite all your efforts to initiate give-and-take bargaining that could enable both sides to meet their rock-bottom requirements, you might try, as a last resort, announcing a deadline for ending the negotiation sessions. Suppose that you have already worked out the basic lines of agreement but are now being held up by one particular point of contention. After long hours of getting nowhere on that issue you judge that a satisfactory agreement could be reached in about one-half hour or so of straight talk. You could act on this judgment by telling the other party that you are willing to devote one more hour to discussing the issues but that if no settlement is reached by that time you will reluctantly conclude that it is impossible to reach an agreement and you will leave.

Making such an announcement is tantamount to issuing an ultimatum. What you would be doing, in effect, is threatening to break off the negotiations if an agreement is not reached within the time limit you specified, no matter how generous the amount of time you are offering. Such an ultimatum should never be made lightly because it can have serious disadvantages along with obvious advantages.

The main advantage of issuing an ultimatum is, of course, that it prods everyone involved in the negotiations to get down to business. The time pressure imposed by a realistic deadline sometimes induces negotiators to lower their demands and to look for openings that may lead to agreement. Above all, it can function as an incentive to cut down on the amount of bluffing.

But imposing a deadline is also very risky. If you miscalculate the amount of time needed to work out a settlement, the deadline will arrive before you are really ready to quit. At that point you can only hope that your opponents will feel the same way and argue that the deadline should be extended. If they do, you can magnanimously give in to their arguments. But if they don't, you are committed to breaking off the negotiations when the time limit arrives. If you fail to keep your word, you will lose your credibility and your opponents are likely to take an even tougher stance than they did before. Yet another problem can arise from misjudging how much more time will be needed. As the deadline approaches, time pressures can mount to the point where severe stress reactions are evoked in your opponents or in yourself. You will recall that it is in just such circumstances that panic or near-panic is evoked, which results in poor judgment and impulsive, ill-conceived decisions. Because of these dangerous risks, we regard issuing an ultimatum as a weapon that should be used sparingly, with full realization of how it could backfire. That is why we recommend using the less dangerous salami tactic first.

When you arrive at an agreement, put it in writing.

In order to avoid subsequent misunderstandings and arguments about the specific terms of an agreement, it is worthwhile to spend the time and effort writing it out. There are two main reasons for doing so. First, as we said before, if the settlement is at all complicated, the people involved will have trouble remembering all the various details. They may end up angrily accusing each other of breaking the agreement simply because one or the other side does not recall the terms accurately. Second, if a large amount of money is involved in a business deal, either the sellers or the buyers might encounter someone who offers them a better deal. They would be tempted to change their minds unless they had fully committed themselves in writing and had signed the agreement, especially if they believe that the signed agreement would stand up in court. The same problems can arise in other kinds of economic transactions. We know of many men and women who thought they had been offered a job only to discover that they had no way to prove it when the other party subsequently decided to back out of the agreement. One man notified his current employer that he was leaving to accept a better position at another firm offered to him after a full day of negotiating the details of his salary, work load, and other such issues. But a short time later he found himself unemployed when he learned that the two officials with whom he had negotiated did not have the authority to make the offer and that the board of trustees had decided not to fill the opening.

If you ever receive a verbal offer like this one, you must assume that a gentlemen's agreement is insufficient, that the offer or agreement is not final until it is put in writing and signed. Remember what the movie mogul Samuel Goldwyn once supposedly said about a purely verbal agreement: "It's not worth the paper it's written on." Remember, too, while you are at it, that you might as well try to have all the detailed "understandings" worded as explicitly as possible, just in case the written agreement has to serve as a legal document.

If you have successfully negotiated a compromise agreement as the representative of a group, be prepared to defend yourself against charges of having sold out to your opponents.

Whenever a compromise agreement is reached by representatives of two opposing groups, members of both groups are likely to feel that too many concessions were made. Some may even condemn it as a betrayal or sell-out. The members are usually in no position to understand all the complicated issues that their representatives were taking into account, nor do they have all the detailed information that led their representatives to regard the concessions as essential for a reasonable agreement. What is reasonable to well-informed persons who have learned how their opponents view the dispute may look quite unreasonable to ardent members who talk only to each other. Consequently any representative who negotiates an agreement with a rival group must be prepared to invest a great deal of time and effort trying to allay the suspicions of the folks back home.

It helps to present persuasive arguments, including new facts learned from the negotiations, in order to explain why the concessions were necessary. It also helps if the representative can point to a well-documented record showing that he or she made strong demands on the opponents, fought hard, and remained tough every step of the way. (This is one way in which the bloody noses we spoke about earlier can be used to advantage.) What does not help is to play up the signs of mutual friendship that emerge between the rival representatives when an agreement is finally reached after long-drawn-out negotiations, as when television newscasts display the conciliatory smiling, backslapping, and exuberant conviviality of the representatives of labor and management shortly after they arrive at a formula for settling a big strike. The representatives, having been isolated from their fellow members for a long period of time while closeted with the rival team, are likely to be regarded with deep suspicion. Have they been won over? Are they still loyal? Are they putting the interests of our group ahead of all other considerations? Impressive avowals of loyalty by the representatives, along with persuasive arguments that appeal to the members who are most concerned with the sectarian interests of the group, may be essential to counteract charges of a sell-out.

Representatives sometimes succeed in heading off the development of such suspicions by shuttling back and forth between negotiation meetings, which are usually located on neutral territory, and group meetings back home. This enables them to familiarize the members with the issues as they arise at each stage of the negotiations and to reassure them that they are striving for a victory for the home team. But clear-cut victories are rare. When the negotiators reach a satisfactory agreement, even the most conscientious shuttlers must be prepared to function as mediators to persuade the members of their own group that the settlement has obtained as much as anyone could hope from the opposing party.

One final point: A certain amount of creativity and horse sense is needed to apply any of the pointers we have extracted from studies of successful negotiations. It should be apparent that a great deal of patience is needed to carry out any tactic effectively when you are in the hot seat as negotiator. All that can be said for the tactics we have recommended in this chapter is that it will probably pay to make a sincere effort to use them in the appropriate circumstances and in a sensible way. Their use should increase your chances of arriving at satisfactory settlements when you negotiate with your spouse, your boss, your opponents inside or outside your organization, or anyone else.

11
Discounting Common Myths

A number of common myths inhibit people from taking the essential steps for sound decision making. In this chapter we discuss what seem to be the most common myths that people cling to when they have to make vital decisions. We have already alluded to them in earlier chapters but they warrant reviewing and more detailed discussion. Each of the eight myths we have singled out are false assumptions that are sources of avoidable defects in the way people go about making important life decisions. All eight are difficult to discard because they are based on ideas that are sometimes valid. Each of the myths has a point that contains a genuine kernel of truth, but the point is greatly exaggerated. Any valid idea generalized to extremes leads to a false assumption.

MYTH 1. The future is a matter of chance or luck, so there's no use spending a lot of time and effort trying to make the best possible decision.

One widely accepted assumption is that there is no point in working hard at making any decision, no matter how consequential it may be for your own future or for that of an organization to which you belong, because the outcome is going to depend on luck. Luck or chance certainly does play a role in the outcome of decisions, and there is no way to guarantee that if you devote the time and effort required by sound decision-making procedures any particular decision will turn out well. Nevertheless, the chances of a desirable outcome can be maximized by following good decision-making procedures. In that sense you can do something that will bring good luck more often and bad luck less often. Each failure to meet one of the main criteria for sound decision making increases the chances that a poor outcome will occur.

What are the criteria? There are eight of them that characterize good decision-making procedures. Good decision makers do the following:

1. They are alert and responsive to potential challenges, both warnings and opportunities.
2. They thoroughly consider a wide range of alternatives. The more effort they make to avoid leaving out viable alternatives, the less likely they are to miss a really good one.
3. They thoroughly consider their objectives and values. They try to consider all objectives, so as to avoid making a choice that will bring unnecessary losses or regret about missing a rare opportunity.
4. They carefully weigh the likely positive and negative consequences of each alternative before choosing the one that appears to have the best chance of achieving their objectives with a minimum of loss or cost.
5. They look for new information relevant to the alternatives. New information can come from other people, personal experience, books, or from television and other mass media.
6. They use the new information to revise their evaluations of the consequences. They don't ignore new information that goes against their initial choice.
7. They reexamine all the information they have gathered before making their final decision. They don't forget to take important considerations into account that they had thought of earlier, even if they have turned up some dramatic new bits of knowledge that strongly sway them in the opposite direction.
8. They make plans for carrying out the decision. These include contingency plans for important problems that might arise when the decision is implemented and for setbacks that might be somewhat discouraging.

There is no need to spend the time and energy trying to live up to all these criteria unless the decision is a really major one in terms of its potential consequences. Even for major decisions, you cannot always expect to be able to live up to all eight criteria before committing yourself. No one can do so consistently because sometimes time pressures are too great or other conditions are present that interfere with sound decision making. Nevertheless, no matter how unfavorable the circumstances may be, it is worthwhile striving to meet as many of the criteria as you can for each crucial decision. The more criteria you meet satisfactorily, the greater your chances of a successful outcome.

Good decision-making procedures are of value even on those occasions when a bad outcome occurs. If people experience bad outcomes after poor decision making, they may ask themselves, "How could I have been so dumb? I should have seen that this would happen." They suffer not just from the undesirable outcome itself but also from strong feelings of regret and shame at having made a stupid decision, which may interfere with their ability to curtail the losses and to make a sound new decision that will enable them to recover rapidly from the setback.

MYTH 2. Deadlines can't be changed.

One common assumption that often proves to be a myth is that you cannot do anything to change a deadline. Employers generally put pressure on a person to whom they offer a job to give their answer by a certain date, preferably within the next five minutes. Obviously it makes it more convenient for them to have the candidate's answer right away so that they can fill the opening without delay or else move on to the next candidate if the first person turns the offer down. For essentially the same reason, colleges, professional schools, and all sorts of mid-career training programs give the applicants they accept a very tight deadline.

But if you are at the top of the list of candidates for a job or an educational opportunity, the people in charge may be quite willing to extend their deadline in order to avoid having to replace you with someone who may be less qualified. So it pays to be a bit skeptical about the common assumption that official deadlines from a big organization cannot be changed. By politely asking the person in charge of hiring or admissions if the deadline could be extended in order to allow you more time to weigh the alternatives, you may be given the extra time you need. Instead of thinking badly of you, managers or officials are likely to be positively impressed about your way of making the choice. And they may think all the more highly of you if you explain that you need more time to collect information and deliberate because you have good competing offers to consider. If you are in that fortunate position, you will probably find it advantageous to talk frankly about your alternatives to the manager or officials who are putting you under time pressure. As a highly desirable candidate, you have a certain amount of power that they will respect.

Even if you have no competing offers and are not sure about how strong a candidate they consider you to be, you probably will have little to lose if you explain carefully that you are requesting a bit more time to take account of the relevant information about the alternatives open to you. When deliberating about whether or not to ask if the deadline can be extended, it is important to realize that although the representatives of big organizations give the impression that hiring and work deadlines are absolute and sacred, they know that most deadlines in fact can be negotiated.

This is worth keeping in mind after starting a new job, especially if you believe that the deadline for any of your work assignments is unreasonable. Your superior simply may not realize how much time it takes and may actually prefer to give you an extended deadline to allow you to carry out the task the way it should be done rather than to have slipshod work that meets an arbitrary deadline. Sometimes, of course, there are strong reasons why a deadline cannot be changed. If so, the superior and the organization as a whole will be better off to know in advance that there is not sufficient time to do a first-rate job. Furthermore, those who judge your work will be less likely to think you are incompetent in the event that you fail to do what they originally expected. If you have informed them in advance about the reasons why the deadline is unrealistic, they can take this consideration into account when they look over your work on a rush job. So for job assignments as well as for job offers it is usually worthwhile to try to negotiate a realistic deadline.

MYTH 3. *Asking questions about an opportunity is asking for trouble.*

A third common myth is that when someone offers you a new job, or an invitation to join a prestigious organization, or any other opportunity, it will be disadvantageous for you to ask questions about the pros and cons of whatever is being offered. Sometimes, of course, employers are annoyed, especially if a prospective employee asks a barrage of questions. But that is not likely if you make a few pertinent requests in a respectful way (for example, "I would appreciate it if you could tell me about some of the drawbacks or difficulties to be expected on this job"). In fact, an employment interviewer may well be positively impressed by your intelligence and self-confidence if you get right down to business in collecting the essential information needed to make a judicious choice.

MYTH 4. Experts almost always agree. If you've asked one, you've asked them all.

A fourth myth applies particularly to decisions requiring expert advice from physicians, lawyers, investment counselors, or other specialists. The false assumption is that asking just one expert is enough, that practically all other experts will agree with his or her judgments and make the same recommendation. It seems thrifty to believe in this myth because it is usually quite expensive to obtain each expert's advice. There is also a psychological gain because when we need a doctor or a lawyer or some other expert we are usually in bad trouble and feel much less tense if we are convinced that the person we are consulting is a good representative of the leading specialists, that he or she knows the right answers and can predict what will happen with great certitude, like a scientist. But despite the monetary expense and psychological discomfort, it is necessary to be realistic, to remember that even if the expert we are consulting is a medical scientist, the advice he or she gives for any individual case requires making a personal judgment, which might be regarded as questionable by other experts.

It is useful to remind ourselves that specialists who are top experts often disagree on what is the best thing for a troubled person to do, each having his or her own good reasons. To find out about these reasons from each expert and to obtain important information that might otherwise be withheld, it is essential to be prepared with a series of specific questions so that after the expert has asked his questions and made his recommendations you are able to reverse the roles by interviewing the expert. (Chapter 8 gives pointers that will help you increase your effectiveness as an interviewer of the experts you consult.) But even when an expert gives satisfactory answers to all your questions and gives reasons that sound very convincing for his or her recommendations, you must still remember that experts are only human and can make bad mistakes, like anyone else.

These same considerations are misused by some people as rationalizations for shopping around until an expert can be found who will give them the advice they want to hear. This kind of shopping around is certainly not recommended when you have to make a decision about starting a lawsuit, investing your life savings, undergoing surgery, or doing anything else that requires the expert advice of professional specialists.

It may take a great deal of tact and skill on your part to be able to obtain an independent recommendation from a second specialist when you need it, without antagonizing the one upon whom you will be dependent for obtaining expert treatment. But once again, if you go about it in the right way, with proper deference and sincerity, you can get a second opinion without antagonizing your lawyer or your financial adviser or your surgeon.

We hope that in the future the vast majority of experts in all professional fields will accept the necessity for an independent opinion, just as many good physicians now do. In the meantime, however, it is up to the perturbed client to make the effort to work out some way of getting that independent second opinion without annoying the one who is going to be in charge of the case.

MYTH 5. Consulting nonexperts is worthless.

When people have to make decisions about an educational, legal, financial, medical, or any other kind of problem that is in the realm of professional expertise, they generally belittle the value of obtaining additional suggestions from nonexperts. The common assumption is that after obtaining professional advice from one or more experts it is worse than useless to listen to what a nonexpert has to say. There is an obvious element of truth in the assumption that one need not bother to listen to old wives tales and that the half-baked judgments of laymen may be based on incomplete information picked up from a television soap opera or misunderstandings of what a genuine specialist once told them.

But if you are appropriately skeptical about the rumors, guesses, and proverbs that people offer when they hear about your dilemma, you can extract something of value from what they tell you. There are two kinds of situations in which the advice of nonexperts can be particularly valuable. The first is in the stage of generating alternatives. People who don't have any preconceived ideas about what the alternatives are can sometimes come up with creative solutions that everyone else misses. Chapter 3 discusses the value of asking nonexperts for ideas about alternatives. The second kind of situation occurs when nonexperts happen to know some crucial bit of information relevant to the situation. They don't even have to be exactly right or to know that they know something important. Something they say can give you a hint or clue that can be checked out by an expert. Chapter 8 gives some striking cases in which this was true.

MYTH 6. *If the members in your well-qualified group of decision makers agree on the same choice without anyone dissenting, you can feel quite secure that it is a sound decision.*

When the members of a decision-making group like and respect each other, they are inclined to assume that the absence of any disagreement about the best course of action is a sure sign of their having arrived at a good decision. This myth is especially likely to distort the members' judgments when at every meeting the leader and the members are amiable, reassert feelings of solidarity, and avoid debating any of the controversial issues that would spoil the cozy group atmosphere. At such meetings, as we pointed out in Chapter 9, there is a strong concurrence-seeking tendency, which we refer to as groupthink: a mode of thinking that the leader and members of a group engage in when their desire for unanimity overrides their strivings to be realistic about appraising alternative courses of action.

Groups, like individuals, have shortcomings. Groups can bring out the worst as well as the best in man. Nietzsche went so far as to say that madness is the exception in individuals but the rule in groups. A considerable amount of social science literature shows that in circumstances of extreme crisis, group contagion occasionally gives rise to collective panic, violent acts of scapegoating, and other forms of what could be called group madness. Much more frequent, however, are instances of mindless conformity and collective misjudgment of serious risks, which are collectively laughed off in a clubby atmosphere of relaxed conviviality.

Groupthink can arise in all sorts of groups, ranging from the highest level of government policy makers (such as President John F. Kennedy and his group of advisers who approved of the Bay of Pigs invasion plan) to everyday work teams, neighborhood committees, and social clubs. In our discussions of illustrative cases we described various symptoms of groupthink. One of the symptoms is a shared sense that the group is so strong and capable that there is no need to worry about taking excessive risks. Nor is there any need to be concerned about whether the chosen course of action is ethically or morally the right thing to do because of an unquestioned belief in the inherent morality of the group ("We are the good guys and whatever we do is for a good cause"). Another type of symptom involves developing shared rationalizations that bolster whatever course of action the leading members prefer. If they decide to take drastic action against a rival group, the members are likely to encourage each other to maintain stereotyped views of the opponents. Worse yet, the group atmosphere discourages any member of a groupthink-dominated group from expressing his or her doubts about the wisdom of whatever course of action the others are pursuing, which leads to an illusion of unanimity and stifles critical thinking about alternatives. When these symptoms of groupthink are present, the members fail badly with regard to meeting the criteria for effective decision making.

From what little is known about the conditions that foster groupthink we recommend a number of steps that a leader might take to prevent groupthink, all of which are discussed in Chapter 9:

- When planning is needed to deal with a challenge requiring an important decision, the members can be selected for the planning group in such a way that there is a good mix of various viewpoints as well as expertise. Different factions should be equally well represented to advocate their divergent positions on the issue.

- The leader should present the problem to the group in an objective manner that does not push the group toward one particular course of action.
- Standard operating procedures can be set up within the group in order to promote open inquiry. The procedures can include starting off with a period of brainstorming during which all members are encouraged to suggest their own ideas and to help each other to formulate those ideas as serious alternatives. Other standard procedures, such as working out scenarios of future consequences and writing out a balance sheet for each alternative, may help to encourage critical analysis after the alternatives have been formulated.
- The tendency to engage in self-censorship of dissenting ideas after a consensus has started to emerge might be reduced by having a period in which each member is expected to be a critical evaluator, with strong encouragement to state openly all of his or her reservations. In order for this to work, however, leaders must be willing to accept criticisms of their own judgments and to urge the members not to soft-pedal their disagreements.
- When alternatives are being evaluated, one or more members of the group can be appointed to be the devil's advocate. The purpose of assigning this role is to probe for weak spots in the most attractive alternatives by raising objections in a devilishly good way that keeps them from being overlooked or overeagerly dismissed as unimportant.
- When the decision involves dealing with competitive groups or opponents, the tendency toward stereotyping them might be reduced by the members trying to put themselves into their opponents' shoes to anticipate how they might react and what countermoves they might make. If the opponents have already given some warnings, it is especially important to examine their communications carefully to try to figure out how the situation looks to them and to construct plausible scenarios of the rivals' real intentions.
- When an organization is confronted with a major policy issue it may be worthwhile to set up two planning groups rather

than one, each carrying out its deliberations under a separate leader. If there is only one policy-making group, it could be divided from time to time into two subgroups to meet separately under different chairmen. The groups or subgroups can be brought together later to hammer out their differences.

• After a group has reached a preliminary consensus about what seems to be the best course of action, it might be helpful to have a second-chance meeting at which every member is expected to talk openly about residual doubts, uncertainties, and reservations, before making a final commitment. In setting up a second-chance meeting, the leader might take as his or her model a statement by Alfred P. Sloan, who was chairman of General Motors. At a meeting of his fellow policy makers he concluded with this statement: "Gentlemen, I take it we are all in complete agreement on the decision here. . . . Then I propose we postpone further discussion of this matter until our next meeting to give ourselves time to develop disagreement and perhaps gain some understanding of what the decision is all about."

MYTH 7. If your opponents make unreasonable, exorbitant demands, there is no point in trying to negotiate.

The danger of arriving at a poorly worked-out decision is just as great, if not greater, when the group you are in is at the opposite pole from the cozy cooperative atmosphere of a groupthink type of group, with the members at sword's point, constantly bickering about incompatible objectives. If you find yourself caught up in internal warfare with obstreperous opponents it is all too easy to fall back on the myth that anyone who makes exorbitant demands and won't listen to reasonable arguments is such a hopeless case that it is a waste of time trying to get that person to cooperate. The same faulty assumption can incline you to decide to slam the door behind you as you walk out on a serious quarrel with your spouse, business associates, or representatives of an organization with whom you have been trying to negotiate.

One important thing that is overlooked when this assumption is made is that negotiations that end up successfully often begin with seemingly irreconcilable clashes. At the outset, the opponents are likely to exaggerate their toughness by making unrealistic demands along with vociferous vows that no compromises will be considered. As we pointed out in our chapter on negotiating (Chapter 10), the first act of a successful negotiation drama is usually characterized by much sound and fury that may signify nothing once the second act (exploring the issues) gets under way. The initial demands that were accompanied by table pounding may be almost completely forgotten during the third act (working out a solution involving some concessions from both sides).

Taking account of the ways in which people in heated disputes mislead others into thinking they are uncompromisingly pigheaded, we have offered the following advice:

- Don't give up hope just because your opponents appear to be hopeless cases.

Here are a few other relevant recommendations we have made in Chapter 10 that could be regarded as a set of reminders for embattled negotiators:

- If you can't present your case, insist on calling in a mediator.
- When deadlocked, try the salami tactic—cutting up the big issues into manageable slices, setting aside the most objectionable ingredients in order to start getting your opponents to accept proposals for concessions on both sides.

Recalling these pointers—which are consistent with conclusions extracted from the research literature on successful negotiating—might help to counteract the faulty assumption that it is useless to try to negotiate with someone who is infuriatingly uncooperative. We also have suggested a few more pointers that may help prevent misunderstandings of the sort that could make you or your opponents become so infuriated and uncooperative as to ruin the chances for successful negotiation:

- Disagree forcefully but not insultingly. Even when they are obstreperous, treat your opponents with basic respect, as future allies.
- Make whatever concessions you are willing to make only when the time is ripe. Hold off until the issues are clear and your opponents show signs of being ready to move toward an equitable

accommodation and even then offer your concessions tentatively, one at a time, with the clear-cut proviso that your opponents must also make some concessions.

- When you arrive at an agreement, put it in writing.
- If you have successfully negotiated a compromise agreement as the representative of a group, be prepared to defend yourself against charges of having sold out to your opponents. Also encourage your opponents to be prepared to defend themselves persuasively against the same charges before they go back home to try to get the new agreement ratified.

MYTH 8. Commitments are almost always irrevocable.

Another common assumption that often takes on a mythic aura is that once you have committed yourself by signing a contract or by announcing your decision to the interested parties, the decision is irreversible. True, as soon as you commit yourself it becomes much more difficult to reverse your choice and you may have to pay a stiff penalty if you do. But if you obtain new evidence that makes you change your mind, it is usually possible to reverse the decision at a tolerable cost.

Sometimes the cost turns out to be much less than one has been led to believe. After signing a marriage contract and going through a wedding ceremony, many a man and woman discover crucial information that had been withheld—for example, that the spouse is a chronic alcoholic, or is subject to psychotic episodes of paranoia, or is a sexual sadist. In such circumstances, there are legal provisions for annulling the marriage. In other circumstances of posthoneymoon disillusionment for which the law makes no annulment provisions, there is always the alternative of getting a divorce, although it is costly not just in money but also in emotional turmoil.

In the case of employment contracts and professional partnerships, there are laws equivalent to those of annulment and divorce, which allow disappointed and disillusioned persons to reverse their decisions. Again, it is not easy because of the considerable emotional wear and tear as well as the material costs. Nevertheless, if you decide that it is the right thing to do, it can be done.

Whenever people encounter severe setbacks after committing themselves to a new course of action—a course of medical treatment, a course of study, or whatever—they feel convinced it is impossible to change. They tend to exaggerate the degree of commitment as a way of escaping from the painful conflict that would be generated if they were to think about reversing their earlier decision. That is to say, people sometimes rationalize when they tell themselves that the commitment is so binding that they have gone beyond the point of no return, that they are trapped no matter how much they want to undo an unfortunate decision.

Of course, a strong sense of commitment sometimes serves the useful function of keeping our regret about a past decision to a minimum each time we encounter a minor setback, such as the first marital quarrel during or right after the honeymoon or the first unpleasant side effects after starting a series of essential medical treatments. Instead of starting to reexamine the whole issue, we realize that we are deeply committed and resign ourselves to sticking with a decision that has temporarily gone slightly sour. This attitude allows us to tolerate the passage of time that may be required for it to become sweet again. But when a person discovers that the soured decision really has turned absolutely rotten, the myth that any such decision is irrevocable does not serve a useful function. The consequences of trying to undo the commitment then should be critically examined so that the person knows in as full detail as possible what the costs will be if he or she were to make a new decision that reverses or undoes the rotten one.

The power of the myths

One reason that it is difficult to correct some of the exaggerated generalizations we have singled out as common myths is that they are tacitly encouraged, if not deliberately promoted, by powerful persons and organizations who have a vested interest in maintaining widespread acceptance of the myths. For example, the managers and personnel officers in big firms that hire large numbers of people are likely to give an exaggerated impression about the rules of their organization requiring an immediate answer, without allowing even a few days' time for careful search and appraisal, from anyone who is trying to decide whether or not to accept a job offer (see Myth 2: deadlines can't be changed). Sometimes the self-serving exaggerations are promoted unintentionally, as is probably the case with many busy physicians who tell their patients that they must decide immediately whether or not to give permission for elective surgery.

Some of the examples we have given to illustrate the most common myths involve personal decisions concerning health and medical problems. The main reason for giving so many examples of this kind is that health decisions have been more fully studied by behavioral scientists than any other type of personal decision. The examples are also of special interest because they are among the most vital decisions any person ever has to make. In fact, such decisions often are literally a matter of life and death. But the most common myths are by no means limited to personal health decisions. The very same misleading assumptions are made by large numbers of people when they have to make all sorts of other vital decisions.

12
Making Sound Decisions: A Summary

It would be wonderful if the art and science of decision making had reached the point where all you had to do when confronted with a vital choice was to ask yourself a standard set of questions and then apply a universal formula that would tell you exactly which choice would be best for your purposes. Unfortunately, there is no such magic formula. But what we do know about arriving at sound decisions is the set of questions that need to be asked and the steps that decision makers need to take in order to answer them in a satisfactory way. In fact, that is what this entire book has been about. In this chapter we present this summary of the essential stages in the form of a useful guide for helping someone to make a sound decision.

Throughout your life you can expect to be called upon for advice about crucial decisions by other persons—by your spouse, your children, your relatives, your friends. If you are a professional in any field your clients constantly ask for help in making decisions. If you are in the business world your boss and your colleagues frequently ask for official help or unofficial advice about the decision problems they face.

Of course, the someone you help could be *yourself*. You can use this chapter when you face a vital decision. The same questions and the same steps can be applied, although it is difficult to overcome your own blind spots.

Words of warning

We intend this chapter to be a brief summary of the essential points in each of the stages of decision making. It should serve to remind you of what you learned in earlier chapters. We do not think that this chapter can be used properly without reading those chapters first. There is more to each stage than just answering the key questions we shall focus on. Reading the earlier chapters, especially Chapters 1 through 7, is necessary to understand the processes well enough to help someone go through all the essential stages of effective decision making.

Another warning is to avoid imposing your values on the person asking for help. Most people ask something like "What would you do in my situation?" They seem to want to know the decision you would make. Why shouldn't you tell them? The reason is that your answer would be based on your own values and your own point of view. You may worsen their decision making because by accepting your advice they may cut down on the amount of consideration they give to the alternatives from their own perspective. They may miss consequences that apply to them but not to you.

There is a better way to answer the question. You can say "What I would do is . . ." and go on to explain *the steps you would use to reach a decision.* This leads naturally into helping them with the essential stages.

A final caution is to avoid imposing yourself on others. If a friend or relative seems to be botching a consequential decision and doesn't ask your help, it is usually better not to interfere. You might offer to help, but unless your friend or relative seems genuinely interested it is better to avoid giving unwanted advice. You might end up doing more harm than good and ruining the relationship between the two of you. But if your help is genuinely desired, you can proceed by asking key questions.

A Preliminary Question

What is the trouble?

Before you can help a friend make a decision you have to have a general view of the situation. You also need to know where your friend is in the stages of decision making so that you can ask the right questions for that stage. But you can't ask "What stage are you in?" because your friend probably doesn't know about the stages. So you ask some general questions and figure out the stage from the answers.

You should be careful about taking the answers at face value. Suppose your friend says he is having trouble deciding whether to sign the contract to buy a house that he likes. He seems to be at Stage 4, in which the decision maker decides whether to become committed to the alternative that seems best. But you may suspect that he is having trouble deciding about commitment because he hasn't adequately searched for alternatives (Stage 2) or thoroughly considered the advantages and disadvantages of the choices available (Stage 3). In that case you should ask the key questions for Stage 2 or Stage 3. But if your friend is grappling with a fresh challenge—a new threat or opportunity—you should begin with the key questions for Stage 1.

Key Questions for Stage 1, Accepting the Challenge

Are the dangers serious?

This is the first question asked when some challenging event brings up the possibility that a person's plans are not going to work out and that he or she is going to have to make a decision about what to do. If a friend comes to you about a problem, she or he has already answered yes to this question and has begun to work actively on the decision. You can then help your friend with the rest of the stages.

What if something has happened to a close friend that you think should be accepted as a challenge but your friend ignores it? For instance, suppose that your friend Chuck, who works in another division of your company, has just had two requests turned down by higher management, one for travel money and one for permission to hire someone to fill a position that was just vacated. Chuck doesn't seem concerned, but you know the higher management well enough to know that these may be signs of displeasure at the way your friend's section is being run.

What should you do? If you are really a close friend, you can ask the key question for Stage 1 and share your concern that this is a challenge that he should respond to.

Is it possible to find a better solution?

When people realize that a challenge indicates real danger, but do not believe that it is possible to find a better solution, they are likely to show the decision-making pattern of defensive avoidance. At some level they realize the danger but they try to avoid it by wishful thinking.

Your friend Chuck, mentioned above, may be showing defensive avoidance. Deep down he may know that he is in trouble, but he is trying to convince himself that the management actions are due to the current financial situation and don't reflect a negative evaluation of him. This rationalization may enable him to ignore the challenge until it is too late to do anything about it.

Can you do anything to help Chuck? You can be supportive and encouraging. Let him know that you think he has the competence to handle the situation. Self-confidence is critical at this stage. If you don't bolster his self-confidence, confronting Chuck with your view of the danger and your concern that he isn't doing anything about it may make him feel worse about his ability to cope with the situation and make him less able to make a good decision.

Is there enough time to make a good decision?

When people are faced with a close deadline they sometimes grab the first alternative that comes along. Their paniclike state prevents them from using the time that they do have to find a better solution.

If a friend of yours is in this situation you can help by being calm and reassuring. If the deadline might be more flexible than it appears, you can call attention to the Myth of Inflexible Deadlines (discussed in Chapter 11) and encourage your friend to try to negotiate an extension. You can also go ahead with the questions for the next stage. This will demonstrate that there is enough time to seek a better decision.

Encouraging positive responses

The three key questions involved in accepting the challenge are somewhat different from the questions for the other stages. These three questions in the form we have just stated them must all be answered yes before the person goes on to the rest of the stages of effective decision making. If the person does not go on, he or she courts disaster by making decisions by default. Thus to help someone you must encourage the person to believe sincerely that the answers are yes if you feel quite sure yourself that those are the correct answers. The purpose in asking the questions is to find out where the person is having trouble and in what ways he or she needs to be encouraged.

All this is very tricky. If psychological resistance is very strong, only people with considerable psychological training should try to help the person overcome his or her internal defenses.

Presenting a challenge to others

There is one kind of situation in which knowledge of these three key questions can enable you to be helpful to someone else without presumptuous meddling. This occurs when it is your responsibility to "break the bad news" to someone, which is a common part of almost every job that involves people. You may have to tell employees that they have been fired, customers that the repairs will cost a fortune, clients or patients that they will have to face new troubles.

When you break the bad news to someone you are presenting information that should serve as a constructive challenge. The way you present the challenge will have a strong effect on the way the person answers the three key questions. The person's answers will determine whether he or she accepts the challenge and begins the steps of active decision making.

To take a specific example, suppose you are a nurse or a doctor in a community health center with the responsibility of telling young women the results of their pregnancy tests. When the test is positive for a young unmarried woman, you want to help her to face the situation realistically and to make a good decision about what is best for her.

Your first goal is to present the factual information about the results of the test and what it means, so that the consequences are clear. You want to make sure that the answer to the first question about the seriousness of the dangers is clearly yes. It is unlikely that any young woman will fail to realize the nine-month consequences of pregnancy, but some may not be fully aware of the shorter-term changes that will occur before that and the longer-term demands after that. Factual information about the expected times of physical changes and likely social consequences of having a child may be helpful.

Your second goal is to encourage the woman to believe that there is hope of finding a reasonable solution to her problem. You can point out that there are lots of options available to an unmarried woman, both with and without the father of the child. You can also try to counteract some of the rationalizations that young women are apt to use to avoid facing the situation squarely, such as thinking the consequences are so far in the future that they don't have to do anything about them for a long time.

Your third goal is to counteract the opposite tendency, the feeling that there is not enough time to make the decision. This can lead to a paniclike state in which the woman picks the most obviously available option, such as getting married or having an abortion, without considering the consequences. There is often time to make a good decision. If the woman had the test early in her pregnancy, she should not have to commit herself immediately to any of the alternatives available before obtaining the relevant information and deliberating about the pros and cons.

An important part of accomplishing these three goals is not just what you say but your whole manner of approaching the issues. You should convey the feeling that although the problem is serious, the woman can arrive at an acceptable solution. You should not expect the woman to begin working on the decision at the moment. She will probably require a while for the news to sink in. You might encourage her to come in again in a few days if she would like you to help her more with the decision. Then you could ask the key questions for the rest of the stages. The same kinds of considerations should be taken into account whenever you are talking about any crucial challenge, whether it involves a personal decision or a business, professional, or administrative policy issue.

Key Questions for Stage 2, Generating Alternatives

What are your goals for this decision?

It is impossible to make an effective decision without being as aware as possible of the goals and the values involved in the objectives for which the decision is being made. When you ask someone this question, you will have to follow it up with further questions to explore more fully the values that person has for the current choice.

Why do you want that?
How can you get it?

These are the why and how questions that can be used to follow up a statement of the objectives to get at the various levels of goals. The why question asks for the next higher level of goal. You can ask your friend this question repeatedly until she or he can't respond any more. The how question moves your friend down to more specific goals that are alternative ways of achieving the higher level goals. The why-and-how technique is described more fully on pages 39–41.

What are all the reasonable alternatives?

After your friend is sure she or he is on the right level, the next step is to generate all the reasonable alternatives. You can help by asking this question and by following it up with more specific questions about types of choices available in your friend's situation. Suggestions for generating more alternatives are given on pages 42–48.

Even when people are making minor decisions they sometimes can benefit from being stimulated to generate more alternatives. Suppose your friend Wilson Ostercampton III tells you that he has just been invited to join the Clovernook Country Club. Will regards it as an honor to be invited to join, but he isn't sure he wants to be a member. He asks you for help in making the decision.

At this point you suspect that Will has considered only two alternatives, join or not join. You also suspect that Will isn't very clear about what he might want to get out of belonging to the country club. So you begin by asking the why question. "Why would you want to join the club?" You find out that one of the major attractions for Will are the tennis and swimming facilities. Further questions reveal that Will is concerned about his health and wants to start getting more exercise than he has in the past. He is not very interested in the social aspects of the club except insofar as it is connected with the sports activities.

Next you ask the how question. "Other than by joining the club, how can you achieve your goals of more exercise and better health?" Will mentions the local community center and the possibility that the facilities of a nearby college may be available to the public. Since Will has not mentioned anything but swimming and tennis facilities, you ask, "How else could you get exercise?" Jogging wouldn't take any special facilities. You find out that Will tried jogging and hated it. He is pretty sure that the only kind of exercise that he would do regularly would be something he really enjoys. But he has never tried racketball or handball and they might be real possibilities.

At the end of the conversation with you, Will is feeling much clearer about what he needs to do to make a decision. In response to the questions you asked he has thought of several additional alternatives to consider and he now knows what information he needs to evaluate them.

Key Questions for Stage 3, Evaluating Alternatives

What might happen if you choose this alternative?

This question should get your friend started on generating the plausible scenarios for the outcome of choosing the alternative. You should encourage your friend to develop a scenario for the best likely outcome and the worst likely outcome. The purpose of generating the scenarios is to explore the advantages and disadvantages of the choice. As these are uncovered by the scenarios, you should encourage your friend to write them down so they won't be lost. Either of the balance sheet formats discussed in Chapter 4 provides a good systematic form for keeping track of the considerations that are uncovered, as well as for becoming more fully aware of the consequences to be taken into account. Chapter 5 includes a further discussion of generating scenarios.

This process must be repeated for each of the reasonable alternatives so that they can all be compared. But the alternatives don't need to remain the same during this process. You can encourage your friend to consider modifying the alternatives to overcome drawbacks revealed by the scenarios or to take advantage of new ideas that arise.

How will you be affected?
How will others be affected?
How will you feel about yourself?
How will others feel about you?

These are the four key questions for completing the balance sheet. They must be asked for each alternative. The first and third questions are primarily concerned with the material consequences of the choice, the kind of things a business person would consider as profits and losses. The other two questions are about feelings that may result from the choice, such as pride, guilt, shame, admiration, embarrassment, and so on. You can help your friend make sure all four areas are covered and entered on the balance sheet. It is not uncommon for people to fail to consider one or another of these areas, with generally undesirable results when negative outcomes occur after the decision has been implemented.

What information do you need?

It is rare for people to have all the information they need to fill out the balance sheet. An important function of the systematic procedures for completing the balance sheet is that it helps identify the essential facts and expert forecasts needed for evaluating the alternatives. As you go through the key questions for the balance sheet, you should help your friend keep track of the missing information so that it can be obtained later.

Suppose your friend Will Ostercampton comes up to you a few weeks after you had talked to him about other alternatives to joining the country club. He thanks you very much for your help. He has tried racketball and found it to be more fun for him and as much exercise as tennis. So now he is primarily considering alternatives that include racketball courts. It turns out that the country club does have air-conditioned courts, a great advantage during the summer. Will is about to say yes to the exclusive country club, but he is not sure that he wants to let himself in for the social obligations that might ensue and he again asks for your advice.

Since Will is concerned about evaluating the alternatives, you ask him the four key questions for completing the balance sheet. When you ask about how others will feel, his only response is that the people who invited him to join the country club would be disappointed if he didn't accept. Then he suddenly realizes that the club might be all white because he cannot recall having heard of any member who is black. His black friends and colleagues will be annoyed with him if he joins a club that discriminates against blacks. Furthermore, Will himself would feel that he was not living up to his own social principles. Will then realizes that it is essential for him to find out what the club policy is. If they do not allow black members Will definitely does not want to join.

Do you need an expert?

This question belongs at every stage. There is always the need for expert information on which to base a decision, most especially when it comes to evaluating alternatives. In addition to asking your decision-making friend this question, you ought to ask yourself, "Do I have enough knowledge to help my friend?" Your friend may be doing a good job working through the stages and may be asking for help only because he or she feels the need for more information about the consequences of certain courses of action. If you lack the appropriate knowledge you will make matters worse by trying to supply the missing information. You can help in these cases by discussing how to find an expert and how to get the most from an expert. (See Chapter 8.)

Suppose your friend Bob Anderson asks you for advice. He hired someone to do a small repair job in his home and it was done so poorly that he refused to pay for it until it is redone properly, which the contractor refused to do. Now he is being sued for ninety-seven dollars plus court costs in small claims court by the person who did the job. Bob is upset about having to appear in court and wants to know what he can do to defend himself against the claim. He is worried that if the judge rules against him and the ruling is publicized he might lose his credit rating with banks and with other commercial organizations in the community, which could have a devastating effect on the new business he has just started. The claim is so small that it is hardly worth hiring a lawyer. Besides, lawyers aren't supposed to be needed in small claims court.

You could try to help Bob by discussing alternatives based on reasonable assumptions about what small claims court is like, such as settling out of court or ignoring the matter and not showing up. But you should realize that your suggestions and evaluations could do Bob considerable harm if your assumptions turn out to be wrong. What Bob needs most is specific information about the procedures in small claims court, the kinds of evidence allowed, and the legal rules about responsibility for poor workmanship. Unless you have that knowledge, the best thing you can do is to help him find someone who does. Maybe the clerk of the court can answer the questions. Perhaps the library has a book on handling one's own case in small claims court that would offer the information he needs.

Key Questions for Stage 4, Becoming Committed

Which alternative is best?

We discussed in Chapter 6 a number of different methods for making a choice. The one we emphasized is the informed intuitive method for selecting the best alternative. You can help your friend to apply this method by encouraging him or her to review all the entries in the balance sheet and then ask this key question. If one of the alternatives seems better than any of the others, she or he should be encouraged to select it as the *tentative* choice but to live with it for a while before making a full commitment, to allow time for second thoughts.

Is the best alternative good enough?

Sometimes none of the alternatives seems to be good enough. Even the best alternative may seem inadequate. One or more of your friend's essential requirements may not be met by the alternative that is otherwise the best. By asking this question you begin a discussion of the overall satisfactoriness of the solution from the standpoint of attaining all of your friend's objectives. The focus is no longer on comparing alternatives, but on judging the best against an absolute standard of adequacy. If the best alternative is acceptable, you and your friend can go on to the next key question.

What if the best alternative is *not* adequate? You can help your friend by going back to the key question of Stage 2, generating alternatives. This time through Stage 2, your friend can make use of all the knowledge that has recently been gained. The particular problems with the old alternatives can help your friend direct his or her search toward new alternatives. You can also suggest reexamining the old alternatives to see if any of them can be modified to work better.

What implementation and contingency plans do you need to make?

An important part of making a crucial decision is working out specific plans for implementing it in ways that will most likely attain the desired objectives. Usually it is also necessary to consider in advance what one will do later on if one runs into trouble when the decision is implemented. It is possible to anticipate for most decisions some of the things that are likely to go wrong. The unfavorable outcome scenarios developed in Stage 3 were designed to identify the most likely problems. After your friend has picked an alternative, you should remind him or her of the problems found in the scenarios and to make contingency plans for them. These plans, in most cases, do not need to be elaborate. Even a little advance planning can greatly reduce the disruption that could be caused by an unanticipated negative event.

Are you ready to make a commitment?

A decision maker ought to feel good at the end of the active decision-making process before making a full commitment. That is to say, the decision maker should feel satisfied both about the choice that is selected and about the processes used to arrive at the decision. If your friend feels uneasy about either of these, then he or she is probably not ready to make a firm commitment to the choice. In that case you might encourage your friend to consider going back to one of the earlier stages of decision making. Perhaps more alternatives are needed or more work on the balance sheet is required. Or perhaps if your friend consults an expert to discuss the residual doubts, he or she will obtain the needed reassurance.

Suppose your friend Christine O'Connell, who has recently graduated from college, is looking for a job in the field of advertising. Only one of the companies she applied to has offered her a job, but in sales rather than advertising. The company feels that people in the advertising department ought to have successful sales experience behind them. They have promised Chris that she can transfer to advertising after six months if she is reasonably successful in sales.

Chris has already done a careful job of constructing a balance sheet for her decision. She is impressed with the company, a small manufacturer of home care and do-it-yourself products. And she doesn't think it is likely that she will find as good a job as this one will prove to be after she is transferred to the company's advertising department. But she doesn't like the idea of a six-month wait. She is concerned that she might not do well in sales and as a result might not get transferred.

If Chris asks you for advice your best tactic probably would be to help her formulate contingency plans for the things that might go wrong. First you could ask her what she could do if she does poorly in sales. Suppose Chris responds with two possibilities. She could sign up for a special seminar in sales techniques offered by a business consulting firm. If this didn't help she could quit the company and resume her search for a job in advertising. Chris might be figuring that she would know within a couple of months whether she had the knack for being a successful sales representative. A two-month delay in looking for an advertising job would not be a serious loss, especially since she feels that she has exhausted all the current possibilities.

Next you could ask Chris about other possible difficulties. Suppose the company doesn't do well. A competitor might introduce a new and better product that would cut deeply into the company's sales. The company would have to contract and might not be able to offer Chris the transfer. In that case Chris might judge that it would be best to follow the same plan of quitting the company and looking for another job.

Finally you could ask Chris if she will be able to afford to quit the job if one of the troubles develops. Chris might respond that she had been planning to move into a better apartment as soon as she gets a job. But now, as she thinks about it in light of the possible unfavorable outcomes, she realizes that she ought to stay in the inexpensive apartment she already has until she is confident that the job is working out well.

After discussing these plans with you, Chris might feel that she is ready to accept the job. It is not what she would like ideally, but it is the best that is available now and she is quite well prepared in case it doesn't work out as well as she hopes. With the new contingency plans clearly in mind, Chris might decide that it is wiser to take the job than to keep searching for something better. She might feel ready to commit herself to this choice.

Key Questions for Stage 5, Sticking to It

How can you stick to it?

Sticking to some kinds of decisions is not hard to do. Indeed, getting unstuck may be much harder. For instance, when you buy and install a television set or any other piece of household equipment it is usually impossible to get your money back. But other kinds of decisions are hard to maintain. Decisions involving changes in the patterns of a person's life are especially difficult. For example, failures are frequent in decisions to stop smoking or to lose weight. If your friend has made a decision of this type you should encourage him or her to make a specific plan for sticking to the decision. Ways of doing this are discussed in Chapter 7.

One way of helping your friend stick to a decision is to help set up a buddy system. You can offer to be the buddy or you can help find someone else suitable for the specific problem. Chapter 7 discusses how to set up a buddy system and makes other suggestions, such as encouraging positive self-talk, which might also help someone to stick to a difficult course of action.

What has gone wrong?

The other kind of situation in which a friend may need help in Stage 5 of decision making is when something goes wrong. You can help your friend treat it as a new challenge and help him or her go through all of the stages from the beginning.

You should remember that there are two common tendencies when people are faced with a sudden crisis. The first is to overestimate the magnitude of the disaster. When something goes wrong people frequently think that the situation is worse than it actually is. The second tendency is to impulsively reverse the decision that led to the trouble. People tend to choose the exact opposite of the original decision. Frequently the exact opposite turns out to be just as bad.

If your friend shows signs of either of these tendencies you can use the key questions from the earlier stages (especially Stage 1) to get him or her to slow down and not make any new commitments until after taking the time to go through the essential steps of effective decision making.

Let's pick up on Chris O'Connell again after she has been working for the manufacturing company for a year. Right now she is disappointed and angry because in spite of their promise to transfer her to the advertising department after six months, the company officials have just told her for the third time that she cannot be transferred. It is not that she hasn't done well in sales—she has done too well. The company business is booming and Chris is one of the top sales representatives. Chris has been given a large bonus for her role in helping to devise the sales strategy that is working so well. But the company thinks they need less new advertising and more sales representatives, so they told Chris that there won't be an opening in advertising for at least another year.

Chris feels double-crossed. She is fed up with the life of a salesperson. Although she enjoyed the travel at first, she is beginning to hate the constant hassle of motels, one-night stands, and restaurant meals. When you meet Chris, she is thinking about quitting the company with an uninhibited blast at the president for his dishonesty. Then Chris asks you what you think.

You could tell Chris that it sounds like she might be overreacting to the situation. To suddenly quit in protest would be an impulsive reversal of her earlier decision. The setback is certainly serious, and her anger seems fully justified, but she needs to make a careful decision about what is the best thing to do. Perhaps she should wait a few days until she is over the immediate emotional reaction to the company decision and then begin going through the essential stages of active decision making to select the best plan for her future.

If Chris still seems inclined toward impulsive reversal, you can use the questions from Stage 1. "Are the dangers serious if you quit your job?" "Is it possible to find a better solution?" Merely raising these questions may enable Chris to see that quitting her job in a way that precludes getting a good recommendation from her employer would make it harder to find another one. She would also lose the possibility of negotiating a better position within the company. After all, she does hold some trump cards. With her successful record she may be able to convince the president of the company to give her the transfer if he sees clearly that otherwise she will leave. You can suggest that the two of you get together in a few days to begin generating alternatives for Chris to consider.

This brings us full cycle. The setback of Stage 5 serves as the challenge for Stage 1. When the challenge is accepted, the cycle of stages begins again. That is the sad fate that all of us have to be prepared to face for any of our decisions. But we can expect to suffer from that fate less often if we go through the essential stages each time we make a crucial decision.

Notes

CHAPTER 1. Going through the Essential Stages

The theoretical framework used in this book is based on the research of Irving L. Janis and Leon Mann. We recommend their book, *Decision Making: A Psychological Analysis of Conflict, Choice, and Commitment* (New York: Free Press, 1977), to readers who want to know more about the scientific basis of the guidelines we present. Chapter 7 of their book gives more information about the analysis of the stages of decision making.

CHAPTER 2. Accepting the Challenge

More information about the defective patterns of decision making is given in *Decision Making* by Irving L. Janis and Leon Mann (New York: Free Press, 1977), chapters 4 and 5. Chapter 13 discusses the research on interventions designed to reduce rationalizations.

CHAPTER 3. Searching for Alternatives

The "Twenty things you love to do" exercise comes from *Values Clarification* by Sidney B. Simon, Leland W. Howe, and Howard Kirschenbaum (New York: Hart, 1972). Their book includes many exercises, most of them for teachers to use with students.

Another book with goal-clarifying exercises is *What Color Is Your Parachute? A Practical Manual for Job-Hunters and Career-Changers* by Richard Nelson Bolles (Berkeley: Ten Speed Press, 1976). Although the focus is on career decisions, the author's life-planning approach is broad enough to include other important goals in life. We recommend this book highly, especially for those who are uncertain about their career choices.

The reader may also pick up some good ideas from many other books and articles on personal problem solving. Some contain suggestions about how to overcome shyness, loneliness, sexual troubles, lack of self-control; others deal with ways of counteracting racial and sex discrimination; still others have something to say about what to do about problems posed by illness, unwanted pregnancy, and financial crises. Among the many use-

ful books we have examined are the following: *Take Charge* by William
H. Redd and William Sleator (New York: Random House, 1976); *How
People Change*, by Allen Wheelis (New York: Harper Colophon Books,
1973); *The Personal Problem Solver*, edited by Charles Jastrow and Dae
W. Chang (Englewood Cliffs, N.J.: Prentice-Hall, Spectrum, 1977).

Means–end analysis is described more fully in Wayne Wicklegren's
How to Solve Problems (San Francisco: Freeman, 1974). This is an excellent book for people interested in puzzles and mathematical or engineering problems.

The quotation from the convict is from Nelson Algren, cited in *Newsweek*, July 2, 1956.

CHAPTER 4. Evaluating Alternatives

Research on the balance-sheet technique is reported in Chapter 6 of *Decision Making* by Irving L. Janis and Leon Mann (New York: Free Press,
1977). The book also provides more of the quotation from Benjamin
Franklin and is the source for Table 1.

The discussion of stress among psychiatrists and psychologists is based
on a systematic study of sixty therapists by B. Farber, "The Effects of Psy-
chotherapeutic Practice upon the Psychotherapist," Ph.D. dissertation,
Yale University, 1978.

The sources for the quotations used in this chapter are as follows. The
first set of quotations is from Seymour Wishman, "A Criminal Lawyer's
Inner Damage," *New York Times*, July 18, 1977, page 27. Dr. Irvine H.
Page is quoted from Michael Clark, "Doctors Who Treat Patients as Peo-
ple," *Parade*, September 17, 1978, page 9. The quotations by Enid V.
Blaylock are from "Lawsuits Draw More Concern Than Patient Care,"
New Haven Register, September 13, 1978. The witticism about the uni-
versity was quoted without source by George F. Will, *Time*, May 29,
1978. The John Stuart Mill quotation is from his *Autobiography*, volume
V, and the reply to Mill is quoted from Bergen Evans (ed.), *Dictionary of
Quotations* (New York: Delacorte, 1968), page 22.

CHAPTER 5. Forecasting the Future

The quotation from Bertrand Russell is from his *Unpopular Essays*
(New York: Simon & Schuster, 1966), page 162. Additional points are
cited from pages 28 and 105 of the same book.

A good, brief book on the formal methods for decision making is *Decision Analysis: An Overview* by Rex V. Brown, Andrew S. Kahr, and Cam-
eron Peterson (New York: Holt, Rinehart, & Winston, 1974). This book
gives a carefully worked-out case history of the use of decision analysis in
business.

A more general discussion of classical decision theory is given in Chapter 4 of *Counseling for Effective Decision Making* by John J. Horan (North Scituate, Mass.: Duxbury Press, 1979). He provides a historical overview and comparison of theories.

More advanced accounts with elaborate examples can be found in *The Structure of Human Decisions* by David W. Miller and Martin K. Starr (Englewood Cliffs, N.J.: Prentice-Hall, 1967) and in *Decision Theory and Human Behavior* by Wayne Lee (New York: Wiley, 1971).

The research on the use of the role-playing technique for constructing scenarios is described in Chapter 14 of *Decision Making* by Irving L. Janis and Leon Mann (New York: Free Press, 1977).

The capabilities and limitations of human reasoning about probabilities are excellently reviewed in *Human Inference: Strategies and Shortcomings of Informal Judgment* by Richard E. Nisbett and Lee Ross (Englewood Cliffs, N.J.: Prentice-Hall, 1980). Most of our discussion of these topics is based on their book and the classic paper by Amos Tversky and Daniel Kahneman, "Judgment under Uncertainty: Heuristics and Biases," *Science*, 1974, *185*, 1124–1131.

CHAPTER 6. Choosing and Becoming Committed

More information on the effects of commitment is given in Chapter 11 of *Decision Making* by Irving L. Janis and Leon Mann (New York: Free Press, 1977).

Ten different decision rules to use with the quantitative methods are explained in *Decision Making: A Short Course for Professionals* by Allan Easton (New York: Wiley, 1976).

The source for the quotation and the statistics about the financial troubles of American families is from an article by Deborah Rankin, "Getting into Debt is Easy, Getting out Less So," *New York Times*, November 20, 1977, page 16. She attributes the final sentence about debt entanglement (in quotation marks) to David Caplovitz, a professor of sociology at the City University of New York.

The figures on dropouts from skydiving are from J. Istel, "Statistical Report," *Parachutist*, 1961, *3*, 11–12.

Other research on skydivers was reported by S. Epstein and N. P. Fenz, "Steepness of Approach and Avoidance Gradients in Humans as a Function of Experience: Theory and Experiment," *Journal of Experimental Psychology*, 1970, *84*, 105–112.

CHAPTER 7. Overcoming Setbacks

A more complete account of postdecisional conflict can be found in Chapter 12 of *Decision Making* by Irving L. Janis and Leon Mann (New

York: Free Press, 1977). The quotations about Boswell and the functions of regret are from this chapter (pages 309–310, 317–318, and 322–323).

For a very readable discussion of the implications of recent social-psychological research on positive self-concept, see E. Langer and C. Dweck, *Personal Politics: The Psychology of Making It*, (Englewood Cliffs, N. J.: Prentice-Hall, 1973).

The use of positive self-talk in the cognitive-behavior modification approach is described by D. Meichenbaum in *Cognitive-Behavior Modification* (New York: Plenum, 1977) and by M. J. Mahoney and K. Mahoney in *Permanent Weight Control* (New York: Norton, 1976). Table 2 has been adapted from Table 3 in the Mahoneys' book.

The discussion of fault trees was influenced by the work of Baruch Fischoff, Paul Slovic, and Sarah Lichtenstein, "Fault Trees: Sensitivity of Estimated Failure Probabilities to Problem Representation," *Journal of Experimental Psychology: Human Perception and Performance*, 1978, *4*, 330–344, and by the work of Michael Scriven, "Maximizing the Power of Causal Investigations: The Modus Operandi Method," in G. V. Glass (ed.), *Evaluation Studies: Review Annual*, volume 1 (Beverly Hills, Calif.; Sage, 1977).

The quotation from H. L. Mencken is from *A Mencken Chrestomathy* (New York: Knopf, 1949).

Details about experiments mentioned in this chapter can be found in the articles listed below:

I. L. Janis and D. Hoffman, "Facilitating Effects of Daily Contact between Partners Who Make a Decision to Cut Down on Smoking," *Journal of Personality and Social Psychology*, 1970, *17*, 25–35.

E. J. Langer, I. L. Janis, and J. A. Wolfer, "Reduction of Psychological Stress in Surgical Patients," *Journal of Experimental Social Psychology*, 1975, *11*, 155–165.

C. Nowell and I. L. Janis, "Effective Partnerships in a Weight- Reduction Clinic," and J. Riskind, "The Client's Sense of Personal Control: Effects of Time Perspective." Both of these articles appear in I. L. Janis (ed.), *Counseling on Personal Decisions: Theory and Research on Short-Term Helping Relationships* (New Haven, Conn.: Yale University Press, in press).

CHAPTER 8. **Consulting Experts**

Consumer-oriented guides to various types of experts are now becoming available, especially in the field of health care. One that we like is *Talk Back to Your Doctor: How to Demand (and Recognize) High-Quality Health Care* by Arthur Levin, M.D. (Garden City, N.Y.: Doubleday, 1975).

Studies of physicians' dissatisfaction and of patients' adherence to physicians' recommendations are reviewed by S. V. Kasl, "Issues in Patient

Adherence to Health Care Regimens," *Journal of Human Stress*, 1975, 5–17, and by I. L. Janis and J. Rodin, "Attribution, Control, and Decision-Making: Social Psychology in Health Care," in G. C. Stone, F. Cohen, and N. E. Adler (eds.), *Health Psychology* (San Francisco: Jossey-Bass, 1979).

An overview of the emerging field of decision counseling is given by I. L. Janis and L. Mann, "Decision Counseling: Theory, Research, and Perspectives for a New Professional Role," in H. L. Pick, Jr., et al. (eds.), *Psychology: From Research to Practice* (New York: Plenum, 1978).

References for the social science suggestions about interviewing are the following:

C. F. Cannell and R. L. Kahn, "Interviewing," in G. Lindzey and E. Aronson (eds.), *The Handbook of Social Psychology*, Volume 2, *Research Methods*, 2nd edition (Reading, Mass.: Addison-Wesley, 1968).

W. D. Crano and M. B. Brewer, *Principles of Research in Social Psychology* (New York: McGraw-Hill, 1973), chapter 8.

S. L. Payne, *The Art of Asking Questions* (Princeton, N.J.: Princeton University Press, 1951).

The surveys on job dissatisfaction are reported by Seymour B. Sarason, *Work, Aging, and Social Change: Professionals and the One Life–One Career Imperative* (New York: Free Press, 1977) and by P. A. Renwick, E. E. Lawler, and associates, "What You Really Want from Your Job," *Psychology Today*, 1978, *11*, 53–65 and 118.

The quotation from John Donne is from his *Devotions*, volume VI.

The quotation from Herman Melville is from *Moby Dick*.

CHAPTER 9. Participating in Group Decisions

An excellent summary of recent research on the advantages and disadvantages of group decisions is given by Albert A. Harrison in Chapter 10 of *Individuals in Groups* (Belmont, Calif.: Brooks/Cole, 1976).

A more extensive discussion of the problems of group decision making with many useful suggestions for effective participation is presented by A. C. Kowitz and T. J. Knutson in *Decision Making in Small Groups* (Boston: Allyn & Bacon, 1980).

A more complete analysis of groupthink is given by Irving Janis in *Victims of Groupthink* (Boston: Houghton Mifflin, 1972). Several historical cases are presented, including the Bay of Pigs disaster. This book also covers the Pitcher, Oklahoma, cave-in and the case history of the group of smokers. The book ends with a chapter on ways to prevent groupthink.

Groupthink is also discussed in Chapter 5 of *Decision Making* by Irving L. Janis and Leon Mann (New York: Free Press, 1977). It includes an account of the San Francisco desegregation planning based on the original study by Steven Weiner.

Other useful information can be found in A. Elms, *Personality in Politics* (New York: Harcourt Brace Jovanovich, 1976) and in B. Raven and J. Z. Rubin, *Social Psychology: People in Groups* (New York: Wiley, 1977).

The evidence about the polarization of opinions in groups is reviewed by D. G. Myers and H. Lamm in "The Polarizing Effect of Group Discussion," which is reprinted in I. L. Janis (ed.), *Current Trends in Psychology: Readings from the American Scientist* (Los Altos, Calif.: Kaufmann, 1977).

The Synectics techniques for running groups are described by George M. Prince in *The Practice of Creativity* (New York: Harper, 1970).

Our discussion of the multiple-advocacy system is based on Alexander George's "Adaptation to Stress in Political Decision Making," in G. V. Coelho, D. A. Hamburg, and J. E. Adams (eds.), *Coping and Adaptation* (New York: Basic Books, 1974), and on his *Presidential Decisionmaking in Foreign Policy: The Effective Use of Information and Advice* (Boulder, Colo.: Westview, 1980).

The inside observer of Kennedy's decision-making group at the time of the Bay of Pigs disaster was Theodore C. Sorensen. The quotation is from his book, *Kennedy* (New York: Bantam, 1966), page 338.

CHAPTER 10. Negotiating

The section on the three acts of the negotiation drama and other parts of the chapter draw upon the comprehensive review of theories and research on negotiation by I. Morley and G. Stephenson, *The Social Psychology of Bargaining* (London: Allen & Unwin, 1977).

Other useful sources are R. Stagner, *Psychological Aspects of International Conflict* (Belmont, Calif.: Brooks/Cole, 1967); J. Z. Rubin and B. R. Brown, *The Social Psychology of Bargaining and Negotiation* (New York: Academic Press, 1975); and G. I. Nierenberg, *Fundamentals of Negotiating* (New York: Hawthorn, 1973).

Estimated business losses from crime are from *Newsweek*, December 3, 1979.

The P. G. Wodehouse quotation is from *Aunts Aren't Gentlemen* (London: Barrie & Jenkins, 1974), pages 100–101.

CHAPTER 11. Discounting Common Myths

The quotation about the shortcomings of groups is from I. L. Janis, *Victims of Groupthink* (Boston: Houghton Mifflin, 1972), page 3.

Alfred P. Sloan was quoted by P. F. Drucker, *The Effective Executive* (New York: Harper, 1966).

Index